WHAT READERS ARE SAYING

I have to admit that I wasn't sure a book that led you through a process dealing with weight loss and hypnosis would work. I was wrong. *From Fat to Thin Thinking* is well written and the information is laid out to comfort your conscious mind allowing the subconscious the freedom to hold onto the hypnosis. I was pleasantly surprised at the overall process and the proof being in the pudding I released 14 pounds in 5 weeks and am still on my course for more. Life is good as a "Weight Master".

— **Tim C. (Released 14 pounds during the *From Fat to Thin Thinking* 30-day process)**

From Fat to Thin Thinking contains the recipe for a totally new approach to weight loss. Rather than offering a "diet" to be slavishly adhered to, it teaches you to recognize the bad habits and old attitudes that have kept you stuck in the weight-loss struggle. You will learn to create a healthy dialog with yourself about food choices; to distinguish true hunger from anger, anxiety, or depression; to eat more protein to curb your cravings for sweet or salty treats; and to nurture yourself as you keep choosing to be the powerful, successful human being you have dreamed of being.

— **Roberta G. (Released 9 pounds during the 30-day *From Fat to Thin Thinking* process)**

I just finished with the 30 days of the *From Fat to Thin Thinking* process and I feel AMAZING. I feel like going thru this process has literally reset the computer in my brain around everything I thought I knew about weight loss, counting calories and weight maintenance. I have released almost 6 pounds and feel my eating is under masterful control. It feels as if a cloud of haziness has been lifted around the secret to eating right and if I just keep applying what I've learned from here on out, I will continue to become a weight master. I have thoroughly enjoyed the learning process and it couldn't have been made easier. Follow along in the book, do the guided meditations and you can do it too! Thank you, Rita, so much, for creating this opportunity for so many of us who as I put it, were lost but now are found!

— **Cheri J. (released 5.5 pounds during the *From Fat to Thin Thinking* 30-day process)**

I was able to release 11 pounds easily using the structure provided by hypnosis and thin thinking. I have used hypnosis with Rita for other major life changes so I was confident that it would be powerful for weight loss. I was not disappointed! I book was powerful and set me up perfectly for the 30-day process.

— **Kristen L. (Released 11 pounds during the *From Fat to Thin Thinking* 30-day process)**

The missing link! Loved this book! I read *From Fat to Thin Thinking* and found it to be a fresh and smart way to approach reaching my weight goals. I have read many diet books over the years, however this not a diet book. This book is personal training for your brain. Fascinating, science-based and effective!

— **Leslie B. (Released 6 pounds during the *From Fat to Thin Thinking* 30-day process)**

Reading *From Fat to Thin Thinking* was uplifting and allowed me to see life from another worldview. It's not about cutting food out of your life; it's about knowing how to eat the right amount for your body. That's all there is to it...Moreover, it's how you treat yourself. Often times we are our worst critic and Rita gives you the tools to love, appreciate, and forgive yourself. This book is probably the only book out there that makes complete sense! It's real, it works, and it's proven. I've released a total of 42 lbs. with Rita Black's *Shift Weight Mastery Process* and now this book *From Fat to Thin Thinking* and I am still releasing. If you want to make a change in your life and you're ready to put aside those fad diets, it's time for you to invest in *From Fat to Thin Thinking.*

> — **Adam A. (Released 42 pounds with Shift Weight Mastery and has kept it off for 3 years***)*

Rita Black's *Shift Weight Mastery Process* has been a compelling force in my life over the last 5 years. It not only has given me control over food, but confidence in my approach to other obstacles. I'm nicer to myself, avoiding self-criticism, and maintaining a positive attitude with myself and others. I'm simply a happier person. All the tools that have helped me are right there in the book *From Fat to Thin Thinking* and the 30 day-online coaching and hypnosis sessions.

> — **Maureen B. (Released 37 pounds and has kept it off for 5 years)**

I made a decision on page 67 of *From Fat to Thin Thinking* to change the way I thought about myself and my struggle with food. As I continued reading it became easier and easier. This book helped me "reframe" all my struggles as part of my success story! (p. 124) My success has only just begun. I have released 22 pounds since I started with the book and the process, and I feel better physically, mentally, and emotionally.

> — **William H. (Released 22 pounds during the *From Fat to Thin Thinking* 30-day process)**

Rita is relatable as you read *From Fat to Thin Thinking*. You feel like you are chatting with a friend, who can share her journey, and you make connections how it applies to your own journey with food. She makes the process of connecting with the inner voices in your head, to become the coach within yourself. I've often thought "if only I was rich enough to have a coach with me daily, and to make my food for me, I could achieve my goal weight. Rita helped me to find that inner coach, and to shift to making better choices. I work in a place with an abundance of free food everywhere. During the 30-day process, I would walk by the snack shelves and tap into that inner coach, to think about my vision and where I wanted to be, and I would consciously choose to walk past. At, the end of the 30 days, I walked past the snacks with greater ease, not even wanting the snacks. I highly recommend "*From Fat to Thin Thinking*" to anyone who believes they have to struggle with food. And, while Rita's book feels like a girlfriend guiding you, she has based her methodology on a scientific methodology of neuroplasticity — scientific research that emerged in the 1980s."

— Bev A. (Released 6 pounds during the *From Fat to Thin Thinking* 30-day process)

From Fat to Thin Thinking is a great book and program. I've never seen such a positive take on looking at our whole life as a weight loss journey and not beating yourself up for past transgressions. Also, I love the anecdotes Rita chose to put into words what everyone who's struggled with weight has gone through and more importantly Rita has gone through. Rita's first-hand struggle with weight makes this book feel truthful and that if Rita could do it, so could you.

— Al H. (Released 13 pounds during the *From Fat to Thin Thinking* 30-day program)

As a veteran Shifter, I found the *From Fat to Thin Thinking* extremely valuable to me to re-enforce the Shift skills and principles as well as help acquaint me with new approaches and insights. I found the meditations invaluable in looking inward to discover my strength and resolve. The author, Rita Black shares her wealth of experience, knowledge and research throughout the book and fully explains the science of weight release that takes away any notion of magic or luck. Follow the rules of science in weight release and it works! I found this and the concept that I was releasing weight for the last time and permanently invaluable for my moral. The book is also full of numerous clear examples of how all this science works with charts tables and real-life examples from her life and that of her clients which makes applying it to your own life much easier and understandable. If you've tried everything else and are looking to finally release extra weight and keep it off permanently, this is the program to look into and the book to have by your side in your journey to permanent weight release.

— **Jan S. (Released 30+ pounds with Shift Weight Mastery and has kept it off over 10 years)**

The book has helped me recognize that there's a rebel, a critic and a coach. I don't have to be perfect but continue in the journey; forgive myself; practice" without the fear of scheme or failure; have a loving relationship with the scale; the science behind releasing weight

— **Albina A. (Released 8 pounds during the *From Fat to Thin Thinking* 30-day process)**

This book changed my relationship with food and weight loss programs. I was able to manage 30 days of this program with life changing skills. I've released 5.4 and feel amazing. I learned how to manage my stressful days as well as keep myself honest with daily food tracking. I'm looking forward to continuing the journey to master my weight release and hit my goal.

— **Jessica M. (Released 5.4 pounds during the *From Fat to Thin Thinking* 30-day process)**

I found the book *From Fat to Thin Thinking* a very informative and effective new approach to releasing weight. It leads you thru the program on a ladder of steps that flows from one idea to the next. It is easy reading and does not require constant visits to a dictionary. I feel it will be an immense help to me in my efforts to become healthier and more active.

— **Herbert L. (Released 9 pounds during the *From Fat to Thin Thinking* 30-day process)**

From Fat to Thin Thinking was a great read that helped me change the way I think about food, my body, and my abilities. I really appreciated the personal anecdotes by Rita throughout the book because it helped give me perspective. Overall, the book filled me with a sense of hope and clarity about how to eat and treat my body and how to treat myself. Labeling and understanding who my inner coach, rebel, and critic were made me better suited to respond to any type of thought I might have. I love that I am in more control and that it feels like an actual "Shift" in thinking and not just a temporary, unsustainable diet.

— **Cynthia C. (released 2 pounds during *From Fat to Thin Thinking* 30-day process)**

From Fat to Thin Thinking is interesting and easy to read. I really enjoyed the and the meditation and the hypnosis. I lost 10.5 lbs., I really feel proud about that. I have a lot more to go but I just feel maybe for the first time that I know I can do it. It's like a light bulb came on and I see the way thru. I don't like the way I feel after I eat junk food so it makes it easier to eat healthier food. I don't feel stressed out thinking I can't eat certain things, if I plan ahead I can have a treat, but it's Weird, I really don't want it, I love that. I can't think you enough for everything you have done for all of us Rita, you're like our angel.

— **Cindy L. (Released 10.5 pounds during the *From Fat to Thin Thinking* 30-day process)**

This is a program that works (and I am proof of this as a long time Shifter) because it is based on researched skills of weight releasers, it makes sense, it has hypnosis to make it easier and it is designed by a dynamic person who supports you daily in the program. Also, the book is well written, makes sense and is enlightening. The many facets of the program give you the tools and motivation to work and release weight.

— **Evelyn N. (Released 30 pounds 10 years ago with the Shift Weight Mastery Process and has kept if off 10 years-released an additional 7 pounds during the book process—now at lighter ideal weight)**

For the first time in more years than I care to mention I am feeling empowered calm and equipped with the knowledge to continue on my mastery journey. Rita has been able to tap into the psyche of an apprentice and mindfully help to guide you towards mastery.

— **Valezra E. (Released 11 pounds during the *From Fat to Thin Thinking* 30-day process)**

I feel great now and I am looking forward to releasing more weight in the coming months. I feel that this is just the start of a transformation that is taking place in my day to day life.

— **Chip C. (Released 11 pounds during the *From Fat to Thin Thinking* 30-day process)**

I now and feeling confident and strong in my journey to my healthy weight. In the past, I've always felt anxious and overwhelmed about reaching my goal weight. Through this process, I have totally done a 360 in the way I am approaching my health and weight release. Reading the book and working through the writing exercises were so helpful. Finally, I was able to go below the tip of the iceberg and gently and lovingly reach issues below the surface that have kept me struggling. The 30-day process gently nudged me to take care of myself and slow down. By setting my goal and focus to 1 pounds a week, I lost the anxious feeling. My whole focus has changed to learning on what my body needs to release weight and feel well. I truly have become an apprentice and I really am enjoying it! I really look forward to reading the daily coaching and also love the meditations.

— **Nancy G. (Released 7.5 pounds during the *From Fat to Thin Thinking* 30-day process)**

From Fat to Thin Thinking has been a tremendous hands-on and comprehensive guide and tool into changing my mind set from the struggle of weight ups and downs…. it has allowed me the power to tap into my Inner Coach and take control of my eating and my life…. giving me peace and freedom from the weight struggle. It is a logical and in-depth process with daily guided hypnosis and encouraging words from Rita. Thank you, Rita!

— Michelle N. (Released 9 pounds during the *From Fat to Thin Thinking* 30-day process)

This is a wonderful program and I would recommend that everyone starts a Shift! I saw my confidence grow and the strength of my inner coach knew no bounds! My daily life became so much more satisfying and this further proved that I was in charge of my food habits and I was good at managing them (as well as my exercise). It is part of your day and it fits in well while not overwhelming you. You are set for success from the first page of the book. And you will always feel supported.

— Kate T. (Released 8 pounds during the *From Fat to Thin Thinking* 30-day process)

The answer to my lifelong struggle with my weight! Shift, is EXACTLY what I needed to help me get past thinking that losing weight was something that I just wasn't capable of doing! It's all here between the book covers. Read it, go through the process and you will master your weight struggles! I never thought I could, either.

— (Julie K.—down 6 pounds in 30 days with *Fat to Thin Thinking* 30-day process—released 30 pounds in total and maintaining 2 years)

From Fat to Thin Thinking

Unlock Your Mind for Permanent Weight Loss

Rita Black, C.Ht.

Creator of the Shift Weight Mastery Process

From Fat to Thin Thinking: Unlock Your Mind for Permanent Weight Loss is more than a book— it is a **hypnosis-based weight loss process** that includes:
1. Audio hypnosis and meditation downloads.
2. A 30-day email based daily support system with hypnosis, coaching and meditation.

The hypnosis, meditation and other parts of the process are available at no additional charge on the From Fat to Thin Online Resource Center that goes with the book. www.FromFatToThinThinking.com

ISBN 978-0-9996782-0-6

FIRST EDITION: 2018
Published by Gramercy House Publishing.

Gramercy House Publishing is a trademark of Shift Hypnosis and Motivational Resources LLC.
www.gramercyhousepublishing.com.

With deep gratitude to my wonderful clients and *Shift Weight Mastery Process* participants who have taught me so much over the years and continue to inspire me daily.

In loving memory of my mother, Catherine June Spiess.

DISCLAIMER REGARDING HYPNOTHERAPY AND MEDITATION SESSIONS—PLEASE READ: It is my experience that hypnotherapy and its approach can provide many beneficial effects; however, hypnosis is not a substitute for proper medical attention. The hypnotherapy and meditation downloads provided in *From Fat to Thin Thinking* are not recommended for persons experiencing mental disorders or illness. If you are unsure if you have a mental disorder or think you might have one, please consult the appropriate professional first. Never listen to or play hypnosis or meditation audio sessions while driving or operating equipment; always select an environment that is safe and secure. The audio products have been developed to assist you and give no guarantee; you are the only person who can provide a guarantee for your own success.

MEDICAL DISCLAIMER: The ideas, concepts and opinions expressed in this book are intended to be used for educational purposes only. This book is sold with the understanding that author and publisher are not rendering medical advice of any kind, nor is this book intended to replace medical advice, nor to diagnose, prescribe or treat any disease, condition, illness or injury. It is imperative that before beginning any weight loss program, including the *From Fat to Thin Thinking* program, you receive full medical clearance from a licensed physician.

Author and publisher claim no responsibility to any person or entity for any liability, loss, or damage caused or alleged to be caused directly or indirectly as a result of the use, application or interpretation of the material in this book. Sorry, but that is what I am legally bound to say in order to be able to offer you my insights. If you do not agree with this disclaimer you may return the book to the publisher for a full refund.

CONTENTS

PREFACE
THE LIGHT OF THIN THINKING

I REMEMBER THE DAY MY "SHIFT" from fat to thin thinking began. I awoke that morning and immediately got on the scale because I was four days into another diet. Was it going to be a good day? For me, if the scale was down, it was a good day. If the scale was up, it was a lousy one. Low and behold, it was down! Ding, ding, ding! The scale said I won! I was two pounds down!

However, instead of celebrating, I stood there as the depths of this 20-year, nightmarish struggle hit me hard. I felt a wave of grief and fear sweep over me. I was awash in the loneliness of my weight struggle and my self-hatred, cruel words, and feelings of deprivation. This was nothing to celebrate.

There I was, standing on the scale like a madwoman in some sort of frenzied need to find my worth in a number. The truth was that even if I did reach my goal weight I knew that I couldn't stay on this stupid diet du jour. I couldn't do it anymore. Forget wanting the thin body part; I just couldn't live in the all-or-nothing, good-or-bad head anymore.

I sat down on the bathroom scale in my Santa Monica apartment and began to cry. I cried and cried. I cried for the times I beat myself up. I cried for the binges I had been on. I cried for my husband and my family and the relationships I had been "phoning in" because my struggle with weight overshadowed everything in my life. I cried because I felt alone and scared. There was no one out there who could help me. There was no diet that was going to put things right. There was no therapist or guru that was going to save me.

I cried and cried for what seemed like an hour. Then in a silent moment, a small voice arose inside of me. It was not harsh like my Inner

1

Critic or seductive like my Inner Rebel. This voice, though faint, seemed nurturing and wise. It was coming from a place deep inside of me.

"Never again," it said.

"Huh?" I asked, not quite sure what I was hearing.

"You are never going to diet again."

How was I going to do this? I had no idea, but I decided in that moment to begin my journey. I got up off the scale and walked out of the dark, dank prison cell of fat thinking and began my shift into the light of thin thinking.

INTRODUCTION
IT BEGINS WITH A SHIFT

I F YOU HAVE YOUR NOSE in the introduction of this book, I'm guessing you are here because you have been struggling with your weight and are frustrated. Who could blame you? The continual cycle of dieting and weight gain is maddening to say the least.

Perhaps you think you are personally at fault for your lack of long-term success in the quest for the holy grail of weight loss? Well, you shouldn't blame yourself but the human brain instead. It's the source of all of this angst!

What if I told you that in 30 days you can make a shift from this mindset of frustration and inconsistency with your ability to lose weight—what I call fat thinking—into a thin thinking mindset that allows you to feel confident and capable and release weight steadily at a rate you decide? And, you'll know you can maintain your ideal weight once you achieve it? Oh yes, and all of this without one millisecond of dieting?

How can I make this daring statement?

For the last 20 years, I have been a clinical hypnotherapist and expert in the psychology of weight management. I help people achieve long-term weight release by making the shift from fat to thin thinking with a hypnosis-based program called the *Shift Weight Mastery Process*.

For almost two decades before I developed the process, I yo-yoed forty pounds up and down the scale and thought my weight problem would never be solved permanently. I looked everywhere for answers—fad diets, vegetarianism, extreme exercise. You name it, and I did it, but I always ended up in the same place—back with my overweight self and feeling like a failure.

Little did I know that the answer was not outside of me. Rather the key to unlocking the prison door of my weight struggle was inside of me. Once I made that profound realization, I was able to unlock the prison door, shed the weight, and walk into a life that was healthy and full of confidence. I would like to offer you the same opportunity to end your weight struggle. I also invite you to see that the starting place does not begin outside of you, in the gym, or on the plate. The journey begins in your mind. The same place that has been the source of your struggle is now going to be your key to long-term, permanent weight mastery.

....

"This program saved my life! I haven't binged since I started it, and I don't even think about food like that anymore. I'm almost 30 lbs. lighter, and I fit in jeans tonight that I haven't wore since 2012! I couldn't believe they zipped up. I credit all of this to shifting my mind out of the jail cell of my fat thinking that I created over years of yo-yo dieting." Laura M. (Released 35 pounds, still releasing.)

....

THE WEIGHT STRUGGLE

On any given Monday, a large percentage of more than 2.1 billion Weight Strugglers[1] wake up and hope to "be good" on their diets.[2]

The typical Weight Struggler begins the morning feeling like a weight-loss saint while eating a healthy breakfast. The Weight Struggler is on top of their diet and is even able to resist, with some heroic exertion of willpower, the doughnuts that Tina, the skinny receptionist, has brought to the office coffee room. Our Weight Struggler even aces lunch when smugly ordering a plate of sinless organic greens with the dressing angelically placed on the side.

But things begin to unravel for the Weight Struggler as the day wears on:

- Maybe it's the afternoon energy dip that leads to impulsively grabbing a mini candy bar from an office mate's desktop.
- Maybe it's the leftover doughnut in the coffee room that screams "Eat me" loudly after that stressful conference call.

---

1 Weight Struggler: A person who has been in a perpetual battle with weight, regardless of whether it's five pounds or 500 pounds.

2 Diet: Any way of eating with the intention of losing weight, including low carb, low fat, Weight Watchers, Jenny Craig, Paleo, clean, vegan, no sugar, and gluten-free.

- Maybe it's the cheese slices nibbled while making dinner and feeling starved.

Whatever it was, our Weight Struggler thinks they have fallen off the pedestal of "being good" on her diet and then feels bad because she "blew it."

FAT THINKING

Then another part of our Weight Struggler's mind follows with "Well, since I've already blown it, today is ruined. I'll start over tomorrow and be perfect."

All of a sudden, like magic, the Weight Struggler feels better, and the rest of the day is a festival of eating everything that is not on tomorrow's diet—more candies, doughnuts, and cheese slices. "Now where were those crackers?"

Or maybe the Weight Struggler's being-good stint lasts longer than a day. Perhaps the stint lasts weeks or even months with sticking to the plan and shedding pounds. One might believe the magic solution, and the cure, has been found with whatever diet has been followed. But even with this apparent success, the Weight Struggler can't quite feel confident. Somewhere in the back of their mind is the fear that the weight loss will not last. Then, as predicted, something happens that causes the diet honeymoon to end:

- A weight milestone is reached, and everyone tells our Weight Struggler how great they look.

- Family from out of town, who loves to eat, comes to visit.

- A stressful patch of life is encountered.

Whatever the trigger is, our weight struggling friend falls off the plan. Now the "being good" phase ends in one's mind, and the familiar "being bad" phase begins. Soon the Weight Struggler is indulging on whatever was missed while on the diet.

Frantic about the gain on the scale, the Weight Struggler tries to recapture the magic. "I have to go back to being good!" The stress of trying to be good again is overwhelming and seems to trigger the "bad" eating of everything in sight. "Come Monday morning," they say to themselves, "I will start over!"

Welcome to fat thinking, where the Weight Struggler's brain has been trained to cycle from a "being good" phase to a "being bad" phase. This Weight Struggle Cycle plays out over and over, putting the Weight Struggler in a constant battle with food, exercise, weight, and, most of all, oneself.

WEIGHT MASTERY

On the same Monday morning when the fat thinking Weight Strugglers are waking up, there is another group of Weight Masters beginning their day. These people have successfully achieved their ideal weight and maintained it for a year or longer.

On any given Monday, the typical Weight Master:

- Does not "start over" on a weight-loss eating plan but rolls out of bed and gets on the scale, confident the number will be within a few pounds of their ideal weight. There are no surprises, no yo-yoing, and no struggle.

- Is confident they will be repeating the same skills today that have allowed for maintenance of an ideal weight for the past year.

- Knows that if the day or evening is stressful, there are other ways to de-stress than reaching into the candy jar. (Even if a piece of candy is eaten, they mentally note it and move on, knowing a single candy isn't going to make them fat.)

- Goes to bed feeling nourished and light because of the day's food and exercise choices. Also feels prepared for another healthy Weight Mastery day tomorrow.

THIN THINKING

The typical Weight Master used to live in the world of fat thinking but made a monumental shift that allowed "thin thinking" to begin. The Weight Master shifted the way in which food and exercise choices were seen and how weight management could fit into their life.

- The Weight Master no longer falls into the "I blew it, so screw it!" trap. They've learned to break though the starting-over habit and to stay consistent even if momentarily going off track.

- The Weight Master doesn't deprive themselves on diets. They have evolved a way of eating that honors their life and tastes and allows them to feel nourished and pleasantly satisfied while maintaining an ideal weight.

- The Weight Master is not expecting to be perfect. They understand that weight mastery is a lifelong process. That feeling of accomplishment feeds into all aspects of life.

Now you might be thinking that Weight Masters must be pretty special. Perhaps they are blessed with strong willpower, are well disciplined, or have inherited a special Weight Mastery gene from Granny's side of the family. The fact is, Weight Masters are not smarter, better, or cuter than you. They don't have better genes than you, either.

You have the ability to be a Weight Master starting right now. The *Shift Weight Mastery Process* is going to allow you to shift from a mind that is wired for fat thinking to a mind that is wired for thin thinking so you attain your healthy weight and confidently maintain it.

HOW TO SHIFT FROM FAT TO THIN THINKING

Research shows that to be successful losing weight and maintaining an ideal weight in the long-term, most Weight Masters had to change not only their eating and exercise choices, they also had to change their thinking. They had to rewire the way they communicated with themselves in order to begin their journey to success. Psychologists call this *cognitive restructuring*. The resulting shift from fat to thin thinking is what I call weight mastery.

Imagine, for a moment, that the fat thinking part of your mind is a prison with electrical wires running through it. Much of your fat thinking behaviors, beliefs, and negativity are programmed into these wires. Trigger a wire and the current of that habit or belief plays out automatically below any conscious thought. The more often you trigger a habit to run through your mind's circuitry, the more entrenched and powerful it becomes.

For instance, imagine it's the end of a long work day. You walk through the door feeling stressed and reach in the kitchen cupboard for a bag of chips. The walking in the kitchen part is the trigger that automatically turns on the preconditioned currents traveling along those fat thinking wires. Here's how it goes after you grab those chips:

- You eat half the bag.

- You feel bad and think *I blew it.*

- Another thought pops into your mind: *I'll start over tomorrow.*

- You eat the rest of the bag of chips. You feel good while you're eating the chips but like a failure when the bag is empty.

Why do you do that? It's not because you lack willpower. It's because the mind has been wired for fat thinking behavior. Once a habit gets triggered, that unhappy cycle plays out automatically. It's hard to fight against, and so the cycle keeps the walls of the mental prison firmly intact.

In order to shift from fat to thin thinking, you need to create a different place, a confident and peaceful home in your mind that is wired for thin thinking habits and beliefs. Here are some thin thinking goals:

- Develop habits and beliefs around food and exercise that are so powerful the excess pounds melt naturally toward an ideal weight.

- Establish a mindful way of communicating with yourself that is focused on self-care and self-respect.

- Easily resist the "start over tomorrow or Monday" trap that keeps the Weight Struggle Cycle going.

The more your mind is wired for thin thinking and the more frequently those wires are used, the stronger and thicker the circuits become. Eventually they are more powerful than the fat thinking wires of that mental prison.

Can we just flip a switch and turn on our thin thinking wiring? It would be great if we could, but first we must create thin thinking wiring, and then use it over and over until it's strong. That is what the process which you are about to embark on is all about.

THE SHIFT WEIGHT MASTERY PROCESS

For two decades, I have spent thousands of hours in the trenches with clients from all walks of life and socioeconomic and cultural backgrounds, guiding them out of their frustrating and painful fat thinking and into healthy and powerful thin thinking. During this time, I evolved a process that allows people's minds to get on the fast track from fat to thin thinking in 30 days.

I have been teaching clients and seminar participants the *Shift Weight Mastery Process* since 2007 in Los Angeles, California. This process has been extremely successful in helping men and women make the subconscious changes in their thinking that are necessary to move past the self-sabotaging thinking and behaviors holding them back from long-term weight mastery.

Weight Strugglers begin with a day-long intensive *Shift Weight Mastery Process* seminar where men and women make the initial shift from fat to thin thinking with a powerful recoding process that incorporates coaching, special mind exercises, and hypnosis.

"What is going on? I dreamt about exercising last night! This process sure is amazing. The hypnosis has given me a new way of thinking (and dreaming LOL) about food and exercise. I am effortlessly letting go of old habits that, for years, have been roadblocks to my success." Micki F. (Released 11 pounds in 30 days, maintaining 3 years.)

Hypnosis isn't mind control but a relaxation technique that allows the stubborn unconscious mind to become more open to change so that old fat thinking habits can shift to thin thinking ones.

The overall impact of the hypnosis and other metal processes radically change participants' thinking about their weight, food, exercise, and, most importantly, themselves.

Seminar participants and clients then continue on their own for 30 days, reinforcing their new thin thinking by listening to hypnosis and meditation recordings and practicing thin thinking skills on a daily basis. They release weight at a rate they decide for themselves. (I use the term weight release because it conveys to your deeper mind that you are letting go of the weight forever.)

MIND-SHIFTING TOOLS
FOR THE SHIFT WEIGHT MASTERY PROCESS

The *Shift Weight Mastery Process* uses three mental techniques to make the shift from fat to thin thinking.

HYPNOSIS

Hypnosis is a relaxed and easy mind state. In this place of trance, communicating directly with the change-resistant subconscious mind is possible. In the 1950s, the American Medical Association (AMA) approved the use of hypnosis. Thousands of people have found hypnosis to be an effective way to stop smoking, lose weight, and make positive changes in their lives.

We think and act with our conscious minds, while the unconscious mind controls our habits and beliefs. In the relaxed state of hypnosis, we can communicate more directly with the subconscious mind. That is why hypnosis can help break through the fat thinking habits and belief patterns in the subconscious mind and create new thin thinking habits and beliefs. This change in thinking allows participants to release weight and have long-term mastery of this area of their lives.

Is hypnosis mind control? Hypnosis has had a reputation as a type of mind control. Maybe you saw somebody barking like a dog at a hypnosis show, and you don't want your mind to be controlled by someone else?

Hypnosis cannot make you do anything you don't want to do. That's because hypnotic suggestions must pass through the conscious mind, which acts as sort of a guard for the unconscious. I tell clients that all hypnosis is self-hypnosis. I give the suggestions, and you accept them. You are always conscious in the state of hypnosis, but you are very relaxed.

Research supports hypnosis benefits. There are many research studies showing that hypnosis can create improved weight management. Here are some examples from three different studies of hypnosis's impact on weight management.

- When comparing control groups to hypnotherapy groups, those exposed to hypnotherapy lost more weight and kept the weight off longer than those who did nothing.

- Hypnotherapy helped people correct faulty thinking and

associations about food and helped them get control over non-hunger-related eating.

- Follow-up sessions with both groups at the eight-month and 2-year marks revealed that only the hypnotherapy group continued to lose weight. The control group regained the lost weight.

MEDITATION

Meditation is the act of spending time in quiet thought for the purpose of relaxation, problem-solving, and reflection.

Research supports meditation benefits. Neuroscientists have shown that meditation helps build new neural pathways in the brain that strengthen willpower, impulse control, and self-awareness. Meditation also helps the prefrontal cortex (our conscious mind) grow stronger by sending more blood to that area of the brain.

Meditation enhances the *Shift Weight Mastery Process*. Daily meditation sessions bring the conscious and unconscious minds together in a state of quiet mindfulness that helps create, strengthen, and achieve a vision of weight release success.

COGNITIVE BEHAVIORAL THERAPY (CBT)

CBT is a form of therapy in which proven cognitive techniques help people become aware of when they make negative interpretations or have behavioral patterns that reinforce distorted thinking. CBT helps people to develop alternative ways of thinking and behaving.

The *Shift Weight Mastery Process* has participants engage in reading, writing, and hypnosis sessions that use CBT techniques to transform negative weight-struggling experiences and points of view of themselves into a more powerful image of themselves as Weight Masters. This builds confidence and enhances self-esteem even before weight release.

"I am a psychotherapist, and I have a great understanding of eating disorders and food issues. I know how many calories foods have. I also know about hypnosis, meditation, and CBT. But I have never experienced all of those approaches together

in one package. I think it was the combination that finally worked for me." Nadine K. (Released 17 pounds, maintaining for 6 years.)

LIFELONG BENEFITS

The *Shift Weight Mastery Process* has proved successful for people because it is not about weight loss alone. Rather, it's about changing the way you think and behave in the area of weight management to achieve Weight Mastery—that is, a confident, healthy, peaceful relationship with food, exercise, and, most of all, yourself.

"You cannot 'unlearn' what you get from the Shift Weight Mastery Process." Sarah A. (Released 37 pounds, maintaining for 4 years.)

Some of the benefits of the *Shift Weight Mastery Process* are:

- **Stopping the "on a diet, off a diet" yo-yo cycle.** Diets are external structures that you "go on," and when the diet is over, so is your resolve. Nothing has changed internally, and so you go back to your old habits and the frustrating "being good" and "being bad" cycle.

   The *Shift Weight Mastery Process* helps you break the yo-yo diet habit and focuses your mind on building a way of living that honors you and your lifestyle. This shift happens from within you, so the results are consistent and long-lasting.

- **Changing the negative beliefs and habits that perpetuate the weight struggle.** Even though you want to change your habits and thinking, your unconscious mind protects those beliefs and behaviors. Your mind is programmed to keep things operating in the same, familiar way!

   The *Shift Weight Mastery Process* uses hypnosis and other powerful mental tools to help refocus your unconscious mind on creating new beliefs and habits that allow you to become slim and masterful.

- **Feeling in charge of weight release and maintenance.** Many diet programs teach how to eat to lose weight but fail to explain the mechanics of releasing weight.

During the *Shift Weight Mastery Process*, you will learn how to release weight at a rate you decide and maintain a healthy weight for years to come. This knowledge allows you to feel in charge of your own weight destiny and, therefore, to be masterful.

- **Gaining confidence and freedom in the weight management area of your life.** Dieters focus mostly on losing weight and rarely on training the mind to keep the weight off. In fact, many diets books give some eating rules and recipes but offer no clear insight into creating a powerful relationship with oneself to attain and maintain an ideal weight.

 The *Shift Weight Mastery Process* delivers mental strategies for long-term success so that you can gain self-confidence as you release the weight and keep it off.

- **Losing weight for the last time.** The word "diet" often implies a short-term period of deprivation and rigid rules that end with achieving a goal weight. Unfortunately, that effort can't be maintained and leads right back to weight gain. Hundreds of research studies show the failure of this type of short-term thinking and behavior.

 The *Shift Weight Mastery Process* creates a commitment to permanent change. It begins with shifting attention to building new habits, skills, and thinking that encourage permanent weight release. More importantly, the *Shift Weight Mastery Process* offers a way to develop a respectful, peaceful, and mature relationship with yourself.

Thousands of participants have experienced "the shift" in their thinking and weight management to become Weight Masters.

Janet S. went through the first official *Shift Weight Mastery Process* seminar in January 2008. After releasing 33 pounds, she confided she had been skeptical about the hypnosis and the program. In 2016, Janet became a Shift Coach and stood up in front of Shift Newbies during a seminar to talk about her experience:

....

"I make healthy choices because I want to, not because I have to. By using the Mind-Shifting Tools, including hypnosis, I evolved a way of feeding myself and exercising that allowed me to release weight and keep it off. I don't ever feel

deprived, just delighted that I love the way I eat. I feel free! Most importantly, I'm confident that I can maintain this way of living for life. I never have to go back." Janet S. (Released 33 pounds, maintaining for 9 years.)

ARE YOU READY TO SHIFT?

The powerful mental training contained in this book, the accompanying hypnosis and meditation sessions, and the follow-up *30-Day Thin Thinking Practice* program create a shift from fat to thin thinking similar to my private and seminar-based *Shift Weight Mastery Processes*. The book process is divided into three distinct parts:

Part I: The Orientation. The initial part of the process is about learning how the mind works around eating and weight and how your shift from fat to thin thinking will happen.

Part II: The Shift. This part of the process initiates the shift from fat to thin thinking and your movement from Weight Struggler to Weight Master. This is accomplished with reading, writing exercises, and listening to hypnosis recordings.

Part III: The Practice. It takes 21 days for new habits to embed themselves in the subconscious. The *30-Day Thin Thinking Practice* provides support and tools (hypnosis, meditations, and daily coaching) to create powerful changes from the inside out and establish a foundation for your Weight Mastery and long-term permanent weight release.

So, the question is, are you ready to shift from fat to thin thinking?

WHO SHOULDN'T USE THIS BOOK?

This process is not for everyone who struggles with their weight. You should not use this book if you:

- Are looking for a quick fix with recipes. Most "diet" books are structured that way. This is not one of them.

- Want someone to give you a specific magic formula for what to eat that will melt fat from your thighs in two weeks.

- Are going to skim through the pages for advice to "try out."

I am going to be frank. To experience the full impact of this process, you must be willing to make the journey. You will have to put your mind and heart into this and not be a spectator-reader. To fully benefit from this process, you have to start the journey by reading the entire book and participating in all aspects of the process. If you cannot commit right now, don't worry. I will always be here waiting for you when the time is right. I just hope you don't wait 20 years like I did!

Not Sure?

You might want to participate in the *Shift Weight Mastery Process* but are saying "I don't have time!" or "This sounds too hard!"

These are the arguments that the resistant, unconscious mind often uses to avoid taking life-changing actions. I encourage you to consider the following self-sabotaging excuses:

Excuse 1: I Don't Have Time

A common challenge is the perception that there isn't time to do healthy things like prepare nutritious meals, exercise, or listen to the hypnosis sessions. The reality is that people make time for what is important. Aren't your health and self-esteem worth some time?

It's true that participating in the *Shift Weight Mastery Process* and becoming healthy, slim, and confident takes time. But the consequences of unhealthy habits and weight struggling will ultimately take even more time. Consider the time that you spend:

- Beating yourself up about your weight and eating and exercise habits.

- Looking for an outfit that you feel good in.

- Endlessly being on diet after diet.

- In doctors' offices with weight-related issues.

That is a lot of time! Participating in the *Shift Weight Mastery Process* won't take any more hours out of your day than you spend surfing the net, catching up on social media, or watching TV. Maybe that time can be invested in this commitment to yourself that will yield a much higher return on your day-to-day life?

Excuse 2: This Sounds Too Hard!

The *Shift Weight Mastery Process* will be stretching you past some familiar places. Certainly, it can be challenging. But isn't carrying around extra pounds already hard enough? For many overweight people, the weight struggle is painful, but it is also familiar. Familiarity may seem more attractive, and, honestly, isn't the struggle with weight one of the hardest things to endure? My guess is that your weight struggle leaves you:

- Constantly feeling bad for being out of control with regards to food.
- Blocked from pursuing other goals and dreams.
- Always trying new diets, cleanses, or food fads and feeling like a failure as each one fails.
- Wondering if the weight struggle will go on for a lifetime.

I don't know about you, but struggling with my weight was the saddest, most humiliating, and frustrating experience I've ever gone through. IT WAS HARD! For me, creating a powerful, thin thinking mindset and releasing weight took focus and time, but feeling free was a dream come true and well worth any effort involved.

WHO SHOULD USE THIS BOOK?

This book was written for people who are hungrier for change than they are for staying in the weight struggle.

This process is for you if you are:

- Tired of knowing what to do but unable to do it consistently.
- Ready to be the answer for yourself and know that you are the magic bullet!
- Prepared to finally feel in charge of your relationship with food, exercise, your lifestyle, and yourself.

Now the big question is, drum roll please, are YOU ready?

GETTING STARTED

Let's get started right here and now with two easy steps:

1. Access the Online Resource Center. Go to www.FromFatToThinThinking.com where you will find the Online Resource Center. There you will get access immediately to the hypnosis sessions for this book along with worksheets, coaching, and other valuable resources to support your *Shift Weight Mastery Process*.

2. Meet me in my office. The first part of the *Shift Weight Mastery Process* begins with The Orientation. After you visit the Online Resource Center, join me in my virtual office and let's get started!

THE SHIFT WEIGHT MASTERY PROCESS

PART I
THE ORIENTATION

Change your life today. Don't gamble on the
future, act now, without delay.

—*Simone de Beauvoir*

FOR BEST RESULTS FOR FROM FAT TO THIN THINKING

1. **REGISTER:** Go to www.FromFattoThinThinking.com and register FREE OF CHARGE. This will allow you access to the hypnosis sessions and other online resources that you will use while reading this book.

2. **PAUSE:** As you are reading the book, please pause and listen to the hypnosis sessions where indicated.

3. **SIGN UP:** When you have completed the book please go to www.FromFattoThinThinking.com and sign up to begin your 30-Day Thin Thinking Practice. Every day you will receive coaching, a daily meditation and hypnosis session to support you in releasing weight and shifting to thin thinking.

CHAPTER 1

WELCOME

FREE YOURSELF FROM THE WEIGHT STRUGGLE

WELCOME. COME INTO MY OFFICE and have a seat in the comfy chair. This is where I introduce all *Shift Weight Mastery Process* participants to the concept of shifting from fat to thin thinking. Relax and enjoy opening your mind. I want to personally welcome you to your journey to long-term, permanent weight mastery. I am excited that you are here and ready to begin.

Let me quickly break down what the *Shift Weight Mastery Process* means.

SHIFT

"Shift" is a powerful word. I've been using it in my hypnosis practice for almost two decades. The idea of moving, evolving, and shaking things up is why you and I are here. I'm going to begin guiding you right now on how to create a shift in your consciousness. You are going to shift from fat to thin thinking. You are going to shift from being a Weight Struggler to a Weight Master.

In order to achieve your <u>loving and reasonable ideal weight</u>, you are not going to begin by looking at food or exercise. Rather, you are going to look at making a shift where the weight struggle begins—in your mind. As you shift from fat to thin thinking, you will achieve your ideal weight and remain there for the rest of your life. As you learned in the Introduction, this is a state I call weight mastery.

WEIGHT MASTERY

When I have a client in a relaxed mind state and their unconscious is open, I will ask them "Why is losing weight so important to you?" The first response is usually "To feel healthier." But I know there is always more, so I push further. "What else is important to you?" The answer often is "To feel good about myself."

Of course, feeling healthy and confident is clearly aligned with releasing weight. It's interesting, though, that when I push a little bit more, a client will tell me that what's most important to them, more than being slim, having high self-esteem, and looking good in their clothes, is PEACE. That's right—peace of mind and freedom from the chaos and pain of the weight struggle.

Weight mastery isn't just about losing weight; it is about achieving a way of living that allows you to feel healthy, confident, and peaceful at your ideal weight. You are now on a journey to shift from fat to thin thinking and achieve weight mastery.

- Weight. Using your mind to build skills and practices that allow you to achieve your reasonable and loving ideal weight.

- Mastery. A committed, respectful way of communicating with yourself that allows you to stay consistent with the skills and practices of long-term, weight release and maintenance.

The mastery part of weight mastery is what brings the peace of mind that Weight Strugglers want so badly. After 30 days, participants in the *Shift Weight Mastery Process* feel transformed by this new inner relationship with themselves even though they haven't yet released all their excess weight.

....

"I never woke up in the morning without that heavy weight in my heart. Now I can truly say I love myself, and I know I have what it takes to go the rest of the way down the scale. Weight mastery is not just about weight and being slim. It is about protecting this wonderful and connected feeling I have with myself." Carrie D. *(Released 9 pounds in 30 days, still releasing.)*

....

PROCESS

Making this shift to thin thinking and achieving weight mastery is a process. Our culture is into quick fixes, but making lasting change is more like an evolution than an overnight turnaround. My own shift to weight mastery was a process that was greatly helped by using the tools of hypnosis, CBT, and meditation. I have been using those same powerful tools to help men and women achieve weight-releasing success for nearly two decades. You will now be going through this powerful process, starting with this orientation. (The Introduction briefly describes these three parts of the process. Here, you'll learn more about them.)

THE SHIFT WEIGHT MASTERY PROCESS: BOOK VERSION

Here is how the process in *From Fat to Thin Thinking* unfolds:

FROM FAT TO THIN THINKING

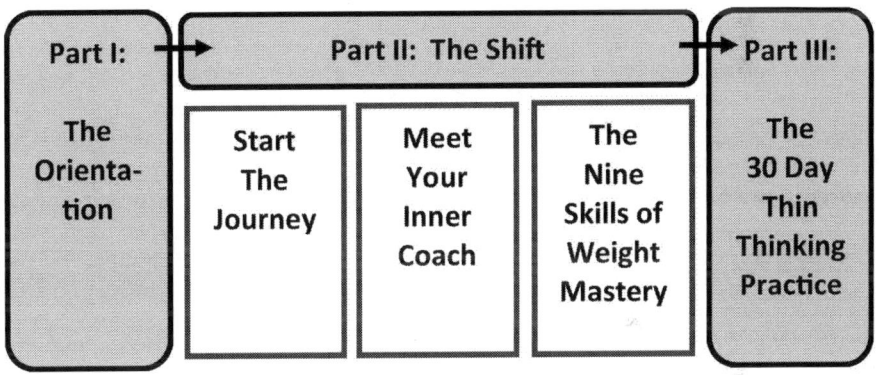

Part I: The Orientation
This first part of the process is divided into two sections and explains how the shift from fat to thin thinking works and how you move from the weight struggle to weight mastery.

Weight Struggle. The mind falls into fat thinking and the weight struggle despite your knowing so much about losing weight. I will use my own weight struggle as an example of how years of losing weight and finding it again led me into a deep, dark prison of despair and fat thinking.

Weight Mastery. I will then look at how to shift a mind wired for fat thinking and trapped in the prison of weight struggling to a mind wired for thin thinking and weight mastery. I will demonstrate how that happened for me. I released over 40 pounds and have maintained a healthy weight for two decades.

By the end of the orientation, you will understand how the shift process works on the deepest level to enable permanent weight mastery.

Part II: The Shift

During the Shift part of the process, you will begin making changes in your thinking with reading and writing exercises and using the mind tools of hypnosis, meditation, and CBT exercises. This part is divided into three sections:

- Starting the Journey: You begin shifting from fat to thin thinking.

- Creating the Connection to your Inner Coach: You engage with your powerful Inner Coach who will be essential in guiding you to weight mastery.

- The Nine Skills of Weight Mastery (Nine Skills): You learn strategies and habits of Weight Masters who released weight and have maintained a healthy weight long-term.

Part III: The Practice

Finally you will embark on thirty days of daily practice called the *30-Day Thin Thinking Practice* which involves meditation, hypnosis, CBT exercises, and coaching that will allow you to reinforce thin thinking while you release weight. The 30-day program is available to you in the Online Resource Center at www.FromFatToThinThinking.com. Practicing for 30 days will start setting new habits deep in your unconscious.

So, without any further delay, let's jump in and begin with understanding why someone as smart and brilliant as you has been struggling with weight in the first place.

TIPS FOR GETTING THE MOST OUT OF THE *SHIFT WEIGHT MASTERY PROCESS*

- Go to www.FromFatToThinThinking.com and sign up. The hypnosis sessions for the book along with worksheets, coaching, and other valuable resources that support your *Shift Weight Mastery Process* are available at this website. I urge you to take advantage of it.

- Set aside some time each day for reading, writing, and listening to the hypnosis and meditation recordings. In order to manage your time, make it the same time every day if possible.

- Skim the book first to get the gist of what the process is about and to satisfy your curiosity. Then, you can dive in and engage fully with each part of the process.

THE ORIENTATION:
WEIGHT STRUGGLE

All the world is full of suffering. It is also full of overcoming.

—*Helen Keller*

CHAPTER 2
WHY AM I STILL STRUGGLING?

THE CONSCIOUS VERSUS THE SUBCONSCIOUS MIND

I ONCE HAD A MALE CLIENT who weighed nearly 400 pounds when he came to a *Shift Weight Mastery Process* seminar. You would think this man needed to be educated about how to eat to lose weight, right? Wrong! He had an impressive, in-depth knowledge of nutrition and exercise. Yet, despite all that he knew, he was still out of control with food and nearly 200 pounds overweight. Obviously, all his knowledge was not helping him.

IT ISN'T ABOUT WHAT YOU KNOW

My guess is that you know enough about food, nutrition, and dieting to write your own diet book. You are in good company. I have had clients in the weight loss and health and wellness professions—personal trainers, nutritionists, family doctors, bariatric physicians, plastic surgeons, and dieticians—who may or may not have had a lot of weight to lose, but they had a dysfunctional relationship with food, exercise, or themselves. Despite the fact that their professions center around helping people lose weight and get fit, they are at a loss when it comes to reigning in their own eating habits.

Like these smart exercise and diet-savvy clients, you may know most of what there is to know about weight gains and losses. So why does research show that nutritional knowledge does very little in the long-term fight against weight? Well, when it comes to weight, the mind has two minds of its own: the conscious mind and the subconscious mind.

THE CONSCIOUS MIND

Your conscious mind is the willpower and impulse control part of your brain. It's the analytical, rational, reasoning, planning, and problem-solving part of you. This is the part of your mind that says "I need to lose weight. Let's make that happen!"

This part of your mind:

- Reads diet books and buys a gym membership.

- Holds the conscious knowledge of what it takes to "be good" on a diet.

- Exerts self-control to say "no" to that impulse to grab the chocolate bar when you're in line at the checkout.

- Has the desire to be thin, the need to feel great in skinny jeans, and the self-discipline to make both happen.

Unfortunately, according to the mind-model theory of hypnosis, this weight-loss rock star part of your mind is only about 12 percent of your brain power **(See Chart A.)**. Yes, you read me right, a measly, teeny 12 PERCENT!!!

Sadly, the part of your mind that drives willpower, controls impulses, and keeps you on a diet leaves a lot to be desired. This is where the story of the weight struggle begins.

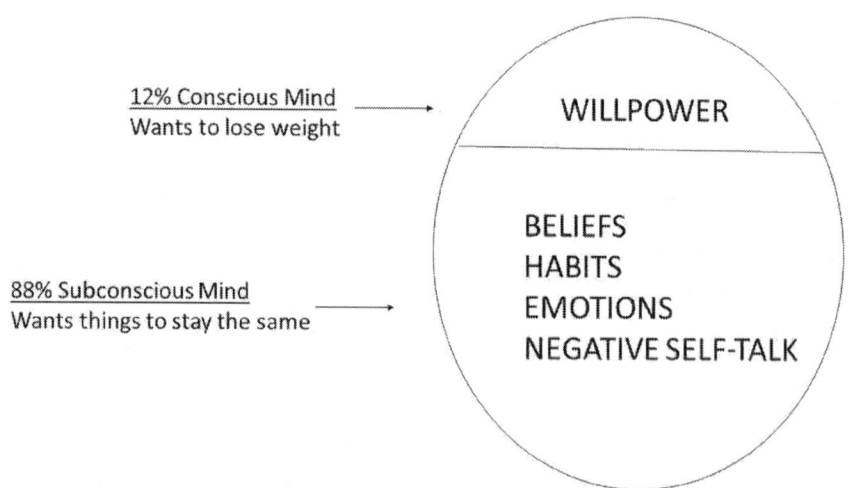

CHART A: The Mind Model

THE SUBCONSCIOUS MIND

Your impulses, desires, habits, beliefs, and emotions spring deep down from your subconscious mind. This is the part of your mind that:

- Perpetuates your limiting beliefs. "It's hard for me to lose weight!"

- Develops habits like eating in front of the television at night.

- Pushes down stressful feelings or emotions with comfort food.

Whatever the patterns of eating that prevent long-term weight release, the unconscious mind is designed to keep things running just as they are. To add insult to injury, the subconscious mind has little to no interest in what the conscious mind wants with regard to weight release.

This old and primitive part of your gray matter helps survival and has put the daily habits that make life happen on autopilot! This, of course, is an amazing feat when you think of all those daily behaviors that you don't have to think about like brushing your teeth, getting dressed, and even starting your car. The downside is that great and powerful unconscious minds want the path of least resistance, which is the status quo. And the subconscious mind doesn't care how many pounds that status quo weighs on the scale or how unhealthy it is!

There exists a powerful unconscious network of circuitry that operates below the conscious "I want to lose weight desperately" mind. These neural pathways of beliefs, habits, and emotions dictate your current weight struggle and continue to grow stronger every time you go on a diet and then fall off it. Every go-around in that vicious and unbeatable neural cycle reinforces these aspects of your subconscious mind:

- Belief that you are a failure at weight management.

- Habits that keep you struggling with weight and falling off every diet.

- Connections between emotions and stress and using food to cope with both.

- The critical way you communicate with yourself.

Researchers at the University of Sydney found that different brain circuits take over as behavior is repeated over and over. The behavior starts in the *neocortex*, the newer mammal brain where conscious thought occurs. However, as a behavior is repeated over and over, it moves to the more primitive brain, the *basal ganglia*, which runs automatic functions like breathing and certain habits.

Once a behavior is moved to the basal ganglia, the amount of conscious thought needed to run that habit becomes almost nonexistent. The pull of habit from the depths of the primitive brain now overrides conscious reasoning. All of which means that the Weight Struggle Cycle of going on and falling off diets and all those fat thinking beliefs and habits continue despite the best conscious-mind attempts to change.

WEIGHT STRUGGLE SUM UP: CONSCIOUS VS. SUBCONSCIOUS

- The constant battle with your weight doesn't originate from a lack of strength or character. The 12 percent conscious part of your mind that wants to eat a healthy salad for dinner is no match for the stronger 88 percent unconscious mind that is used to reaching for the cheese and crackers after a long day.

- Our willpower cannot win the battle against our habits and beliefs in the long-term, which is why short-term, external solutions like diets do not work. We have to shift our thinking on a deeper level.

Let's seek to understand a little more about our precious but limited 12 percent conscious mind resource—**WILLPOWER**—and why it is so elusive when it comes to helping us manage our weight.

CHAPTER 3
IF IT'S MONDAY, I MUST BE ON A
DIET
THE TRUTH ABOUT WILLPOWER

"I DON'T HAVE ANY WILLPOWER!" I hear this all the time from clients, and I am sure you have certainly felt this. You are right to a certain degree; the daily amount of willpower we have is limited. The impulse control ability of the conscious brain allows you to get what you want, keeps you from what you don't want, and helps you keep moving forward when the going gets tough. But remember, that is only 12 percent of the mind's overall power. Research shows that willpower is used up quickly by many physical and emotional factors, including:

- Decision-making
- Stimulation from our environments
- Stress and emotions
- Lack of sleep
- Poor nourishment
- Dehydration

HOW WILL BECOMES POWERLESS

Daily willpower is at its most potent when you awaken in the morning. That is why breakfast and lunch are not usually a struggle when dieting. By the middle of the afternoon of a day of running errands or working and being stimulated by phones, computer screens, people, traffic, work, and kids, the sand in your willpower hourglass runs out. That's when bad decisions are made, like reaching into the candy jar, deciding to go home instead of to the gym, and sitting in front of the TV and eating mindlessly.

I have a saying, "If we all went to bed at five 'o clock, we would be thin!" But you probably don't go to bed that early, and so your willpower is likely to give way to preconditioned habits and beliefs. The conscious knowledge of what to do to lose weight dissipates as you eat food to soothe, sedate, and reward yourself. Then, when you eat something bad, the tendency is to think *I already blew it, so I may as well start over tomorrow.* This hope springs eternal from the idea that somehow willpower will be stronger tomorrow. Unfortunately, as you have probably noticed, to your dismay, it rarely is.

Diets also work against that willpower reserve. Just the idea of restricting food and focusing on what to eat and not eat creates a lot of stress, which wears your willpower down.

My Mother, the Nutritionist

I learned very early on that the "struggle with weight" had very little to do with knowledge about food and nutrition. My mother graduated with honors with a bachelor's degree in nutrition from the University of California, Berkeley in 1950. She then earned a scholarship to complete her master's degree at Cornell University. If anyone knew about food and the impact it had on the body, it was my beautiful, sweet mother.

As a child I loved spending hours with her in the kitchen. I watched her cook as she told me the nutritional makeup of the healthy family meals she was preparing. "See this green pepper? It has vitamin C, which protects against colds. That's why it's important for you to eat it." I was in awe of her nutritional prowess.

Yet, as much as my mother consciously knew about nutrition, she became a victim of her own weight struggle. She prided herself on her tall, slim physique, and she watched what she ate until we moved from Portland to Seattle in the early 1970s. The move was tough on my mom. Staying at home to take care of three small kids and living in the city of gray skies, cut off from friends and family, Mom turned to food for solace and comfort.

Distraught by the pounds that were creeping onto her, she tried to cut back and diet. I often came home to see her standing in the kitchen with a cake on the counter and a fork in her hand. "Come and help me even up the edges," she would say as I joined her with a fork. "We won't eat a slice," she said with a seductive wink, "but a few bites aren't going to hurt, right?"

It was painful to watch my strong mom so out of control and helpless as she got more frustrated and ashamed of herself. She gained sixty pounds over a few years. Her deep knowledge of the chemistry of food and understanding of what it did in her body was little help against the emotional stress that ate away at her willpower. That same stress drove her to eat comfort food despite her best intentions of trying to be "good" on a diet.

WEIGHT STRUGGLE SUM UP: WILLPOWER

- Willpower, on its own, is no match for a powerful, fat thinking, subconscious mind.
- Willpower gets quickly sapped over the course of stimulating days, making it easy to fall back into old behaviors that perpetuate the weight struggle.
- This "lack of willpower" reinforces a sense of failure.

Let's now leave the conscious willpower mind and dive down into the subconscious to understand more about the very root of your fat thinking and weight struggle—your FAT THINKING **BELIEFS**.

CHAPTER 4
I STRUGGLE, THEREFORE I AM
FAT THINKING BELIEFS

ONE OF THE FIRST QUESTIONS that I ask a client is "When do you believe your weight struggle began?" The answers are as varied as the stars in the sky. Some people swear they started struggling the moment they were born! Sometimes it was their childhood years or early twenties when they headed off to college and stopped being so active. Others didn't struggle until later, after their first child, during their thirties, or around menopause. Some believe their trouble started because of things that happened, such as a tragedy in the family, the diagnosis of a medical condition, or a promotion to a sedentary position.

Many admit that when they look back at pictures of themselves when they believed they were fat, they see with hindsight that they weren't fat at all or at least they were a lot thinner than they thought. "Why did I think I was fat? I was beautiful. I wish I could go back in time and tell myself that now!"

HOW THE BELIEF SYSTEM EVOLVES

For better or for worse, your beliefs filter how you experience reality. From birth until your early to mid-twenties, your subconscious mind is imprinting information about you and your family, including your morals, cultural rules, and the surrounding world. Your parents, friends, teachers, and life experiences all take part in this process. The subconscious mind takes all this overwhelming and sometimes chaotic information and forms it into beliefs that help you experience reality in a consistent way.

Once beliefs are in place, the unconscious mind creates a "critical filter," a system that sorts through the billions of bits of information bombarding it every hour of the day. This filter allows the unconscious mind to reject information that collides with your personal reality, morals, and ethics and reinforces what your beliefs say is true.

Our beliefs and critical filtering system come together to form a belief system, the stories that define our personal sense of who we are in the world. Many belief systems work well, helping us achieve success in school, make friends, find a good job, and function highly in the world. But when we keep struggling with weight, we come to see ourselves as a Weight Struggler. This self-image is like a prison, holding us captive by the rope-like wires of all those fat thinking stories we have come to believe as true.

You Can't Diet Negative Beliefs Away

At the root of fat thinking is the belief that you are the problem—that somehow you are flawed and need to be fixed. Therefore, you reason, the solution must be outside. Maybe a diet will help you escape that pain.

The problem is not really solved, because even if the diet does fix the weight issue temporarily, the beliefs and habits that existed in the brain before the dieting started now rear their heads with a vengeance. The weight went away but the unconscious wiring didn't, and so you begin to fall back into old habits and eventually regain the lost weight.

Soon, the weight problem is an ongoing struggle, and negative assumptions like these take hold:

- When I am sticking to a diet, I am good; when I am not sticking to the diet, I am bad.

- If I diet and get thin, I will be happy.

- I am lazy because I don't like to exercise.

This is how the Weight Struggler belief system evolves. Over time these beliefs take root in the unconscious mind and grow strong, feeding on the evidence that you are a failure at this thing called "weight loss."

Struggling in Seattle

I remember the moment when my first fat thinking belief was created. I was sitting in my second-grade class on a rainy January in 1972. My family had recently moved from Portland to Seattle, and I was the new kid in town. As the teacher was presenting the lesson, my eyes were wandering around the Fairview Elementary classroom. I caught a glimpse of a few of the other girls and boys sitting in their chairs, and I noticed something. Their thighs fit nicely within the seats of their chairs.

I looked down at myself, and to my horror, my thighs hung over the sides of my chair! I immediately felt bad. "There is something wrong with me, I'm different. My thighs shouldn't be so big. Look at Karla's thighs, they fit in her seat just fine, but look at mine! I wish I weren't so fat."

At that moment, a little fat thinking belief light bulb went off in the back of my mind. "Hey, I'm different, there is something wrong with me, I am not like the others."

As my mother's weight struggle grew, my own fat thinking began to blossom as well. I was also learning, just as she did, that being in the kitchen, away from the chaos of daily life, was a comfort. Food for me quickly became a fast friend as I learned to bake and cook and eat and eat and eat. I would come home from school where my weight was frequently the source of ridicule by the other kids ("Hey, Thunder Thighs!"), make a batch of cookie dough, and eat half of it before the cookies hit the oven. I would go lay down upstairs in a sugar stupor, waking up just in time to join the family for dinner, eating seconds and thirds and dessert, of course.

I can't control myself, I thought, as I lay in bed at night feeling full and fat.

That fat thinking belief wasn't alone for long. It was soon accompanied by others. Fat thinking beliefs breed like rabbits, and soon I had a whole head full of them.

"Skinny people have it easy. If I were thin, my life would be easy like theirs."

"I don't fit in and have to try to be thin so people will like me."

When I was twelve, I was in enough pain about not fitting in to finally take action. I put myself on the Scarsdale Diet, which was very popular at the time. I ate a weird breakfast of a half piece of dry toast and a half a grapefruit. For lunch and dinner I was allowed all the meat I wanted, so I piled my plate high with roast beef but nothing else.

For a month I stuck to the Scarsdale Diet to the letter. It felt good to be so in control, even if I was sick of all the meat. I got on the scale and had lost fifteen pounds. You think I would be happy, right? You think that the diet success would be a fairytale ending for me. But even though I was at my weight goal and even had earned a few compliments from friends and family, I still had the same negative belief system around myself and my weight. I was in a slimmer body that didn't feel like mine because I had lost the weight so quickly. I got off the scale and instead of going and living happily ever after, I began to eat.

To my horror it was as if the switch in my head had been flipped, and I proceeded, zombie-like, to fill my mouth with any food I could get my hands on. Any food, that was, except food that was allowed on the Scarsdale diet. I tried to stop myself and "get back on the plan," but this drive to eat was bigger than me. I ate until I was eighteen pounds higher on the scale within a few weeks. I was back to my weight-struggling self, believing I was always going to have a weight problem and feeling so ashamed that I never wanted to show my face in public again.

WEIGHT STRUGGLE SUM UP: Beliefs

- Your fat thinking beliefs create your Weight Struggler reality.

- Fat thinking beliefs are acquired over time, over failed weight-loss attempts, reinforcing the weight-struggling belief system circuitry.

- The wires of fat thinking belief layer one on top of the other to become a Weight Struggle Prison. Your beliefs keep you struggling, and the struggling keeps the beliefs alive.

Now that you understand how fat thinking beliefs create a Weight Struggler's reality, it's time to explore another unconscious player at the heart of fat thinking—FAT THINKING **HABITS**.

CHAPTER 5
SEE A COOKIE, EAT A COOKIE, REPEAT
FAT THINKING HABITS

You're trying not to do it, but it's hard...real hard.

Think of the agitation you might feel when you are sitting in front of the TV at night, trying to fight the urge to go into the kitchen and microwave that bag of popcorn you eat around the same time every night. "Must have popcorn! Must have popcorn!" your subconscious screams like a hysterical child.

The feeling is urgent, it's unbearable, so you give in and get up, go to the kitchen, grab the bag, and throw it in the microwave. As you watch the bag expanding and hear the familiar "pop, pop, pop" of the exploding kernels, you begin to calm down a bit, knowing what you want is coming soon.

The microwave dings. You rip open the bag, and the steam poofs out as you reach in to grab the fluffy bits of white starch and put them into your mouth. The sharp taste of salt and the heady flavor of chemical butter explodes in your mouth. Immediately, there's a feeling of relief as the agitation falls away and your brain's reward center gets a hit.

Now what happens? You head back to the TV and eat the rest of the popcorn mindlessly, not even really experiencing the mouthfuls until you reach the bottom of the bag. The popcorn is all gone, and a sinking feeling and some guilt creep in. You blew your diet again, and you didn't even really enjoy that popcorn! Why did you do it? You said you weren't going to tonight and the night before and the night before, and yet you keep doing it again and again and again. What the heck is going on?

THE RINGING PHONE OF HABIT

Your brain is wired to pick up a ringing phone.

1. Phone rings.

2. Respond by going to pick up the phone.

3. Pick up phone and feel relief when ring goes away.

This familiar sequence of events in the unconscious mind is called HABIT.

Have you ever noticed that for some reason if you don't pick up a ringing phone, that trill drives you crazy? Your body feels agitated, and your mind can't focus because of that stupid ringing phone? What happens when you pick up the phone or the phone stops ringing, especially if it has been ringing for a long time? YOU FEEL RELIEF! You relax and can think again. That's because the initial cue—the ringing phone—stimulated the brain to begin the routine of picking up the phone, and when it is picked up, you get the reward: The phone is answered, the habit cycle is complete, and your mind can relax again.

In one study, monkeys were habituated to press a lever to receive a reward of sweet juice in response to seeing shapes on a computer simulator. The researchers noted that once the monkeys saw the cue on the monitor, they began craving the reward. The monkeys became agitated, even depressed, when the juice was not delivered. That was because the "expectation" of the perceived reward was not happening.

When you are sitting in front of the TV, the habit cue rings: "There is popcorn in the cupboard waiting to be popped and eaten." The ring is very hard to resist. Your deeper mind thinks you must fulfill that habit, and it becomes agitated until you give in and go pop the corn. The irony is, as soon as you complete the routine and eat the first bite of popcorn, there's a sense of relief from the agitation. Your mind has moved on to other things, but you are still mindlessly eating popcorn and watching TV, not even enjoying the calories being stuffed into your mouth.

HOW HABITS BECOME ESTABLISHED

The mind, in its infinite wisdom to support your survival by being efficient, puts the behaviors it perceives as important to survival on autopilot and then drives you to fulfill those behaviors. After a new behavior is repeated a few times, it moves from a conscious-mind, deliberate action to an unconscious-mind, automated habit driven by a series of neurological responses that become very hard to change.

It doesn't take too many repetitions to establish a habit either. Researchers including Bernard Balleine from the University of Sydney and Simon Killcross of New South Wales in Australia recorded rats' brain activity as they learned a new habit. The behavior sequence went like this:

1. The sound cue of a "click" signaled a rat to begin traveling a maze.

2. The rat scurried through the maze to the end.

3. The rat found the reward of sugar water or some other reward.

The first few times, a rat's brain activity was high during the entire sequence as it learned the ropes. After a few times, the brain activity was still high in response to the cue at the beginning and the reward at the end, but during the routine maze running, each rat's brain activity significantly decreased. What happened during the middle routine part of the experiment? Very little brain activity, only a few expert cells were handling this part of the habit!

Think of how many habits men and women perform rather mindlessly each day. Many are helpful to health and survival. It's just that other fat thinking habits are wired into the brain, too, like mindlessly munching popcorn in front of the TV. Those fat thinking habits keep the weight struggle going.

WHY BREAKING A HABIT IS DIFFICULT

Often habits are hardwired into the mind with a perceived additional reward known as secondary gain. The mind associates the habit with something else it values. This happens with all different sorts of habits, both positive and negative. Here's how it works around a fat thinking habit:

- OBSERVATION: Your mind sees the popcorn and you relaxing and zoning out in front of the TV.

- ASSOCIATION: It marries the popcorn and relaxing in front of the TV together.

- SECONDARY GAIN: Eating popcorn symbolizes relaxation and zoning out.

Of course, popcorn has no sedative powers, but try telling that to your unconscious mind that keeps agitating you to go make the popcorn because it needs to relax from all this agitation of wanting the popcorn!

So, dieting and trying to avoid negative habits don't work because the wiring for that habit still exists. Plus, there is the deeper secondary gain that the habit gives us. Taking away the habit and trying to cope without it causes raw, out of sorts, and vulnerable feelings. You miss the fat thinking habit even though consciously you know it isn't good for you.

FREEZER BURN

I gained over 25 pounds my junior year in high school when I developed a very specific fattening habit while trying to lose weight.

I was working at Kidd Valley, one of the best hamburger stands in Seattle. Here is where I got in trouble. I went to work after school at four o'clock. I would be starving because I was trying to diet and be good all day. My dinner break was not until seven. Although I tried to not eat anything, I usually didn't succeed because I fell prey to a sneaky ritual.

After I fried up an order of breaded mushrooms for a customer, I set one fried mushroom aside for myself. I would slip into the walk-in freezer when no one was looking and scarf it down. The first bite was an explosion of juicy and flavorful mushroom juxtaposed with the crunch of the fried battered crust that made my mouth sing. I also got a moment in the cool of the freezer, away from the hot oil and the maddening crowds of customers clamoring for food.

As soon as the first thrill of the bite was over, I didn't even experience the rest of the mushroom as I crammed it into my mouth and headed back out to the fry station. This little ritual started out innocently but became a hardwired habit that went like this:

- **CUE:** Someone orders the mushrooms.

- **ROUTINE:** Fry up the mushrooms and take one for me, sneak into the walk-in fridge, and pop the mushroom into my mouth.

- **REWARD:** The first heady bite of mushroom.

- **SECONDARY GAIN:** The quiet and cool relief of being in the freezer.

After the first mushroom of each shift, I felt bad for breaking my diet. *Oh well*, I thought, pushing that negative feeling down. *I may as well eat more mushrooms now since I blew it. I'll try again tomorrow.*

And guess what? Thinking "I blew it so I may as well eat more..." became its own fattening habit as well! Soon I was habitually going off my diet with whatever I could get my hands on, mistake milkshakes, fries, and double bacon cheeseburgers. Yes, the fried mushroom was the gateway habit for all the bad "I am off my diet now" habits that fell into place after that first mushroom trigger. So even though I began each day on a diet, I ended each day being pulled into a string of habits that got me to my highest weight yet.

WEIGHT STRUGGLE SUM UP: HABITS

- Our fat thinking habits get triggered and play out automatically under conscious thinking and drive our behavior.

- When you try to take the habit away, your mind gets agitated, ringing like a phone that wants you to answer by engaging in the habit.

- Changing a habit is difficult because the subconscious mind perceives the habit as something valuable that fulfills a need.

So, you can see how willpower is no match against the hardwiring of beliefs and habits. Now let's look at another big piece of the puzzle of our fat thinking circuitry—**STRESS AND EMOTIONS.**

CHAPTER 6
FEEL HAPPY, EAT. FEEL SAD, EAT.

STRESS AND EMOTIONS

M Y GUESS IS THAT ONE of the challenges you have faced is stress and emotional eating? You are not alone. According to the American Psychological Association (APA), 43 percent of women surveyed said they ate in response to stress in the previous month. Many women said that eating in response to stress didn't make them feel better, only more guilty and bad about themselves and their bodies. So, even though the rational mind knows a bagel isn't going to solve the fact that a boyfriend didn't send a Valentine card or that the chocolate cookie isn't a cure for having to sit down and do taxes, the Weight Struggler eats when she's upset anyway.

EMOTION, STRESS, AND THE BRAIN

Our mind and body evolved to move from 0 to 100 milliseconds to get us out of danger as fast as possible. This fight-or-flight response enhanced survival back in the day. When fear or danger happens today, the same amazing survival mechanism occurs. The hormone cortisol floods the system, and the reptilian brain literally shuts down the conscious, rational-thinking brain. It says "Hey, there's no time to think—JUST MOVE THOSE FEET!" Almost instantly, every bit of energy goes to preparing us to flee as fast as possible.

The problem is that the reptilian brain does not know how to differentiate between a lion and bumper-to-bumper traffic, the yelling boss, or a bad hair day. The mind interprets any change in "normal" as a threat, triggering release of cortisol to prep the body for a lightning-fast getaway. Stress also shifts the brain into a reward-seeking state, because it associates the reward state to "feeling better."

Eating may be a calming reward, but eventually it also makes the Weight Struggler feel bad. Only 16 percent of women in the APA survey reported that the food they turned to for comfort actually helped.

CINDER-STRUGGLER

In the summer before my senior year, I quit my part-time mushroom job and joined Weight Watchers. I had never been so heavy in all my life. I felt ashamed as I got on the scale in front of the nice lady who reminded me of my grandmother and she called out my weight. "192 pounds!" It was a humiliating moment. Had it really come to this?

I was only 16, but I felt like I was 100 years old. My body ached and I didn't move well. I didn't fit into any cute clothes like those my friends wore, and I had never been out on a real date. I hung out with guys, but no one looked at me as girlfriend material. I was just the funny fat friend.

I needed to do something. I thought I couldn't go into my senior year looking and feeling like this. My struggle was consuming every waking minute of my day. So, I embraced the Weight Watchers plan and stuck to it. I had to make it work, and I found I had enough willpower to "be good" on the plan week after week.

I was losing weight and feeling excited about my progress. I cherished my weight loss card that showed each week's weight victory. I was in control, and as long as I was "good," I would keep getting my weight loss payoff. There were other payoffs too. I could wear normal-sized clothes. People seemed to treat me with more respect, too.

The dark side of this rather magical time of being a star Weight Watcher was that I still felt like a Weight Struggler on the inside. Would I be able to keep this charade up forever? I pushed the dark thoughts aside and just kept going with the program.

CINDER-STRUGGLER GOES TO THE BALL

I hit my weight goal of 134 pounds in Weight Watchers in the spring of 1982. I remember being called up in front my weekly meeting for my goal weight award and feeling so proud, emotional, and like I had arrived. This amazing feeling lasted less than 24 hours.

The very next day I was sitting in the lunchroom, selling tickets for the senior breakfast with the other girls on the committee when I was asked to the prom, in front of the entire lunch room, by the captain of the swim team. We were in the spring musical together, but I didn't know him well. I sat there dumbfounded, mouth gaping, as the lunchroom fell silent and waited for my response. "Yes," I said rather meekly but loud enough to cause a roar among those listening. I felt dizzy. Was this really happening?

Now you would think after two stunning wins like hitting your goal weight and being asked to the senior prom by one of the most popular guys in school would have you feeling on the top of the world, and I did… for a moment.

I walked home from school on cloud nine, my heart racing. My emotions were soaring so high that I couldn't take them all in. When I got home, I went immediately to the kitchen and without even thinking began to eat everything. I pulled crackers and peanut butter out of the cupboard along with chocolate chip cookies and milk from the fridge. It seemed like I had a bottomless hole to fill. I tried to stop it, but any conscious-mind protests were run right over by my subconscious mind's need to eat my way back to calmness and an emotional status quo.

Over the next few weeks before the prom, my emotions were all over the place, and so was my eating. I tried to get back to that magical spot on the Weight Watchers plan where I was before the prom invitation. I could be good for a few days, but then the dam would break, and I would binge away all the unfamiliar feelings. I was like a gazelle running from the lion of emotions swirling inside me.

I made my prom dress from a cool Vogue pattern four weeks before the prom. On the night of the prom, I discovered I couldn't zip the dress all the way. I had tried it on the previous week and it fit. It was snug but it worked. Now that zipper wouldn't close! I panicked and began to cry.

My wonderful mother thought fast on her feet and never once brought up what we both knew—I had gained weight. The stress eating had driven me out of my prom dress. Mom handed me a jacket that went pretty well with the dress and covered both the partly unzipped back of my dress and my humiliation.

Anyone who saw me that night at the prom would have seen a girl dancing and having fun. Inside, though, my heart was broken. I had proven yet again that my Weight Struggler beliefs were true. I was a failure. My bad habits hadn't gone away; they were just temporarily dormant. Now they were back with a vengeance. There I was like Cinderella. The clock hadn't struck midnight, but I was already turning back into a weight-struggling pumpkin.

WEIGHT STRUGGLE SUM UP: STRESS AND EMOTIONS

- When struggling with weight, mounting feelings create an internal fight-or-flight reaction that bypasses the conscious mind and its weight loss plans and sends us running to those old calming and comforting eating habits.

- I'm fond of saying, "Life never lines up for us to do well on a diet forever." There are always going to be major events in life, holidays, vacations, and ups and downs that create stress and emotions, both good and bad. We eat as a response to these emotions and get side-tracked off our diet and fall back into our old fat thinking habits and beliefs.

Now that you have been introduced to how our fat thinking circuitry of beliefs, habits, and emotions create powerful walls to hold us in a Weight Struggle Prison, I would like to introduce two parts of the unconscious mind that manage this prison and are responsible for keeping the on-again, off-again, diet cycle going—**THE INNER CRITIC AND THE INNER REBEL**.

CHAPTER 7
YOU BLEW IT, SO SCREW IT!
THE INNER CRITIC AND THE INNER REBEL

"I THINK I MAY BE CRAZY. I think that there is something definitely wrong with how my brain works. Can you help me?" clients often ask me. I always respond, "Tell me more."

"I have had the same weight issues forever. It doesn't make sense because I know what to do! I eat healthfully for a while, but then it's like there is this other part of me that just gets, I don't know, bored, frustrated, or stops doing what I am supposed to do. It feels like there is a part of me that always wants to be thin and healthy but another part of me that wants to be bad, to shut down, and eat. What is wrong with me?"

Have you ever felt like there might be something wrong with you? Like you had multiple personalities when it came to weight management? I know I did. Well, the good news is there is nothing wrong with you. Everyone has different aspects of themselves that influence their thinking and actions in life. Some of them are negative and some are positive.

The bad news is that right now there are two parts of your mind running the fat thinking beliefs, habits, and emotional responses that are leading your struggle with weight. I call these two parts the Inner Critic and the Inner Rebel.

THE INNER CRITIC SAYS, "YOU BLEW IT."

The idea of an Inner Critic as a negative voice is a commonly used term in psychology. For the Weight Struggler, the Inner Critic wants what is best, hates weight issues, and wants to be "normal." The Inner Critic acts like the mean, never satisfied drill sergeant who sees that it's his job to encourage survival by being strict and controlling. In the Weight Struggler's mind, the Inner Critic formed as fat thinking evolved as a survival mechanism to help keep the Weight Struggler in control.

This fat thinking Inner Critic communicates in two essential ways: overwhelming expectations and negative self-talk.

Overwhelming expectations are distorted and impossible to follow through on. The Inner Critic will do anything and say anything to whip you into shape, such as:

- "You must be perfect on this diet!"

- "You cannot touch one bit of sugar this week—none!"

- "You need to lose 20 pounds by the end of this month!"

Negative self-talk occurs when you don't live up to the Inner Critic's impossibly high expectations. The Inner Critic gets upset and says:

- "Why did you eat that? You blew it!"

- "You are so lazy, why didn't you exercise?"

- "You gained two pounds? Ugh, failed again! You are never going to lose weight."

Pretty nice inner dialogue, huh? Our Inner Critic speaks more cruelly to us than anyone would dare to speak to a bitter enemy. The Inner Critic motivates with fear, and, therefore, is not a powerful force for change. In fact, the Inner Critic keeps the Weight Struggler small and thinking that the Weight Struggler is the problem. The Weight Struggler is deficient and needs to be controlled and fixed.

Let face it, the Inner Critic is exhausting and overwhelming, leading that wonderful survival-oriented unconscious mind to create another aspect of consciousness. This one—the Inner Rebel—helps you cope and escape from that tyrannical dictator, the Inner Critic.

THE INNER REBEL SAYS, "SO SCREW IT!"

The Inner Rebel developed as an escape route from the harshness of the Inner Critic and it's overwhelming expectations and negative self-talk. The Inner Rebel wants release from the tension of "being good" and to give in to impulses.

Some psychological terms for the rebel are the "addictive voice" or "inner child." Whatever the title in the outer world, the Inner Rebel sees food as fun, survival, and comfort. Yes, the Inner Rebel just wants to shout, "Screw it! Be bad. Have fun. Live life!"

The Inner Rebel seduces you away from exercise and a healthy eating plan with negative self-communication:

- "Everyone else gets to eat that and have fun, why can't I?"

- "I don't want to get up and exercise. I want to stay in bed where it's warm."

- "But eating chocolate is the only way I will feel better!"

- "What the hell? You already ate one so you might as well eat the rest."

- "What a hard day! You deserve a reward."

- "Relax today. You can start again Monday and be perfect."

The Inner Rebel isn't bad per se, the Inner Rebel is just trying to get back to the status quo and offer protection from the stress of the Inner Critic's restrictions and expectations. The problem, unfortunately, is that the Inner Rebel is going about it the wrong way. Sure, release from the Inner Critic's dictates is a momentarily relief, but ultimately guilt and disappointment arise from eating too much.

The Inner Critic and Inner Rebel are constantly pushing and pulling this way and that. "Be good!" says one. "Come on, be bad!" says the other. No wonder the Weight Struggler ends up feeling overwhelmed and a bit crazy!

THE CHEAT SUMMER

The summer after my freshman year at New York University, I returned to Seattle for the summer to work and attend my big brother's wedding.

My first year away had been an adventure of being independent and away from home in the Big Apple. Even though I was homesick and lonely, I had the constant companionship of my two closest friends, my Inner Critic and my Inner Rebel. They were always with me wherever I went.

My weight continued to creep up as I began eating to cope with the pressure of studying and the stress of socializing. By spring I decided I better get serious. I went on a strict diet with my friend Kim who had been thin her whole life until she gained the well-known "freshman 15."

We supported each other. We walked to our classes instead of taking the subway. We ate only salads during the week, and rewarded ourselves with a cheat day on Sunday.

Our diet was successful. Kim lost 15 pounds, and I lost almost 30. I wanted to lose five pounds more to look great for my brother's wedding. I was slim, but I still didn't like the way my body looked in the mirror. "You can do better," my Inner Critic whispered in my ear.

I remember my Seattle homecoming and how happy I was to be back for a few months. My family was excited to see me and complimentary of my new trim, sophisticated New York persona. "You have wasted away to nothing," my dad said. "Here," my mom said, "I made all of your favorites for dinner!"

As I looked at the table full of lasagna, pork chops, and German chocolate cake, my Inner Rebel started the seduction. "Well, I know it's only Saturday, but maybe since you are home and your mom made all this amazing food, you should make today your cheat day instead of tomorrow."

I ate the homecoming feast and then some, feeling free to eat whatever I pleased, and on Sunday…well, I kept right on eating.

Monday I woke up, feeling gross and bloated. I was sure I had gained all the lost weight back, but I hadn't. I was five pounds from where I was when the plane landed.

"See, now you have ten pounds to lose before your brother's wedding, you big dummy," my Inner Critic sneered. "Don't you have any self-control? No breakfast for you, just start your day later with a salad. Pull it together!"

I sighed and began my salad week. I also started my new summer job behind the counter of an Italian delicatessen in Seattle's Pike's Place Market. Talking all day with customers about what amazing Italian dishes they were going to cook and being in the heart of an international food market didn't help my wired brain shut off thoughts of food. I was good for a few days on my lettuce regime, but I was always hungry and thinking about delicious food.

My Inner Rebel whined, "Look at those cannoli! Why can't we try just one?" My Inner Critic snapped back, "Because you're fat, and those will make you even fatter. They aren't on our plan so just suck it up and move on. Salads only, remember? Salads only!"

By Thursday my Inner Rebel was feeling stifled. "Come on! I am bored. I want to try some of these amazing foods. Let's make today our cheat day, and we can try some of the amazing foods around the market."

The trend is obvious, right? I started each week with good intentions about sticking with my Inner Critic's restrictive regime. Somewhere toward the weekend, though, my Inner Rebel would find a way to escape and eat whatever I'd missed out on during the week.

This went on for weeks until one month before I returned to school I was 35 pounds heavier than I was at the beginning of summer. My family and friends at my brother's wedding didn't mention their dismay at my weight gain, but I could see it in their eyes.

Instead of giving up on my diet, I tried harder. "If you lose a pound a day before school begins, you will almost get back to where you were in June," my Inner Critic pronounced.

What do you think happened? Did I lose a pound a day? No, of course, I didn't. The stress from that pressure just made my Inner Rebel push back more and escape with food.

I can remember the horrifying feeling I had as I got out of the cab in front of my dorm in Greenwich Village. I was ready for my second year of college, but I was nowhere near ready for the looks I got from my dorm mates as they helped me get my luggage out of the cab. Unlike my parents and friends out west, these were New Yorkers who said what they were thinking. "What happened to you, Rita? Oh, my God!" they exclaimed as they looked me and my 40 extra pounds.

I sighed. "I don't know. I went home. The food's good there." My dorm mate Cindy said, "If I were you, I would stay in New York next summer!"

WEIGHT STRUGGLE SUM UP: INNER CRITIC AND INNER REBEL

- About 80,000 thoughts whirl though the mind each day. For the Weight Struggler, many of these thoughts are negative and sabotage any move forward toward success.

- The Inner Critic's expectations are high, as the Inner Critic sees only an out-of-control beast that needs to be tamed and put on a diet.

- The Inner Rebel just wants to let go, keep things the way they are, and indulge in whatever craving or enticing treat comes along, saying, "You deserve it, right?"

- The harsher the Inner Critic is, the more the Inner Rebel pushes back, eating more and more to escape the oppression.

These two characters are the root of those "Being good, being bad" thoughts. Their constant pushing and pulling are what I call the Weight Struggle Cycle. And the back and forth between the Inner Critic and the Inner Rebel only reinforces the Weight Struggle Cycle's power.

Now, there is one last piece of the Weight Struggle puzzle to orient you to—**THE WEIGHT STRUGGLE CYCLE.**

CHAPTER 8
ON OR OFF, ALL OR NOTHING,
GOOD OR BAD

THE WEIGHT STRUGGLE CYCLE

HOW ARE YOU DOING? I hope the Weight Struggle chapters have given you a better understanding of the elements that are creating your personal weight struggle. Now I would like to put all of those elements together and walk you through the Weight Struggle Cycle. This frustrating and self-sabotaging cycle embodies the circuitry of limiting beliefs, habits, and emotions and is run by the Inner Critic and Inner Rebel.

The Weight Struggle Cycle gives us that frustrating feeling of being trapped in this all-or-nothing, good-or-bad, on-or-off-a-diet cycle that makes us feel like we are in this never-ending un-merry-go-round with regards to weight.

Take a closer look at the cycle because soon you are going to learn to escape its prison. In order for you to escape, you need to know how the cycle works.

The Weight Struggle Cycle is broken into two phases:

1. The "Being Good" Phase
2. The "Being Bad" Phase

These phases can be broken down into a sequence of steps that get played out on a subconscious level.

THE WEIGHT STRUGGLE CYCLE: THE "BEING GOOD" PHASE

Here we are at the top of the Weight Struggle Cycle. It usually begins as the Weight Struggler emerges from a being bad phase of going off track and overeating.

Step 1: The Initial Impulse to Lose Weight.

The first step in the cycle is the habitual "I have to lose weight!" reaction to feeling a negative emotion. The trigger to that unpleasant feeling can be external or internal, such as:

- The number on the scale.

- Someone says something about your weight.

- You have an indulgent weekend of overeating and drinking.

- A doctor's warning.

- Realizing a wedding or reunion or the beach season is happening soon.

Step 2: Find Some Method to Lose Weight ASAP.

This next step involves finding a quick solution to get us out of the pain of feeling overweight or out of control and back in charge. This kind of thinking makes us vulnerable to extreme diets or other weight loss methods (fasts, cleanses, exercise regimes, or pills) to get the weight off. Often, we never really stop to think if the method is sound from a health perspective or is reasonable for our lifestyle.

One client confided to me: "If you gave me a bucket of dirt and some water and said I would lose 20 pounds by just eating it, I would have done it to lose the weight and get out of that place of pain!"

Steps 3: Start a Diet and Feel in Control...For a While.

This step in the cycle may go on for hours, days, weeks, or even months if the Weight Struggler gets into a "being perfect" groove. There may even be a kind of diet high—that is, a feeling of being in control—on top of the world! Yippee!

As long as the diet and exercise regime goes smoothly, the Inner Critic is quiet and offers praises for the "good" behavior. And, as long as the scale keeps going down, all is well in the fat thinking world.

Step 4: Willpower Fades.

The next step in the cycle occurs when the will to maintain the diet or exercise plan weakens, as it does in situations like these:

- The Weight Struggler feels deprived of old habits and gratification.

- The Weight Struggler can't eat what everyone else is eating.

- The diet is too restrictive and hard to follow.

- The scale stops going down, and the Weight Struggler doesn't know why.

- Stress and life commitments interfere.

Even short-term successes like these can challenge the Weight Struggler:

- The Weight Struggler loses some weight and fits back into clothes.

- Others say the Weight Struggler looks good.

- The Weight Struggler reaches a more acceptable number on the scale.

In this case, the pain that drove the Weight Struggler to diet has faded. Therefore, his resolve to stay on the diet starts to diminish as well.

With either of these scenarios, the Weight Struggler moves quickly to Step 5.

Step 5: Going Off "Being Good."
Somewhere in the "being good" phase, as willpower or resolve diminishes, the Weight Struggler will inevitably eat some "bad food" (that food being whatever the Weight Struggler's Inner Critic deems is off limits.) The explosion of sugar and/or fat in the Weight Struggler's mouth causes a chain reaction of pleasure. It's as if fireworks are exploding in the brain!

The fat thinking part of the brain kicks into action, and the phone starts ringing again for more of the fattening food. It doesn't take long before the pleasure of enjoying the food gives way to the Inner Critic's shaming admonishments. "Look at what you did! You were doing so good, and you blew it!"

Step 6: Feeling Bad.
It's upsetting to feel like we have blown it when trying to diet. Then the need to seek shelter from the Inner-Critic-induced feelings of guilt and shame arises. That stressful ringing phone of habit now expects and wants more of the fattening and comforting food, leaving a perfect opening for the Inner Rebel to step in and begin his seduction.

THE WEIGHT STRUGGLE CYCLE: THE "BEING BAD" PHASE

There are a few important moments between the "Being Good" phase and "Being Bad" phase. In this short but important time frame, we have a choice to get back on track or give up. Weight Masters will stop, take a breath, and get back on track. This is the key to consistency and weight mastery. (You will be learning how to do this soon—I promise!) Weight Strugglers move on to Step 7.

Step 7 Screw It, Start Over Tomorrow.
This is the most common habit that's wired into the Weight Struggler's brain. There's an almost immediate sense of relief at being off the diet hook and having the license to eat without guilt and shame.

The more times the Weight Struggler falls off a diet, the more the "I blew it, so screw it!" response is reinforced in the Weight Struggler's mind, making the cycle almost impossible to avoid. The pleasure in the release and relief from the restriction of the diet is undeniable. The problem is what follows in the next step.

Step 8 Eat: with Reckless Abandon.
The eating train has left the station and is moving forward with the powerful habit of "eat tonight because tomorrow is deprivation day!"

Without even fully experiencing the taste of food or its initial pleasure, the Weight Struggler gives oneself permission to eat "whatever," which usually means whatever foods have been off limits.

Next, after the Inner Rebel is satiated from eating all that bad food and is groggily sitting in the corner, the Inner Critic wakes up, refreshed and ready to bring on reality. The Weight Struggler now feels guilty and anxious about being so out of control, and reboots the cycle.

WHY DOES BEING BAD FEEL SO GOOD?

So you ate something you shouldn't have and spoiled your eating plan? You promise to start over tomorrow, and all of a sudden you feel great! Here are some reasons why:

1. The promise for future goodness absolves present badness. When our mind anticipates our being good in the future (like going on a strict diet Monday), the neurotransmitter dopamine floods our brain and makes us feel good. In our mind we feel virtuous, as if we were already being good even though it's Sunday night and we are polishing off that last slice of pizza!

2. You pick up the agitating ringing phone of "start over tomorrow." Remember your old friend habit and how a cue, like a ringing phone, triggers the urge to pick it up? "Feeling bad" acts as a trigger that compels us to "start over." Pretty tricky, huh? Just like picking up the phone brings relief from the agitation of the ringing, the mind mistakes the feeling of relief for pleasure or relaxation.

3. You get to break the bonds of a restrictive diet and eat whatever you want! When surrounded by tempting high fat, sugary foods, you may feel a huge wave of additional arousal as your pleasure neurotransmitters become stimulated. Dr. David Kessler in his book, *The End of Overeating*, calls this phenomenon "hyper-stimulation."

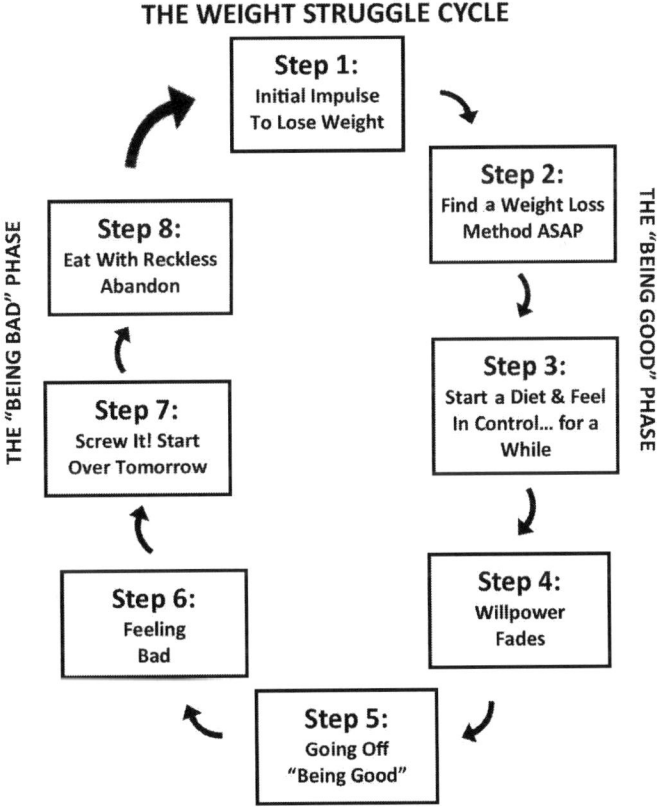

Chart B: The Weight Struggle Cycle

The entire Weight Struggle Cycle may last hours, days, or months, but it all boils down to one thing: fat thinking. It drives the perpetual weight struggle. No diet or exercise regime, magic pill, or combination of foods will cure it. Every time the Weight Struggler goes through the cycle, it becomes stronger.

MAKING THE SHIFT TO WEIGHT MASTERY

Now you understand that it is not necessarily your own personal short-comings that have prevented you from long-term weight success but that over time your mind has become wired with:

- Beliefs

- Habits

- Negative self-talk

The part of your mind that has been wired for fat thinking has grown strong over time. That is why no matter what you do, you keep coming back to the same place of weight struggle. Luckily, as your mind has been wired for fat thinking, you can now shift it to thin thinking and weight mastery.

> ### WEIGHT STRUGGLE SUM UP: THE WEIGHT STRUGGLE CYCLE
>
> - The Weight Struggle Cycle consists of two phases: "Being Good" and "Being Bad." These two phases are made of a pattern of steps that are driven by fat thinking beliefs, habits, and emotions.
>
> - The Inner Critic and Inner Rebel keep the Weight Struggler moving through the steps of this cycle again and again and again.

The next chapter begins the Weight Mastery part of The Orientation and examines how the mind can be shifted from fat to thin thinking and details the specific steps of **DECIDING TO START THE WEIGHT MASTERY JOURNEY**.

THE ORIENTATION:
WEIGHT MASTERY

Ah, mastery… what a profoundly satisfying feeling when one finally gets on top of a new set of skills… and then sees the light under the new door those skills can open, even as another door is closing.

—*Gail Sheehy*

CHAPTER 9
THE DARKEST HOUR IS JUST BEFORE THE "DUH!"

DECIDING TO START THE WEIGHT

MASTERY JOURNEY

W HEN YOU READ ABOUT OR speak to a man or woman who has been successful with weight loss in the long-term, there is usually a defining moment at some point in their "story" where they made a decision to come at their weight from a different place. Instead of struggling with their weight, they decided to take personal ownership for the changes they needed to make in order to get healthy and release weight. In an instant, he or she shifted from being a victim of their weight problem to a master of their weight release journey.

Statistics from the Bureau of Justice show that 77 percent of released prisoners eventually end up back in prison. Is this because the prisoners love prison? No, but prison is what they have become used to, so when they're on the street with nowhere to go and no new way of thinking of themselves in the world, 77 percent get pulled into the same behaviors that landed them in prison in the first place.

Living with a weight struggle is like living in a prison of self-abuse and dysfunction. Unfortunately, painful as it may be, this relationship becomes familiar, even comfortable. Dieting seems to offer a way out, but usually the pull of the unconscious mind, which only knows the familiar beliefs, habits, and emotions of the weight struggle, exerts a powerful pull.

The Weight Struggler is a victim of beliefs that the answer to becoming thin is external. Somewhere out there, something in a pill, a diet, a combination of foods, or an exercise regime will end the struggle.

Psychologists say a person who believes the solution to a problem lies outside of them has an *external locus of control.*

In contrast, a person with an *internal locus of control* believes she has the ability to create the outcomes in life and that her destiny lies in her own hard work and determination. Therefore, the first step toward weight mastery is to make the decision to shift from an external locus of control to an inner locus of control. That is what happened to me on that March morning in my thirtieth year when one small but powerful decision shifted my mind and my weight destiny forever.

MY LIFE IN PRISON

Throughout the 20 years I struggled with my weight, many different and exciting things were happening to me. I received a college scholarship; moved from Seattle to New York; met my husband Simon, fell in love with him, and married; lived with him in London; moved to sunny Los Angeles; and finally settled down.

From the outside, my life appeared happy and normal. Inside, though, was another matter. My fat thinking mind was relentless, keeping me in a weight struggle that never let me fully participate in my life. You could say I was a fairly functional hostage of fat thinking.

My husband and I were close, but my thoughts and obsessing about my weight definitely got in the way of our being intimate. My finances were not the best, because I spent a hell of a lot of money on diet food, products, and schemes. I was obsessed: Thinking about my weight, my body, trying to fix my weight, failing to fix my weight, and then trying something else to fix my weight. At 30, my weight struggle was becoming a full-time career.

I did think I was going insane, but even going to therapy didn't help shift me out of my fat thinking prison. After a few years in therapy, I did get to the root of why I ate. My therapist and I explored my childhood, my insecurities, and my emotions. But unfortunately, I still overate, felt bad, tried to cut back on calories, failed, and stayed in the same old rut of what I now know was a Weight Struggle Cycle.

The Overeaters Anonymous (OA) community offered some relief, but I found the first of the twelve steps of OA—"I am powerless over food"—depressing. How could I feel powerless over something I needed to do in order to live?

I believe in this first step for those with substance abuse disorder or who are addicted to gambling. You can live without drugs and alcohol and leave gambling behind completely. But it didn't make sense to admit powerlessness over food.

I also struggled with the idea of abstinence and having to begin abstaining all over when you had a slip-up. I seemed to go even deeper into an all-or-nothing attitude. My Inner Critic and Inner Rebel must have had a heyday with that one. "I blew my abstinence! I am never going to get OA right. Oh well, I will start again on Monday and be perfect in OA. So, I might as well eat everything that isn't on my abstinence plan until then."

A lot of people find help in therapy and OA, but those roads to freedom were just not the ones that helped me. After trying OA, therapy, and every diet on the planet, I was convinced of three things:

- I am insane.

- I am a failure.

- There is nothing or no one in the world that can help me.

PRISON BREAK

I remember the day my initial "shift" happened. I awoke that morning and immediately got on the scale because I was four days into another diet. Was it going to be a good day? For me, if the scale was down it was a good day. If the scale was up, it was a lousy one. Lo and behold, it was down! Ding, ding, ding! The scale said I won! I was two pounds down!

However, instead of celebrating, I stood there on the scale as the depths of this 20-year nightmarish struggle hit me hard. I felt a wave of grief and fear sweep over me. I was awash in the loneliness of my weight struggle, self-hatred, cruel words, and feelings of deprivation. This was nothing to celebrate.

There I was, standing on the scale like a madwoman in some sort of frenzied need to find my worth in a stupid number. The truth was that even if I did reach my goal weight I knew that I couldn't stay on the stupid diet du jour. I couldn't do it anymore. Forget wanting the thin body part, I just couldn't live in that head anymore, that all-or-nothing, good-or-bad head.

I sat down on that scale in my bathroom in Santa Monica and began to cry. I cried and cried. I cried for the times I beat myself up. I cried for the binges I had been on. I cried for my husband and my family and the relationships I had been "phoning in" because my relationship with my Weight Struggle Cycle had been more important. I cried because I felt alone and scared. There was no one out there who could help me. There was no diet that was going to put things right. There was no therapist or guru who was going to save me.

I cried and cried for what seemed like an hour. Then in a silent moment, a small voice arose inside of me. It was not harsh like my Inner Critic or seductive like my Inner Rebel. This voice, though faint, seemed nurturing and wise. It was coming from a place deep inside of me.

"Never again," it said.

"Huh?" I asked, not quite sure what I was hearing.

"You are never going to diet again."

I sat quietly and listened.

"Stop looking outside for the answer. You have to create the answer within yourself. But first you have to decide not to diet. Decide to become successful and strong instead. You have got to be the source of your own change. You have got to do this…and you can. I believe in you."

I understood this voice from an emotional place. I felt a serenity and calm sweep over me.

This was another part of me that was coming to the front of my mind and communicating so powerfully with me. This new voice wanted to guide me, believed in me, and wanted me to embark on a new path altogether. This was the voice that I now call my Inner Coach.

My Inner Coach was urging me not to diet, not to be a victim of my weight ever again. My Inner Coach was guiding me to leave the weight struggle behind and take back my power from all the diets and other things that I had given it to. I decided to begin my own journey forward.

A few months previously, I had successfully stopped smoking with one session of hypnosis. Until then, I had tried and failed to quit for years, However, once I decided I was a non-smoker in the state of hypnosis I focused on being a non-smoker. There was no tension in being a non-smoker, just the ability to move forward into freedom.

So, I concluded, my Inner Coach was guiding me to decide to shift from my usual way of thinking, which was keeping me overweight and struggling, to a new way of thinking that allowed me freedom and health. In this new way of life, I would focus on feeding myself and moving my body in a way that allowed me to be healthy and slim. I didn't have to be thin to love myself. Rather because I loved myself, I deserved to take good care of myself and learn to master this area of my life and be confident and free.

I needed to shift my relationship to myself, too. I moved from giving my power to diets and food to giving the power to myself. How was I going to do this? I had no idea, but I decided in that moment to begin my journey. I got up off the scale and walked out of the dark, dank prison cell of fat thinking and began my shift into the light of thin thinking.

WEIGHT MASTERY SUM UP: DECIDE TO START THE WEIGHT MASTERY JOURNEY

To begin making the shift from fat to thin thinking, you need to DECIDE to commit to the journey out of the weight struggle and into weight mastery. This puts the power in your hands by shifting your mind from that of a passive victim of circumstances to active creator of your own destiny. This changes how you perceive yourself and your behavior.

MAKING YOUR SHIFT In the Start the Journey section of this book. I will guide you through four distinctive mental shifts, using reading, writing, hypnosis, and visualization exercises. This will allow you to step out of the painful but familiar weight struggle, shut the door on the prison of fat thinking, and move forward on your journey to weight mastery.

....

"I love that I am now in control of my weight destiny. I would never think of myself as a victim of circumstances in other areas of my life, but I now see how much of a victim I allowed myself to be with my weight. The moment I decided to master my weight instead of struggling with it was the moment I knew I would succeed." Kayesha W. (Released 83 pounds, maintaining for 6 months.)

....

Once you have made the decision to leave your weight struggle behind, you are going to need an inner resource to guide you to that new way of thinking and reinforce weight mastery in your subconscious mind. Let's look at how you will begin—**THE INNER COACH**.

CHAPTER 10
SHOWING UP FOR YOURSELF
THE INNER COACH

WHEN ON A JOURNEY OF change, bumping into some obstacles is unavoidable. Weight Strugglers often allow these obstacles to be stumbling blocks, and the struggler gives into the voice of the Inner Critic who says, "You failed again!" Instead of learning from mistakes, the Weight Struggler vows to start over, hoping to do better next time, without ever learning anything except to be more self-critical.

The key to success for most Weight Masters is to shift their negative "I give up!" self-talk into a problem-solving, self-motivating way of speaking with themselves. I call this more evolved self-talk communicating with your Inner Coach.

This way of communicating with yourself creates a powerful inner dialogue that is focused on creating a vision of support and respect. Having a good relationship with your Inner Coach creates a secure and stable foundation. It allows you the respect and freedom to make mistakes, learn from them, and progress forward to weight mastery.

IN SEARCH OF...

The days that followed my decision to shift my thinking were a little foggy at first. The good news was that I wasn't dieting or obsessing about my weight. I wasn't even struggling, because I was now coming from a different place. I wasn't a victim anymore. I was learning and seeking answers for myself. I was, without really knowing it at the time, a student of Weight Mastery. I felt sure that the key to success was listening to this new voice I was finding inside of me.

I remembered a time when my husband Simon and I were living in London a few years earlier. Simon worked for an investment firm while writing his second novel. His boss was a charming man who had a lovely wife. Joan loved to entertain. She often invited us over to their luxury flat in Chelsea for lavish parties where we all smoked cigarettes, drank gin and tonics, and ate super-rich foods. Ah, the good old days!

On one occasion I noticed Joan wasn't smoking and she had also lost weight. I asked her, "How did you do it, Joan? It's so hard to quit smoking, and it's so hard to lose weight. It's almost impossible to do both at the same time. What's the secret?"

"Well," she confided, "I hired someone to follow me around all the time and talk me out of smoking when I wanted to, and pretty soon I quit the habit."

"That's amazing! What about the weight?" I asked.

Joan smiled and replied, "Well, once I stopped smoking, I did start gaining a bit of weight because I was snacking instead of smoking. There was no way I was going to get fat and outgrow my wardrobe. So I asked the same person to come back and follow me around, coaching me to stop eating at inappropriate times. He helped me with portions and motivated me to exercise. Pretty soon I had these new habits down, and voila, I am now doing it on my own," she said, proud of her cleverness of coming up with such an out-of-the-box solution.

I was green with envy. I wished desperately that I had the money to hire someone to follow me around and to tell me when to eat, talk me out of snacking, and encourage me to exercise. If I had a coach following me 24/7, I could be thin and stay thin, too.

BUILDING MASTERY WITH AN INNER COACH

As I began my new Weight Mastery life, I realized what I was developing was something like having this 24/7 coach inside of me. This coach kept me focused on moving toward the kind of life I now saw for myself at my ideal weight. One that was self-respecting, healthy, light, and, above all, free!

Instead of criticizing myself and going on restrictive regimes, I used my Inner Coach to evolve a way of eating. I would honor the tastes I liked as well as satisfy my nutritional requirements and my needs for pleasure, too. And I would still lose weight! I focused on eating enough to feel satisfied but not so much that I felt overly full. I began tuning into the reality of my body and balancing how much food and exercise I needed to create a slow, steady, and pleasurable weight release.

When I went overboard and ate something that seemed bad or ate too much, instead of saying "You blew it, so screw it!" and throwing my eating plan under the tracks, I forgave myself right in that crucial moment. I got myself back on track, knowing the damage done couldn't be worse than going back to that place of struggle.

I thought about teachers I had in high school who believed in me. When I turned in less than stellar work they didn't say, "You blew it! Start 10th grade over!" They showed me where I needed to improve so that I could learn how to do the task better.

My Inner Coach became like those teachers that knew I could succeed. My Inner Coach knew I could succeed at weight mastery, too. My Inner Coach was dedicated to helping me become that person who could live her life at 140 pounds.

By staying connected to my Inner Coach at all times I found something I never had before—CONSISTENCY. I was able to keep taking care of myself and tending to my new skills of feeding myself effectively, moving my body, and staying connected. It felt great and every day I was more confident in my new way of life. Plus, I was developing a wonderful relationship with myself. This broken part of my life was being healed, so was my body, and so was my heart!

INNER EVOLUTION

Months passed. The weight was coming off slowly but surely. I gave myself permission to eat nourishing foods as well as fun foods. However, I ate only enough to satisfy my hunger.

Some days I went overboard, but instead of beating myself up, I figured out how certain foods caused me to want to eat more. (These were the sugary, refined carbs.) I learned that those same foods made me feel sluggish and hungrier when I ate too many of them. I also realized that when I ate more lean protein and beans I felt fuller faster and more even-keeled. I began eating less white foods like sugar and those made of flour.

I avoided them not because some diet guru said I had to, but because I felt better. My eating plan seemed to work for my body.

These revelations came because instead of being stuck in the Weight Struggle Cycle, I was constantly tuning in, making little corrections, and creating new thin thinking wiring that bypassed the old habits. I was focusing on changing from the inside in order to change my outside.

An inner conversation with my coach might go like this: *"Wow I just ate four pieces of pizza, why did I do that? I forgive myself. I won't blow it. I am a smart and good person, so why did I do something like that, knowing it doesn't work for me?"*

Thinking back to before I ate the pizza, I realized that I hadn't had time for lunch. I went to the party starving, and when I sat down to eat, one slice was not going to be enough. What is the lesson I learned? I need to eat something and not feel starved when I am going out, especially for pizza!

This new way of communicating with myself was revolutionary—so freeing and peaceful. Sure, I had bad days when my Inner Critic and Inner Rebel threw me around a bit. But their power over me had changed. With the new and more powerful voices in my head, I could hear behind the harshness of the Inner Critic and the seductions of the Inner Rebel and hear their fear.

They weren't strong and powerful entities that could push me around anymore. They were frightened little children. The more I learned to comfort myself from within, the less these voices reared their heads. They, too, seemed to be comforted by having a new powerful leader—me. And they were just as interested as I was in the path to weight mastery.

WEIGHT MASTERY SUM UP: CONNECTING WITH YOUR INNER COACH

There are many ways that developing an Inner Coach helps you use your mind to begin thin thinking and moving toward weight mastery.

Your Inner Coach:

- **Calms you down.** When you communicate calmly and powerfully with yourself, you take yourself out of the stress that would habitually take you to food in the past.

- **Enables you to learn new habits and beliefs with 100**

percent of your mind. When your Inner Coach asks questions about what doesn't work and what could work better, you engage both your rational brain and your imagination (in your subconscious) to creatively solve problems using 100 percent of your mind.

• **Keeps you focused on moving toward what you want.** Your mind doesn't work backward but is constantly moving forward. This is why negative thoughts like "I don't want to be fat" don't work. Your Inner Coach is constantly moving you in the direction you want to go, as in "I am moving toward being slim, healthy, and confident!"

MAKING YOUR SHIFT In the Creating the Connection with your Inner Coach section of this book, you will be led through a writing exercise and hypnosis session to help you discover your own powerful Inner Coach. During your *30-Day Thin Thinking Practice*, you will develop a working relationship with your Inner Coach. You'll set goals, plan meals and snacks, strategize, problem-solve, and learn as you move toward your ideal weight. You and your Inner Coach are a powerful team. This relationship will be the heart of your weight mastery.

. . . .

"Finding my Inner Coach has been such a life-changing experience. The ability to have positive and rational conversations with myself about weight management is a revelation!! I never realized how capable I am at releasing weight without a diet." Charlene M. (Released 6 pounds in 30 days.)

. . . .

Now that you have been oriented to your Inner Coach, your guide to weight mastery, let's look at **THE NINE SKILLS OF WEIGHT MASTERY** that are going to build the foundation and structure of your Weight Mastery Home.

CHAPTER 11
WHO I AM TO BE I AM ALREADY BECOMING
INTRODUCING THE NINE SKILLS OF WEIGHT MASTERY

Y OU WILL BE HAPPY TO know that success leaves clues, and I have spent a lot of time studying the forensics of long-term weight release. Over the years, I've searched for answers to questions like these:

- Why are some people able to achieve their ideal weight and keep it off and others can't?

- What are the Weight Masters doing...and not doing?

- How are Weight Masters thinking that allows them to have that personal triumph?

I have boiled my findings and observations down to nine skills that Weight Masters have in common. I will share these skills with you at the end of this chapter. For now, I would like to give you a chance to see the humble beginnings from which these seemingly miraculous people came.

The National Weight Control Registry Study qualifies individuals who have released a minimum of thirty pounds and kept those pounds off for one year or more as Weight Masters. Here are some traits Weight Masters have in common:

- Most of them had been overweight since childhood.

- 91 percent said they had a history of dieting and failing. Some gained and lost as much as 270 pounds.

- They lost an average of 66 pounds and kept it off for an average of five years. (16 percent maintained for ten years and some maintained for as long as 67 years)

So you see, even if you have failed once or many times in the past, this research proves that you, too, can become a Weight Master. Masters come from a wide cross section of society. Race, gender, economics, intelligence, and location do not determine success for becoming a Weight Master. There is plenty of room for you to join us!

BREAKING THROUGH

My journey to Weight Mastery kept going. My weight continued to melt off as my Inner Coach helped me use my new thin thinking instead of impulsively acting out. My Inner Coach asked me questions like *"If you eat that cheeseburger, how will you feel three hours from now?"* If my inner reply was *"Full and disgusting, but I want it anyway,"* my Inner Coach might inquire further with a curious tone, *"Could you eat a few bites of it and then choose something more nourishing like fruit?"*

The way this worked was that I got a taste of what I wanted but didn't feel gross and bloated. I wasn't the Inner Critic saying "No, you can't have it!" or the Inner Rebel demanding, "I need it all!" There was a part of me working to find a place of moderation. My new lifestyle was taking hold, and everything seemed to be wonderful until…I hit my first plateau.

Behind every problem is an opportunity and a solution. In the journey to my ideal weight, I was forced to see that everything, even a plateau that goes on for two months, is an opportunity for finding a solution. So even though I hit a plateau, I stayed committed. My thin thinking was more important to me than a number on the scale. As I hovered at 165 pounds for over eight weeks, I learned to dig deeper and ask more questions to create long-term solutions.

Was this the weight I was going to be? I was making healthy choices, exercising, and being consistent. I hadn't binged or started over in five months, which was a miracle to me. What more could I do?

Was there something wrong with my body? Had the years of weight loss finally killed my metabolism? I wasn't greatly overweight anymore, but for health, and admittedly vanity's sake, I wanted to release about 20 more pounds. Grrrr, what could I do better?

I had a friend who was a personal trainer by day and waitress by night. She had been very supportive of my journey and often gave me helpful tips. When I hit my plateau, the first thing she suggested was that I record my food, something I hadn't done before.

"Yeah, it helps," she said. "We forget what we eat sometimes. You probably are eating more than you need to. Also, now that you have lost 23 pounds, you need fewer calories than before just to maintain the loss. To keep losing, you may have to cut back even more. It really is just physics. If you have stopped losing you have to either eat even less or exercise more, and you probably won't get a sense of how much until you record your food and exercise."

"Okay," I said reluctantly. I started writing down what I ate and how much. Sure enough, at the end of the week, when we looked at the amount of calories eaten and the amount of calories burned in exercise, it was clear why I was maintaining weight and not releasing it.

Wow, that was like a kick to the stomach! Here I was thinking I was eating pretty small amounts of healthy foods and exercising a fair amount. Reality had a different idea of how much food and exercise my leaner body needed to keep releasing. I needed to burn about 500 calories more a day with either eating less or exercising more or a combination of both to begin releasing weight again at the rate of about a pound a week.

All of a sudden, I felt resistant to change. *Hmmmm,* I thought. *My thinking is resistant to eating less or exercising more or both. How do I change my thinking around this and keep practicing this new food-tracking skill?*

Here was another turning point in my journey where I had to dig deeper into my commitment.

SHIFTING WITH HYPNOSIS AND THE NINE SKILLS

That is when I decided to begin studying hypnosis and reading about the mind. I began with my old cassette recorder and made tapes of suggestions I could give myself in the state of self-hypnosis. Hypnosis had helped me become a non-smoker. Why not use this powerful mind tool to help me become a Weight Master?

I gave myself suggestions about the amount I needed to eat daily in order to continue releasing and that I could let go of the fear of eating less. I also made exercise more appealing. I worked on seeing myself as a fit and toned person. I used hypnosis to help me believe I was going to succeed even though the evidence from my past and my old beliefs said that I should give up.

I listened to a hypnosis recording in the morning to help plan for the day. In the afternoon, I took a few minutes to meditate and refocus my tired mind on getting through the challenging part of the evening. I listened to a longer hypnosis session as I went to bed at night. These relaxed mind sessions allowed me to focus strongly, and within a few days, my attitude changed. I easily stayed within my new eating and exercise plans and began releasing weight again.

The other breakthrough in awareness that helped me bust through the plateau was understanding that achieving and maintaining my ideal weight wasn't mysterious and magical. My weight success was directly aligned with the skills I practiced day in and day out.

Some of the things I associated with "being good on a diet" were skills that I could hone. Take writing down my food, for instance. At first it seemed cumbersome and "diet-y." But it took on a new meaning when I was using it as a way to be in charge. Tracking my food and exercise calories also gave me an idea of the rate with which I released my weight. Instead of dreading it, I enjoyed developing this skill. It became a fundamental part of my long-term weight release.

Being curious and discovering common behaviors that worked for Weight Masters helped me to see that long-term success was about developing skills and problem-solving. I could develop new slimmer habits to replace the fattening ones. I could see from the success of others that there were certain skills that helped create Weight Mastery—a slim, healthy body and a thin thinking mind. The key is to use these skills regularly.

The Weight Skills

The basic three weight skills are practical and essential tools for long-term weight release. These are the skills that will help melt fat and, if you keep practicing them, keep the weight released from coming back. The research on Weight Masters shows that:

- 98 percent of them modify their food intake. Some lose weight rapidly and some more slowly.

- Many Weight Masters don't follow a diet, and if they do, they eventually modify the structure of the diet to their own lifestyle.

- 78 percent of them eat breakfast.

- Most Weight Masters release weight with a low-fat, lower-calorie way of eating.

- Many Weight Masters use vegetables and fruits as a way to eat more with less caloric density.

- 94 percent of them increase their physical activity.

- 90 percent of them continue to exercise an hour a day to maintain their ideal weight once they obtain it.

It seemed to me that what I call weight skills are the first and most important three steps to being a Weight Master. For weight release to happen, each of the basic skills must be mastered. They are:

1. Living your Life within your Calorie Budget for Weight Release and Maintenance

2. Building a Consistent Relationship with Exercise

3. Creating a Masterful Relationship with Food

The Environmental Skills

Most people make an average of 277 food decisions a day. Weight Masters eliminated many of those choices simply by taking control of their environments and not being victimized by them. This is a huge distinction from relying upon willpower alone.

The research on Weight Masters shows that:

- 74 percent of them monitor their food and exercise during their weight release.

- 50 percent of them continue recording their food to maintain their ideal weight.

- 75 percent of them weigh themselves weekly.

- Many avoid having trigger foods in their environments whether it is the kitchen, the car, the office, or all three.

- Success rates more than double when the person releasing weight has support.

I call the ways in which Weight Masters manage their external world Environment Skills. These skills may look like some of the behaviors you engage in when you're on a diet, but there is a big difference between developing each of them as a skill to practice daily and being a compliant or being a temporary user.

The difference in the shift from fat to thin thinking relies on these skills:

4. Self-Monitoring

5. Stimulus Control

6. Creating a Weight Management Support Team

The Mind Skills

The skills of using your thin thinking mind are the most important of all. With these skills, you create a new way of communicating with yourself that frees you from self-sabotaging patterns. Research on Weight Masters shows that they:

- Learn to problem-solve challenges rather than give up.

- Become adept at censoring negative self-talk.

- Develop strategies to bypass impulsive cravings.

- Break the "I blew it, so screw it!" Weight Struggle Cycle.

These are the thin thinking skills that I extracted from the Weight Masters research:

7. Communicating with your Inner Coach

8. Managing your Inner Critic

9. Managing your Inner Rebel

I realized on my journey that unlike diets that few people can sustain, the Weight Mastery skills work better and better with practice. Occasionally mistakes happen, but the Weight Master has learned to keep going forward. There is no starting over with mastery—just learning and practicing without the fear of shame or failure.

I practiced these Nine Skills daily, using hypnosis to help my mind ingrain these new habits and behaviors so they became a part of me. This was a huge step forward on my journey to Weight Mastery! As I began my clinical hypnosis practice and started helping others, I also incorporated the idea of Weight Mastery and skill building into my practice with clients.

WEIGHT MASTERY SUM UP: THE NINE SKILLS

The Nine Skills are the core common practices and habits of Weight Masters—taken from research studies such as The National Weight Control Registry, the National Institutes of Health's evidence-based guidelines, as well as my clinical observations of what has consistently yielded long-term success for my clients on the Weight Mastery journey.

The Nine Skills of Weight Mastery:

1. Living your Life within your Calorie Budget for Weight Release and Maintenance
2. Building a Consistent Relationship with Exercise
3. Creating a Masterful Relationship with Food
4. Self-Monitoring
5. Stimulus Control
6. Creating and Maintaining your Weight Management Support Team
7. Communicating with your Inner Coach
8. Managing your Inner Critic
9. Managing your Inner Rebel

- Weight mastery comes from focusing on building these skills within yourself and engaging the brain in a different way. When you think of weight mastery as an ongoing learning process, the way you approach weight management changes.

- Hypnosis helps open up your change-resistant subconscious mind. It helps replace old useless patterns with wiring for new healthy ones.

- Meditation helps create mindfulness of our current thoughts and an ability to shift the focus of your thinking toward a vision of the Weight Master that you are becoming.

MAKING YOUR SHIFT In The Nine Skills section of this book you will learn about these mastery skills and be given strategies to apply them to your daily life. The *30-Day Thin Thinking Practice* part of the process is designed to allow you to incorporate these practices into your life and have them become an easy and habitual part of you and your life.

Good news! You will never have to be perfect on a diet again in order to release weight permanently. Weight success is about embodying skills and practicing them over time. This practice will build your confidence, grant you independence, and instill a feeling of accomplishment. Isn't it about time you feel good about your ability to manage yourself in this area of your life? Don't you deserve to be the boss of your own healthy, fit body and the life that supports it? I know this was the shift for me that finally made the difference and it can now be the same for you.

··

"I found that the Shift Weight Mastery Process not only gave me the skills to release weight but also to keep it off permanently. Eating regular foods, I was able to release 8 pounds during the 30 days even though I was on vacation for eight of them." Veronica L. (Released 78 pounds, maintaining for 2 years.)

··

Now it's time to move forward and put all the pieces of weight mastery together and look at **THE WEIGHT MASTERY JOURNEY**.

CHAPTER 12
FROM FAT TO THIN THINKING

THE WEIGHT MASTERY JOURNEY

ARE YOU BEGINNING TO SEE that the path to having a slim and healthy body is an inside job? That the steps to weight mastery begin inside your mind and not outside of you in a diet?

Unlike the Weight Struggle Cycle that keeps you in the un-merry-go round-feeling of yo-yoing from good or bad, on or off, all or nothing, the steps of weight mastery form a long-term journey forward for the rest of your life.

THE WEIGHT MASTERY JOURNEY

The following list of steps is in the order with which you begin your journey.

Step 1 The Weight Struggle Cycle.
At the beginning of the journey, you are typically starting in the prison of your own fat thinking, limiting beliefs and habits—stuck in the Weight Struggle Cycle. At this point, your mind is wired to keep things playing out in this frustrating all-or-nothing, good-or-bad, yo-yo weight pattern.

Step 2 Start the Journey.
Now you make the powerful decision to leave your victim-based, Weight Struggler mindset behind and take control of your weight mastery. By making four mental SHIFTS (Forgive, Decide, Vision, 100% Belief) in this process, you begin breaking up the old fat thinking wiring that has kept you stuck by changing your mental focus and seeing yourself in a new light. You take yourself out of your Weight Struggler Cycle prison

and start out on the road to weight mastery as an open-minded and open-hearted apprentice.

Step 3 Meet Your Inner Coach.

Now that you are beginning your journey from fat to thin thinking, you need a guide, an inner voice of reason and wisdom that can inspire you and lead you through releasing your weight and achieving your ideal weight and weight mastery. This new way of communicating with yourself is focused on problem-solving, learning and adjusting, and improving old fattening behaviors. This new rational, self-respecting, strategizing, and solution-thinking way of interacting with yourself gives you consistency and long-term staying power. So that even in those moments when you want to give up and say, "I blew it, so screw it," this part of you can "show up" and help you keep going and staying consistent.

Your Inner Coach has been with you all along, but its voice has been masked by the louder voices of your Inner Critic and Rebel. This step in the Weight Mastery Journey allows you to hear that voice, connecting you to your Inner Coach to create a new inner communication system that will guide you to success.

Step 4 Practicing the Nine Skills of Weight Mastery.

During the *Shift Weight Mastery Process*, practicing the Nine Skills builds a foundation for thin thinking. Remember, these skills are the behaviors and mental processes of people who have achieved significant weight releases and have maintained their weight for more than a year.

Consistently practicing Weight Mastery skills may sound overwhelming, but think of all the skills involved in, say, driving a car. With practice, those driving skills become automatic, and you barely think of them consciously. The same is true of the Nine Skills of Weight Mastery. They evolve from something you have to think about specifically to becoming a part of who you are.

When you become masterful at anything in life, you use the skills involved in that activity continually to maintain them. Likewise, no matter how long a Weight Master has been maintaining a healthy, ideal weight, the Weight Master continues to use and hone the Nine Skills.

Step 5 The *30-Day Thin Thinking Practice*.

It takes about 21 to 30 days to create the roots of new habits and beliefs. The *30-Day Thin Thinking Practice* was designed to give you the support and structure to begin shifting from fat to thin thinking. Once you begin to think of yourself as the Apprentice, with your Inner Coach as your guide, you will begin to use your Nine Skills within the *30-Day Thin Thinking Practice* and begin "building your Weight Mastery Home." This is the foundational network of thin thinking wires—the new habits, beliefs, and systems that will support your weight release, help you achieve your ideal weight and maintain it.

During these 30 days you will use daily meditation and hypnosis to program these changes into your deeper mind so that they become permanent. By the end of the 30 days you will:

- Be releasing weight at a rate you decide.

- Feel free of the cravings and fake hunger of out-of-balance eating.

- Have begun breaking the Weight Struggle Cycle..

- Be engaged in daily habits and self-supportive communication that allows you to stay consistent on your continuing journey forward.

Research shows that when you reinforce new healthy behaviors, the less prominent the neurological pathways of bad habits will become. By day 30, your new thin thinking wires will be established and getting stronger as the old, fat thinking wires weaken and fade.

Step 6 Continue Releasing Weight, Reach Your Ideal Weight, and Maintain a Healthy Weight.

This step is pretty straightforward. So why has releasing weight and maintaining the loss been so hard in the past? Because when you diet, you usually focus solely on losing weight and not on establishing the mastery habits and communication skills that allow you to be successful in the long run. By embarking upon a journey to weight mastery you are changing the lens with which you see yourself. You are no longer one who struggles but one who is consistently mastering a healthy, slim, and confident lifestyle that allows you to live life at your ideal weight and be your best you.

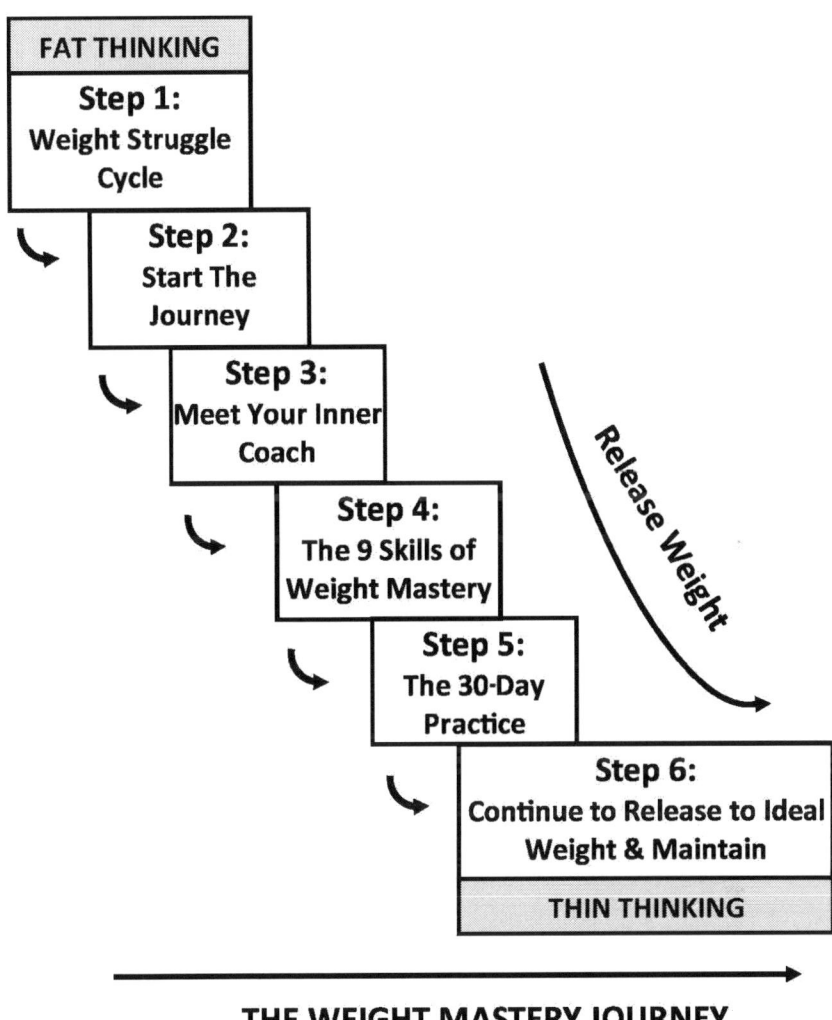

THE WEIGHT MASTERY JOURNEY

Chart C: The Weight Mastery Journey

NEVER STOPPING, NEVER "STARTING OVER"

So there you have the Weight Mastery Journey! You can see that it is quite different from the Weight Struggle Cycle. There is no stopping and starting over as with the Weight Struggle Cycle. The Weight Mastery Journey keeps you moving forward toward a slim and healthy body and confident thin thinking mind. (**Chart C**)

SANITY OVER VANITY

I like to say "Choose sanity over vanity." What I mean is that although releasing weight is wonderful, ultimately it is your rational, respectful, and confident relationship with food, exercise, and yourself that is the most thrilling part of weight mastery. Yes, the skinny jeans are great on the outside, but it's who you have become that is more beautiful and interesting on the inside.

I began my journey over 20 years ago when I made the decision to take back my power and said "No more!" to diets. I saw a vision of what my life could be—slim, healthy, and free. Little did I know that this journey would open the door to a new relationship with myself. Not only was my weight going to change for the better, but everything else in my life would improve as well.

The day I stood on the scale and saw I had reached my goal of 140 pounds, I didn't celebrate. It was a busy day. My life was full. Indeed, I now had a life! I was training to be a hypnotherapist, knowing that what I wanted to do was help people take back their power and shift into weight mastery.

A few months later, I still weighed 140 pounds. This was a plateau I was enjoying being on! After years of rushing to the scale and hoping that my weight would be down, I was quite at peace with it reading the same weight day after day. Sure, the glamour and thrill of the dramatic weight losses were gone, but so was all the drama and pain.

I will be honest and say that the scale has moved up and down three to five pounds over twenty years. There have been days, weeks, and even months that didn't look so good, and my eating habits started to swing back to some of my old ways. But because of my relationship to my Inner Coach and my commitment to continuing to practice the Nine Skills, I was always able to stay on my Weight Mastery Journey. I'm 5' 9" tall, and my weight has ranged from 139 to 144 pounds for two decades.

WEIGHT MASTERY SUM UP: THE WEIGHT MASTERY JOURNEY

- Unlike the Weight Struggle Cycle that keeps you in a frustrating cycle of "on" or "off" behavior, the Weight Mastery Journey is focused on continually honing the weight, environment, and mind skills that allow you to release weight and keep it off long-term.

MAKING YOUR SHIFT During your *30-Day Thin Thinking Practice,* you will incorporate the Nine Skills into your life and learn to depend on your Inner Coach. Over the 30 days, these new practices and healthy living habits will become second nature. You will lose weight and the old struggle will soften.

The 30-day program of daily writing exercises along with the hypnosis and coaching resources available online will help keep your mind in thin thinking mode as you begin releasing weight and feeling confident in your new emerging weight mastery.

"After years of struggling and feeling like a failure I can finally check this one off my list." Dina E. (Released 45 pounds, maintaining at 3 years.)

My personal Weight Mastery Story has caught up with the present time. Let's take a moment in this final chapter of Part I, The Orientation, to be inspired to continue on to Part II of the *Shift Weight Mastery Process—* **START THE JOURNEY**. This is where things get exciting, so follow me.

CHAPTER 13
IT'S YOUR TURN

START YOUR SHIFT WEIGHT MASTERY PROCESS

You HAVE NOW HEARD ALL about me and my shift. You've also learned how your mind works in this area of your life and why you struggle despite knowing what to do to manage your weight. Now you're ready to start your own journey and step out of the Weight Struggle Cycle. I couldn't be more excited for you.

You have separated yourself from the pack of Weight Strugglers who keep looking for the fast and easy weight-loss solution. They want the change to happen to them rather than creating a change within themselves. In Part I, The Orientation, you learned that the key to your weight-release success is in your shift from fat to thin thinking. You are now ready to get up from the virtual "comfy chair in my office" and begin unleashing your powerful mind for thin thinking.

OPEN YOUR MIND AND HEART

The *Shift Weight Mastery Process* recodes your mind step by step. Don't worry. It isn't mind control. You will be doing your own recoding. I've written this book to lay everything out for you in a way that makes it easy and fun. I've made all the mistakes and taken all the wrong turns so you don't have to.

The *Shift Weight Mastery Process* has many graduates who have been living their lives at their ideal weight for years. They made the choice to make this journey and gave it their all. Now they are continuing to reap the rewards day after day, month after month, and year after year.

I'm going to repeat what I said several times in The Orientation.

You have to be all in with this process. If you skim, skip, or leave out sections, I cannot assure you the success I know you can have. Why would you skimp on yourself? Are you ready to leave all of the frustration with your weight behind once and for all? Give yourself a huge gift, the gift of life outside the Weight Struggle Prison. The key is in your hand, and you can unlock the door by giving yourself the chance to SHIFT 100 percent.

GOOD STRETCH MARKS

There will be times as you complete the next two parts of this book when you may feel stretched beyond where you normally would stop. There might be times when you feel confused. You may have feelings that are outside your normal realm of experience. You may feel confronted, sad, ecstatic, overjoyed, overwhelmed, and even pissed off. I invite you to not only welcome everything that arises on this journey but to embrace it all.

These stretching points are good! Let me remind you that the mindsets and behaviors that have seemed comfortable to you have also kept you exactly where you are—struggling and frustrated.

Don't back down when you have uncomfortable feelings. Stretch past them. Be stronger, more courageous, and more determined than you ever have been in your life. You are about to stretch into a new way of thinking and behaving that not only will give you health at a lighter weight but also self-esteem and freedom.

FINAL NOTE OF ENCOURAGEMENT

I cannot share with you the awe and gratitude I have for my own weight struggle. It opened a door into my life for mastery that I would have never opened if I had been naturally thin.

In the creation of my own weight mastery, I became the person I always felt and dreamed I could be. I consider myself far luckier than all of the naturally skinny people of the world. I wake up every day feeling grateful for the opportunity to become more masterful as I continue this journey.

I respect you so much for opening the door in your heart and stretching it wide to make this powerful journey for yourself. Remember, I am here with you every step of the way. Alone we diet, together we SHIFT!

Let's move forward and get going with Part II of your process: The Shift. We are going to dive in with **START THE JOURNEY**.

PART II

THE SHIFT

Progress is impossible without change, and those who
cannot change their minds cannot change anything.

—*George Bernard Shaw*

THE SHIFT
START THE JOURNEY

Happiness is not found in things you possess, but
in what you have the courage to release.

—*Nathanial Hawthorne*

CHAPTER 14
BEGIN WITH A BREATH

THE SHIFT BREATH

I WANT YOU TO KNOW THAT you have just crossed your first mental hurdle: You have begun! I know it may seem crazy to shift out of a struggle that may have spanned years or even decades of your life with a 30-day process, but your mind is equipped to adapt very quickly once you put it on a new road.

This part of this process is specifically designed to get you started on the journey of shifting out of the weight struggle into weight mastery. You're going to make these specific mental shifts.

1.   Forgive Yourself

2.   Make Your Decision

3.   Create your Weight Mastery Vision

4.   Shift to 100 Percent Belief

INSTRUCTIONS: START THE JOURNEY

- **Grab a journal or notebook and a pen and plan to actually use them!** During this part of the process, there will be specific points where you stop to engage in thinking and writing. Please do not pass over these exercises because writing helps your mind process. Give yourself the value of the experience.

- **Go to the Online Resource Center at www.FromFatToThinThinking.com.** There you will find additional resources to augment your Start the Journey process. Head over there now to get started before you begin reading.

- **Download the "Start the Journey" hypnosis recording** that you will listen to at the end of this section. This will also be found in the Online Resource Center.

TAME THE LOSER

Maybe you're a little impatient and saying "C'mon, Rita, let's get to the part where I lose the weight. How do I do that?"

I invite you to thank that impatient part of you for sharing and know that this is the fat-thinking dieter wiring in your mind. It wants a quick fix and to keep doing what it knows how to do best.

Before beginning the weight release part of the process (It's coming, I assure you!), you need to prepare yourself to be mentally ready for it. Besides, you know where that other diet path leads you. You've been there, done that a million times. Try saying "Thank you fat thinking brain, you have worked so hard. Why don't you take a little nap while I proceed with my Weight Mastery Process? That nap is long overdue!"

Start right now by taking a deep breath and being present. I call this deep breath the "Shift Breath."

THE SHIFT BREATH

Try this:

1. Breathe in through your nose to the count of five.

2. Hold for a count of two.

3. Breathe out through your mouth to the count of six.

Ahhhh. I hope that felt nice. In addition to feeling nice, the Shift Breath literally intercepts whatever old fat thinking neural loops are active in your unconscious mind. The Shift Breath creates a pause, a moment of relaxed suspension outside the mind's old wiring. This allows you to be present in the moment.

Once present, you can easily access your rational mind. That is where you can engage in powerful thin thinking. This deep breath also creates a complete oxygen exchange that massages your central nervous system. In short, the Shift Breath is very calming!

You can use the Shift Breath to interrupt an old behavior or thinking pattern and shift out of it.

- You find yourself mindlessly reaching for a cookie on the counter—PAUSE—SHIFT BREATH—put the cookie back, and continue on your way.

- You find yourself speaking negatively to yourself. "You are never going to be thin!"—PAUSE—SHIFT BREATH—Replace it with a new positive belief. "I deserve to be healthy and slim."

- You are about to mindlessly start quickly eating a meal— PAUSE—SHIFT BREATH—take a moment to notice the meal, smell it, appreciate it, and begin eating slowly and mindfully.

- You are stressed and tired at your desk, thinking that chocolate is the cure—PAUSE—SHIFT BREATH—tune in to yourself, your emotional state, and take a few more SHIFT BREATHS— feel yourself beginning to relax and also notice that need for chocolate disappearing as you give yourself what you really need—a break!

Try the Shift Breath again. This time, breathe in through the impatient, fat thinking loop that just wants to get to the weight loss tips and go on another diet. Inhale to the count of five. Bring yourself to the you who is present and ready to forge a new path to permanent weight release. Pause to a count of two. Exhale through your mouth to a count of six.

Well done. Now you're present and in the moment ready to begin thin thinking. Go to Shift 1—**FORGIVE YOURSELF**.

CHAPTER 15
FORGIVE YOURSELF
BEGIN WITH AN OPEN HEART AND MIND

"WHY WOULD I FORGIVE MYSELF?" is a question I hear from many men and women at the *Shift Weight Mastery Process* seminars. I know they're also saying to themselves, if not out loud, "If I were stronger, had more willpower, and wasn't so weak, I wouldn't be overweight. I don't need to be forgiving myself; I need to be tougher on myself. If I forgive myself, then things will get worse and all hell will break loose."

The reason I begin with forgiveness is that Weight Strugglers live in a relatively constant state of disappointment about themselves and have a fairly high dose of disrespect. They have let themselves down in the weight department so many times that there is little trust left. Like a cheating lover or a lying friend, they learn to close their hearts to themselves as a protection from the pain of their relationship with themselves.

If you've been struggling with your weight, my guess is that you look at your past sins broadly, bundling them all together in accusations like these:

- I never follow through.

- I have no discipline.

- I give up too easily.

This distrust also causes stress. And, as you've learned in this book, stress keeps your mind stuck in a prison. Researchers have found that when people adopt a compassionate approach to themselves, they are also willing to take responsibility for mistakes. Compassionate acceptance makes a person more likely to learn from the experience, too.

In order to make this journey, you need to learn to create a powerful and connected relationship with yourself, one built on trust and respect.

CASE STUDY: LAURA BREAKS DOWN THE WALL

Laura, a lovely, fair-haired woman in her late forties, had been a Weight Struggler for 30 years. She raised her hand during the Forgive Yourself discussion at the seminar and asked, "Why would I forgive myself? My inability to get a handle on my weight has pretty much ruined my life. I have developed pre-diabetes, I don't have a social life, because I don't feel good about the way I look. Yet, despite my unhappiness, I'm not able to put down the fork. If I forgive myself, isn't it just sending my subconscious a message that my lack of discipline is okay?"

"Thinking that would make rational sense, Laura," I answered. "But when we are upset with ourselves, it's hard to want to be on our own team. Try this. Take a deep breath and close your eyes. Think of a loved one or friend with whom you have been angry. Allow yourself to feel that anger. Notice how that anger creates a wall of resentment between you and the other person. Now, imagine him or her asking you for a favor. How do you feel about their request?" I asked.

Keeping her eyes closed and staying with the exercise, she said, "I am thinking, 'Why would I want to do this person a favor?'"

"Exactly, you don't want to cooperate." I continued, "It is exactly what happens when you hold anger at yourself for your weight struggle."

"Take another breath and imagine forgiving that person, not for any reason other than to forgive her because it makes you feel better. Breathe into that feeling and imagine that wall of resentment between you and the person melting. Do you feel more connected to that person? Let that warmth and peace well up within you. Are you there?"

Laura nodded. I kept going. "Now imagine this person asking you to do her a favor. Notice your willingness to help that person. Take a deep breath and open your eyes. How do you feel?"

Laura smiled. "I am so much more willing to help someone with whom I feel connected." Tears welled up in her eyes as she said, "I have been so mad at myself. It's like I have had no room for myself in my heart. I have put a part of me in a dungeon, because it is so dysfunctional and bad."

"Do you see how you could break down that dungeon wall with some compassion? You need 100 percent of Laura to go on the journey of weight mastery. Can you forgive and accept all of yourself and trust that you can be successful?"

Laura could and did! By the time she completed the *Shift Weight Mastery Process*, Laura had released ten pounds. Over the following year, she released another 38 pounds.

"I understand that my success is not about me being good but of having a profound, accepting relationship of myself, the strengths and weaknesses. The more I accept myself, the more I can lovingly work with my weaknesses and make them stronger. I have a big space in my heart for myself that I never had before, and this space is what makes my thin thinking stronger." Laura D. (Released 48 pounds, maintaining for five years).

FORGIVE YOURSELF EXERCISE

This exercise melts the barrier of ill will and distrust that you're holding within. Replacing those criticisms with self-love and acceptance permits you to move forward on your journey to weight mastery.

Use your journal and pen for this exercise. Please make sure you do this, and don't cheat yourself of this valuable experience.

1. **MY ANGER AND RESENTMENT WITH MYSELF AND MY WEIGHT STRUGGLE**

Make an Anger and Resentment List of the ways that you feel you have failed or let yourself down with regards to your weight. Write down in your journal whatever pops into your mind and don't self-edit. Let the answers surface from your unconscious. (You can use the Anger and Resentment Prompts I have listed below if you need guidance.)

NOTE: Leave a blank line below each Anger and Resentment listing in your journal—you will be writing something else there in a moment.

ANGER AND RESENTMENT PROMPTS

- **Physical** Are there any physical or medical issues that you have as a result of your weight struggle? Are you upset with yourself for having that issue? (This may be an obvious lifestyle-related, medical issue, such as type 2 diabetes, arthritis, high cholesterol, or kidney stones. Or it may be an issue that's a result of your weight-loss attempts, such as bariatric surgery or liposuction.) *For example: I am mad at myself for having bad knees as a result of my weight.*

- **Emotional** What emotional challenges have you experienced as a result of your weight struggle? Has your struggle caused you shame or depression or made you to feel like a social outcast? *For example: My weight has caused an intimacy issue between me and my husband.*

- **Quality of Life** In what ways has your weight struggle kept you from living the life of your dreams? Have you put off pursuing a life-fulfilling goal because you want to wait to be thin before giving yourself permission to do it? Do you lack confidence because of your weight struggle? *For example: I have put off going back to school until I lose 30 pounds.*

2. MY FORGIVENESS OF MYSELF AND MY WEIGHT STRUGGLE

Take each item that you listed in your Anger and Resentment List and write a Forgiveness Statement below it. After writing each Forgiveness Statement, use a Shift Breath to bring the forgiveness in and let the resentment out.

For example:

- Anger and Resentment List Item: I have back pain due to my struggle with weight.

- Forgiveness Statement: I forgive myself for having back pain due to my struggle with weight. (Shift Breath—inhale in forgiveness—exhale out resentment)

NOTE: You may not feel like you have fully forgiven yourself in the writing or breathing exercises. That is okay! I assure you that change is happening. There will be an opportunity for you to do this on a deeper level in the upcoming Start the Journey Hypnosis Session.

It may feel a bit strange to forgive yourself, but I assure you it's addictive, especially when you begin to experience peace in your mind and heart along with the health and slimness that comes with it.

WEIGHT FORGIVENESS AND ACCEPTANCE

Now that we are on a forgiveness roll, I invite you to do one last courageous bit of forgiving. Write down whatever you weigh today, and forgive yourself for your weight. Accept that this is where you are right now, and it is okay.

Our shame about weight is often enormous—perhaps more weighty than the weight itself. That's why this process is designed to help you learn to use your weight in a way that removes the emotion, guilt, and pressure.

Please write down your current weight in the space below. If you don't know it because you have thrown away your scale, then take a guess. As you dive deeper into this process, I will ask you to weigh yourself. It will help your mind stay in thin thinking and lessen any fear or dread about knowing your weight (There will be more on this later.). For now, take a deep Shift Breath and write down your weight or your honest guess.

My current weight is:

During the *Shift Weight Mastery Process,* you are going to do what I describe as "love yourself down the scale." This is one of my favorite sayings. Weight Strugglers often are trying to lose weight so they can love and accept themselves when they achieve their ideal size or weight. This disconnects Weight Strugglers from loving themselves as they are right now in the current moment. What a crime!

You deserve your love and respect today—not sometime in the future. By giving yourself love, you create an acceptance of who you are. This opens up your fat thinking mind for deep change. Therefore, the last step in this exercise is designed to help you accept yourself today.

LOVE YOURSELF DOWN THE SCALE EXERCISE

Repeat each of the following statements out loud to yourself. When you finish the statement, take a Shift Breath, bringing the energy of the statement inside your mind and heart. If powerful feelings come up, repeat the Shift Breath a few times. Please let any emotions surface in your awareness. Notice any resistance to an emotion and stretch through it. You are creating new thin thinking wiring!

- I forgive my current weight and accept it. It is where I am today. (Shift Breath)
- I deserve to love myself no matter what I weigh. (Shift Breath)
- I forgive myself for struggling with weight. (Shift Breath)
- I accept that I am ready to move forward with myself on my journey of weight mastery. (Shift Breath)

Congratulations. You are now ready to move on to Shift 2—**MAKE YOUR DECISION**.

CHAPTER 16
MAKE YOUR DECISION

TAKE BACK YOUR POWER

WHERE WOULD YOU LIKE TO spend the rest of your life?

A. Living in a Weight Struggle Prison? Stuck in the perpetual confines of the Weight Struggle Cycle, day after day, year after year.

B. Living in a Weight Mastery Home? Living a comfortable, slim life of weight mastery with confidence, health, freedom, and wisdom.

If you would rather live in a Weight Mastery Home, you must make the decision to leave your Weight Struggle Prison and begin building your new home of weight mastery.

Why is making the decision to be a Weight Master so important? It allows your mind to commit to a different path and move forward on that path. I want you to be certain about your decision and have complete ownership of it, so let's weigh your options (no pun intended).

THE WEIGHT STRUGGLER VICTIM FILTER

You learned that when you are stuck in fat thinking, you view weight through a Weight Struggler's belief filter.

- Weight loss is hard.

- I don't have time to be healthy.

- Other people get to eat yummy things and be thin—why can't I?

- Why bother?

The Weight Struggler filter of life chips away at the struggler's faith in their ability to be successful. The Weight Struggler is always looking outside of themselves for a solution, giving power over to other people, diets, fasts, and cleanses.

If you're locked into the Weight Struggle Cycle of "going on," "falling off," "being good," or "being bad," you've become a victim of your own fat thinking.

- I have no willpower!
- I am lazy.
- I will always struggle.
- I shouldn't even try!

How exhausting and painful the Weight Struggler filter is!

THE WEIGHT MASTERY FILTER

According to Mark Lewis, professor of developmental psychology and author of *Memoirs of the Addicted Brain*, new neural pathways form at the expense of others that are no longer needed. So when you begin to forge thin thinking beliefs and habits and reinforce them over time, they become dominant and the fat thinking beliefs and habits weaken.

When you decide to commit to the path of weight mastery, you refocus your mind's attention on a different empowered way of seeing yourself, your body, food, and exercise. You are no longer a victim of your weight.

- I decided to make my weight and health a priority. I am in charge.
- I create the time to exercise and get healthy.
- I am designing a way of eating that I enjoy and that helps me become and stay slim.
- My health, confidence, and peace of mind are worth it!

THE MIND OF THE APPRENTICE

Now I know you may be thinking how can I be a master at weight? Fear not, your mastery journey doesn't require that you start as a master. All masters at one point began as an apprentice.

Guess what? When you decide to become an apprentice of thin thinking and weight mastery, there is no starting over because you were "bad" or went off your diet. Can you imagine a medical student getting a D on an exam and saying "I blew it! I am going back to day one of medical school and starting over!" No, they look at what didn't work, make corrections, and move on so that next time they will know how to avoid mistakes.

As an apprentice of weight mastery, you choose to see the world and your experiences as chances to learn, improve, and try things out. If something doesn't work, you can try something else. As an apprentice, you can become confident in your ability to sustain your weight release and maintenance long-term, because releasing weight isn't something you are doing on the outside. It is something you are becoming from the inside.

CASE STUDY: MIKE'S DECISION

"What if there are some upsides to my weight struggle?" Mike, a 38-year-old, high school history teacher asked during a *Shift Weight Mastery Process* seminar. He had experienced a health scare and wanted to shed eighty pounds.

"I obviously want to master my weight, but this relationship with the struggle has been going on forever. I admit sometimes it's easier to hide out behind the weight."

"I am glad you mentioned that," I said. "There are upsides to the struggle, like hiding out. We don't have to live up to others' expectations. We can be invisible."

I asked Mike, "Do you have 'bad' students who have become accustomed to bad grades and are afraid to change, even though they know that better grades would make their future so much brighter?"

"Sure," he said smiling. "I see what you are getting at. These kids are like me, hiding out because they are afraid of the extra work it takes to be a good student. I can literally see their minds freaking out at the idea of the homework and studying they would have to do to get a good grade just as I am freaking out at the idea of working for weight mastery."

"So with your students who struggle, do you just let them keep failing?"

"Of course not. I try to help them by teaching in a fun way. Giving them new material a little bit at a time, so they aren't overwhelmed. If they can fall in love with learning the subject rather than being a good student and getting an A, then they usually do start enjoying themselves. If they improve, it builds their confidence, and they can turn themselves around."

"So, Mike, what if weight mastery wasn't about getting an A, but it was about learning about managing your weight in a way you could enjoy and do, bit by bit? What if you could make mistakes but keep moving forward and improving? Suppose you then began to lose weight and feel better physically and emotionally? Wouldn't you be more confident? Could you look at it that way?"

Mike smiled. "Okay, if I expect my students to do it, I can do it, too."

Mike made the decision to become a Weight Master and committed to first being an apprentice. He dropped by my office, while riding home on his bike, a few months after hitting his goal weight. He looked happy and completely transformed.

....

"I finally was able to become a learner rather than a struggler. I took it slow and didn't go for the A. I kept learning and making mistakes, but instead of starting over, I kept learning. I learned how to live in a way that keeps me eighty pounds lighter than I was before. That was a pretty good lesson that I know I can't unlearn." Mike J. (Released 80 pounds, maintaining 3 years.)

....

MAKE THE DECISION EXERCISE

Okay! Now it's time for you to decide on the path of the life you want to live.

Weight Struggler

- Victim mentality
- Stuck in yo-yo Weight Struggle Cycle
- Run by fear and shame
- Seeing mistakes as failure

Weight Mastery

- Apprentice mentality
- Consistent weight release and maintenance in the Weight Mastery Journey
- Run by self-support and self-respect

- Seeing mistakes as opportunities to learn and improve

Remember either choice is valid. You know which one I am hoping you will choose, but make the decision from your heart.

Take a deep breath and drum roll, please…what path do you decide on? Circle your choice!

THE WEIGHT STRUGGLE JOURNEY The journey of Weight Struggler stuck in the perpetual Weight Struggle Cycle.

THE WEIGHT MASTERY JOURNEY The journey of an "apprentice" of weight mastery living a slimmer life, full of learning, adventure, confidence, health, and freedom.

If you chose The Weight Struggle Journey, I understand and no hard feelings.

If you chose The Weight Mastery Journey, congratulations! You are now an apprentice of weight mastery and are ready to move to the next step.

When you begin your life, you get a birth certificate. When you graduate from school or training, you get a diploma. When you begin your life as an apprentice of weight mastery, you need to make it official with yourself. How many diets have you started as a knee-jerk reaction to feeling fat and then you forgot you were on a diet the second the brownies were presented?

This contract represents a powerful decision. No matter what, you are now an apprentice on a lifelong journey to release weight and master the skills and mindset that will keep you at your ideal weight for the rest of your life.

APPRENTICE OF WEIGHT MASTERY CONTRACT

9/6/23

I, (name)_____Lisa Eckberg_____am now an apprentice of weight mastery.

By being an apprentice, I commit to learning, evolving, and improving my relationship with food and exercise, my body and myself.

I am shutting the door on the prison of my weight struggle, choosing the path of weight mastery instead. I am ready to begin my journey, and by signing this contract, it means that I will never turn back or start over.

I will participate fully, keep an open mind (and heart), stretch, and push myself past where I normally stop, because where I stopped kept me in the struggle and living the same predicable outcome over and over again. I also promise to have fun and enjoy the journey as I release weight and achieve weight mastery!

Sign here: Weight Mastery Apprentice: _Lisa Eickberg_

Date: _9/6/23_

Good work, Apprentice. Take a deep Shift Breath and seal the deal. If it's okay, I will call you "Apprentice" from now on? Being an apprentice of weight mastery gives me such joy and a wonderful daily attitude. I am glad you are now initiated into this powerful club. Move forward now with confidence to Shift 3—**CREATE YOUR VISION OF LONG-TERM WEIGHT MASTERY**.

CHAPTER 17
CREATE YOUR VISION OF LONG-TERM WEIGHT MASTERY
CREATE YOUR PATH TO SUCCESS

NOW THAT YOU HAVE DECIDED to be a Weight Master, it's as if you are standing right outside the prison door of your weight struggle and are facing your pathway to weight mastery. You are now going to light the entire path ahead with different visions for each part of your journey. Say the two following statements to yourself in your head:

1. **Fat Thinking Statement.** "I am going to try to lose some weight for my beach trip next month. I hope I can be good, because I don't want to be the fat whale beached on the sand."

2. **Thin Thinking Statement.** "I have a vision of standing in the waves 30 days from now in my red bathing suit. I feel strong and lean, having released eight pounds. My arms are firm and my tummy feels tighter. I enjoy running on the beach feeling free and confident in my slimmer body. I jump in the water and play with my kids. I feel good in my skin."

Can you see how the first statement turned off your mind, while the second one engaged it? That is because the fat thinking statement is filled with negative imagery. In contrast, the thin thinking statement subconsciously creates a detailed vision of you in a positive light. It's a vision that prompts a good feeling.

A WELL-LIT PATH TO YOUR DESTINATION

A 2013 study funded by the National Institutes of Health concluded that overweight and obese women ate less when they imagined themselves as slimmer in enjoyable future scenarios before they ate.

What is a vision? It's like a big billboard in your mind of where you want to be. By creating a vision of how you ultimately want to see yourself look and feel, you direct your unconscious mind to be like a map—a step-by-step guide from your location today to tomorrow. If you don't have an end point, the application in your mind can't do its job properly.

When you envision your life at your ideal weight, both your conscious mind ("I wish to create this outcome.") and your subconscious mind ("I can feel what achieving this goal is going to be like.") engage with each other. With 100 percent of your mind working in synchrony, you begin to figure out how to achieve your vision.

Having a vision creates excitement, too. Your subconscious experiences a reward, so your brain gets a little hit of dopamine, which prompts a strong sense of pleasure, which it wants to obtain again.

When you are stuck in fat thinking, you don't have an appealing vision, and there is no reward. You not only don't imagine what you want, but most of the time you also are defensively living life, "hoping" and "trying" to lose weight, armed only with willpower. Remember willpower is only 12 percent of your mind's power. The fat thinking approach to weight release is like trying to make your way through thick brush without a path and only a very dim flashlight.

What Is Ideal?

What weight would you like to live at for the rest of your healthy life?

The words "ideal weight" sound nice and dreamy, don't they? It may be a few pounds away or two hundred pounds away. Wherever you are, give your mind the opportunity to figure out what your ideal weight is.

I've heard many people in my clinical practice tell me goal weights that are extreme or unrealistic. I ask them, "Why did you choose that weight?" They often reply, "Well, it seems like a good number." I can tell they haven't thought about what it might take to sustain that lower weight. Some clients in their 50's tell me an ideal weight that was what they weighed at 16!

I like to use the term "loving and reasonable ideal weight." What I mean by that is a weight that you can comfortably maintain with the amount of food you feel comfortable eating on a daily basis and the amount of physical activity you can realistically sustain.

Ideal doesn't necessarily mean stick thin. For many men and women, the ideal weight is going to be a slimmer, healthier, more toned version of themselves. Understand, though, that your basic body shape is not going to change when you release weight. If you have wide hips, you will still have wide hips.

I think it is important to be clear that a Weight Master embraces reality and loves his or her body for what it is. Having a loving and reasonable ideal weight releases you from unrealistic expectations that will only set you up for disappointment down the road.

I had a client who at 70 said that it was hard to make the shift because she would start saying "Who cares? No one is looking at me anyway. I might as well eat those brownies."

Who cares? You care! Don't you want to live in a body you appreciate and love and care for? More importantly, don't you want to live in a mind free of the frustration of a weight struggle?

My ideal weight—the weight I have maintained for 20 years is about ten pounds above some of my more extreme goal weights of the past. However, I find this weight allows me to keep myself out of the health risk zone and feel light and slender, toned, healthy, and strong. I'm not stick thin or emaciated.

My current shifted weight is the natural by-product of the amount of exercise I do and my eating healthy and nutritious meals for the most part. It allows for the fact that I have a husband, kids, and an active social life and I love to cook and entertain. My weight supports my life, and my life supports my weight. That is what I call my loving, reasonable ideal weight. I urge you to think about this as well, when you think of your ideal weight.

If you are feeling challenged because you have no idea what your ideal weight might be then you might Google "Body Mass Index (BMI) chart." There are many programs that help you figure it out. You input your height and weight, and an online calculator gives you a good estimate of a healthy weight range for your height and age.

Also, the American Diabetes Association defines "Ideal Body Weight" as:

MEN: 105 pounds for the first five feet plus six pounds for every additional inch above.

WOMEN: 100 pounds for the first five feet plus five pounds for each additional inch above.

Research shows that even if you release only ten percent of your current weight, you will be improving your health immensely. So set a goal that inspires you rather than scares you and work with that. You can always adjust later.

IDEAL WEIGHT EXERCISE

Close your eyes and imagine being at a weight that feels healthy, stepping on the scale, and seeing that number. How does that feel? Good, comforting, unbelievable? How does your lighter, slimmer body feel standing on the scale? Take a deep Shift Breath and open your eyes. You can adjust your ideal weight goal at any time if that first number feels unrealistic.

My ideal weight goal is: ____155____ lb

Now that you have your ideal weight in place, you can engage your mind in very specific visions of yourself at various points along your weight release journey and beyond. In forming a vision for yourself, you're also etching new neural pathways in your brain that begin making thin thinking circuits to the desired outcome.

THREE VISIONS, ONE JOURNEY

These three visions work together to create a mental pathway to your slender, healthy, and long life.

1. **Short-Term Vision**

This vision is a definable milestone that is possible to reach in the near future. I recommend setting a short-term vision milestone no further out than three months. Your milestone could be a date, an amount of weight release, or a certain fitness goal (e.g., walking your first 5K.) However, your first milestone, my dear apprentice, will be finishing your *30-Day Thin Thinking Practice*!

2. **Ideal Weight Vision**

Have you ever thought about the actual difference in the "you" that supports your fat thinking weight and the "you" that is living the life of your thin thinking, slender self? Your ideal weight vision is the future "you" when you achieve your ideal weight.

I know it may be hard to imagine that image right now, especially if your ideal weight seems like a faraway goal. But by beginning to create a vision in your mind, you also begin to make it real. It's not some far-off goal in the back of your mind that is easily dismissed.

3. **Lifelong Mastery Vision**

I like to think of this particular vision as the stuff heroes are made of. By making this journey to permanent weight mastery, you are becoming a hero. This is a vision of you having sustained your loving and reasonable ideal weight over a long period of time.

Imagine how impactful achieving your ideal weight and sustaining that weight release over five years (for example) will be not only to you but your family, friends, and community. This vision is really exciting because it changes how you perceive yourself not only in the area of weight but in the area of leadership as well. When you release weight and keep it off long-term, you become a source of inspiration for others around you.

CASE STUDY: SANDY'S SALSA STORY

Sandy was stuck in a place that you may have experienced. She was focusing on what she didn't want. "I don't want to be fat. I haven't thought about what my thin life will look like. I can't do anything until I get out of this suit of blubber I am wearing. I can't look for a better job. Who would hire me looking like this? I can't date right now. Who would want me?" Others at the seminar nodded with understanding of Sandy's frustration.

I explained to Sandy and the group that not wanting to be fat was not an effective way to use the mind. "The mind doesn't process negatives. So by concentrating on what you don't want, you are creating more of it."

"When you say 'I don't want to be fat,' your mind is attending to the words "want" and "fat." Instead, I explained, "You want to concentrate on what you do want. That way the mind can see it and start to move you in that direction."

I asked Sandy to close her eyes and take a deep Shift Breath. As she did, I said, "Imagine you have achieved your ideal weight. Tell me what you see. Where are you? What do you look like?"

Sandy replied with her eyes still closed, "I see myself at a club dancing.

I am wearing a cool red dress. I'm confident and enjoying salsa dancing on the dance floor. I am even dancing with someone!" She opened her eyes and asked, "Is that a good vision?"

"Dancing is a great vision because your dancing will also be a great way of maintaining your ideal weight once you achieve it. How does that vision make you feel now?" I asked.

"I'm excited and determined. I love to wear beautiful dresses, to be feminine and to dance. I don't let myself do any of those things, because I am ashamed and mad at myself. I don't think I can have fun until I get skinny," she said.

"Really? That's too bad. Here is my invitation. Start dancing now."

"What?" she cried. "No way! I can't go out when I have 40 pounds to lose."

I argued, "Dancing is a great way to burn calories, and guess what? You don't have to go out to a club, start dancing at home. Don't wait until that magical day when you get on the scale at your ideal weight to move your body in the free and fabulous way you described. You have to love yourself down the scale. Give yourself permission to live today. The more you enjoy the journey, the more you will want to keep going."

Sandy took my advice and during her *30-Day Thin Thinking Practice* began dancing at home as her daily exercise. As she danced around her apartment, she was releasing weight in a fun way that was in line with her vision. She released ten pounds during her 30 days and kept going toward her ideal weight vision. Eventually, she ventured out to dance at clubs on the weekends.

On one of those weekends, Sandy went with her girlfriends to a local club. She was 20 pounds from her goal on that Saturday night when she met Roger at the free salsa lesson. Both beginners, Sandy and Roger became friends and would meet to dance twice a month to practice their moves. Then they started dating officially. By the time Sandy reached her ideal weight vision, she and Roger had been dating for three months. She celebrated fulfilling her ideal weight by buying a red dress and dancing with Roger at their favorite club. Sandy has continued dancing into her long-term weight mastery for almost three years now.

....

"Until I saw and felt what life could be like, there was never really any joy in losing weight. My vision opened my eyes to the fact that my weight release

journey wasn't just about losing pounds. It was about bringing my dreams to life, which helped me sustain my ideal weight. It has been the most creative endeavor in my life!" Sandy G. (Released 38 pounds, maintaining 4 years.)

What would it be like if you made your ideal weight so real in your mind that when you achieved your goal, it seemed like a natural part of who you are. You were practicing being this ideal weight all along? Let's get started.

VISION SHIFT EXERCISE

This exercise requires writing down your three visions, so please grab your journal, and on a new piece of paper, leaving plenty of space beneath each vision name, write Short-Term Vision, Ideal-Weight Vision, and Long-Term Weight Mastery Vision.

NOTE: You will also be guided by me in the Start the Journey Hypnosis Session to imagine these three visions. Writing them down now will help you use them later in that hypnosis session.

Important Tips for Creating Your Visions

See it. Be patient with your imagination. Sometimes you can see certain things more clearly than others.

Feel it. Sometimes you cannot see your vision as well as you can feel it. If this is true for you, pay attention to the feeling part of the vision. For instance, ask yourself, "What will it feel like to slip easily into a pair of pants I couldn't get into last year? What would it feel like to have my daughter put her arms all the way around me?"

Hear it. You may be able to engage other senses like hearing. For instance, "What will it feel like to hear how proud my husband is that I am finally healthy?"

Create Your Short-Term Vision

Imagine a specific place and time 30 days from now. You have completed the *Shift Weight Mastery Process*. Close your eyes and imagine it fully, as if you are really in that place and time. What are you wearing? Where are you? Who are you with? Or, are you alone? What are you doing in the scenario? How much weight have you released? How do you feel? How does your body feel? Open your eyes.

Write what you see in your vision. Do not worry about spelling or how it sounds. Write from your heart.

_____

_____

Take a deep Shift Breath and bring your 30-Day Short-Term Vision deep within you. Allow it to be the new map that guides your unconscious mind.

Create Your Ideal Weight Vision

Imagine a specific place and time in the future when you have achieved your ideal weight. Imagine it fully as if you are really in the place and time right now. What are you wearing? Where are you? Who are you with? Are you alone? What are you doing? How much weight have you released? How do you feel? How does your body feel? What is your life like now that you have achieved your ideal weight? What dreams are you living? How have your relationships with yourself, your family, friends, and others improved? How has your health improved? How has your self-confidence improved? How have your finances improved?

Open your eyes. Write what you see in your vision. Do not worry about spelling or how it sounds. Write from your heart.

_____

_____

Take a deep Shift Breath and bring your Ideal Weight Vision deep within you. Allow it to be the map that guides your unconscious mind.

Your Long-Term Weight Mastery Vision

Imagine yourself in a specific place five years from now. You have maintained your ideal weight. What are you wearing? Where are you? Who are you with? Are you alone? What are you doing in the scenario? How do you feel emotionally? How does your body feel? How is life different after maintaining your ideal weight for five years? How has that affected your health? Your confidence? Your self-esteem? Your feelings of peace and self-mastery? How has your long-term release affected others in your life? How do they view you differently? Has your mastery affected them in a powerful and positive way? How has your weight mastery affected your community? How are you a leader for health in your own life?

Open your eyes. Write what you see in your vision. Do not worry about spelling or how it sounds. Write from your heart.

Take a deep Shift Breath and bring your Lifelong Weight Mastery Vision deep within you. Allow it to be the map to guide your unconscious mind.

Good work. With your powerful mastery visions lighting the way, you can see clearly for miles! Take those first steps out onto the path. The path is solid and strong. Now let's move on to Shift 4—**100 PERCENT BELIEF**.

CHAPTER 18
100 PERCENT BELIEF
MOVE FORWARD WITH CONFIDENCE

O NCE UPON A TIME, YOU did not know how to walk. Walking upright is a complicated system of strength, balance, coordination, and skill. Today you walk without thinking too much about the mechanics of each step.

Watching a toddler learn to walk is fascinating. They are fearless in how they get up, fall down, and get up to try again. What keeps them going? Belief. They see other people walking, and their little brains say, I can do that, too."

The toddler doesn't say, "I have failed 20 times to stay on my feet today, which means I am never going to walk!" No, he keeps on believing he will walk no matter what with 100 percent conviction. And guess what? The toddler learns to walk!

How many diets have you started with the 100 percent belief that you were going to be successful at taking the weight off and keeping it off for the rest of your life? Does that number begin with a zero? Does it end with a zero as well? I thought so.

Okay, Apprentice, take a breath and reflect. So far you have forgiven yourself for struggling, decided to embark on the journey to weight mastery, and imagined your visions. You need one more thing—fuel to get there and build your thin thinking home of weight mastery. That fuel is belief.

CURRENT WEIGHT SUCCESS BELIEF EXERCISE

Let's hop right into this exercise. You're going to read the question below and produce a number in response. It's crucial that you take the number that first pops into your mind. The number will be your UNCONSCIOUS answer, your immediate gut response to the question. (If you think too much about it, your answer is conscious and will not serve its purpose.) Ready?

CURRENT WEIGHT SUCCESS BELIEF EXERCISE

On a scale of 0 percent (no belief in success) to 100 percent (no doubt that you will be successful), what percentage represents your belief in your Weight Mastery success at this moment? Enter your belief percentage here: __75__ percent

Good! If you said, for example 63 percent, that would mean that 63 percent of you believes in your ability to succeed with weight mastery and 37 percent has no belief that you will succeed. I call this 37 percent Limiting Beliefs.

Get to know a little bit about the gap between your Limiting Belief percentage and 100 percent belief. The limiting beliefs holding you back are roadblocks to your future success. You are now going to shift right over all of those barriers.

EXCUSES, REASONS, AND STORIES, OH MY!

Before the printing press existed and before movies were made, ancient tribal people sat around campfires and told stories passed down to them from one generation to another. Stories still help us understand history, how things happen, and the rules of the culture we live in.

Chances are you have in your mind a story of all the reasons you struggle with weight: The who, where, when, and why of it. Your weight tale helps you process and make sense of your struggle. You become attached to it, as painful as it may be. Your story probably has some elements common to other Weight Strugglers' stories. For example, here is my story.

RITA'S WEIGHT STRUGGLE STORY

The beginning of my story. In second grade, at the age of 7, I realized I had a weight issue when I noticed my thighs were bigger than those of the other children in my class.

The first diet or attempt to stop the weight struggle. My first diet was the 1970s Scarsdale Diet of toast, grapefruit, and all the meat I could eat!

The biggest humiliations. I couldn't fit into my prom dress. My roommates almost didn't recognize me after the rapid weight gain of my freshman summer.

How the weight struggle made me feel like a failure. I felt weak. I was a failure. I thought I must be crazy because I knew what to do to lose weight, but I didn't do it. My mind and body seemed to be broken, since I always failed!

Limiting beliefs of why I will never succeed. My limiting beliefs were: I like food too much. I don't have time to exercise. I hate sweating. I need lots of food to feel full. I can never be thin when I am like this.

You can see my Weight Struggle Story was quite a page-turner! Even though there was a lot of pain in my story, I was very comfortable and familiar with the reasons I would not succeed. More importantly, there was absolutely no room for any belief! I couldn't succeed with this struggle story hogging up all the space in my head.

My Weight Struggle Story was not only about my past. It was about creating my future, too, because my beliefs and assumptions were what I brought with me on any weight loss attempt.

It's time to explore your own Weight Struggle Story. Dig down deep and discover what weighty tales you have spun and what power they currently have over your future success.

WEIGHT STRUGGLE STORY EXERCISE

Answer the questions below quickly. Try not to edit yourself, and let your responses flow.

MY WEIGHT STRUGGLE STORY

Take a piece of loose paper or a new page in your journal and write on the top: "My Weight Struggle Story." Take all the space you need to write your answers to each of the questions below.

The beginning. How old were you when your Weight Struggle Story began?

___

How did you first know you were overweight? How did you feel about being overweight?

___

What were the many ways in which you tried to solve your weight struggle? List the diets, fasts, cleanses, and any exercise programs you did to release weight and the results.

___

What was the biggest humiliation associated with your Weight Struggle Story?

___

In what ways has your Weight Struggle Story made you feel like a failure?

___

What limiting beliefs do you have about your ability to release weight successfully?

___

Are you beginning to see the way our Weight Struggle Story holds power over us? Weight Strugglers carry that heavy history with them wherever they go. Every weight loss attempt becomes another chapter in our story with failure the predictable ending.

EVIDENCE FOR FAILURE OR FODDER FOR SUCCESS

Did you know that Abraham Lincoln lost races for the Illinois State Legislature, Illinois House Speaker, US Congress, US Senate, Vice President, and US Senate before running for and winning the office of President of the United States? Do you think Lincoln let losing all those races define him as a failure, or did he use those races to build his belief in his ultimate success?

In the National Weight Control Registry (NWCR) study, 91 percent of Weight Masters failed many times, losing and gaining an average of 270 pounds, before finally becoming successful. Instead of using past failures of their struggle story as proof that they would never be successful, they shifted how they saw their past. They reframed their histories of weight struggle as a part of their journeys to weight mastery.

The term reframing means reimagining how you interpret an action or thought so that it can empower you instead of taking your power away. By reframing your Weight Struggle Story, you can shift your belief in your long-term weight release success skyrocketing to 100 percent.

CASE STUDY: DANA'S DOUBT KEPT HER DOWN

Dana is a pretty brunette and a successful person. She's a mother of two children, has a wonderful marriage, and enjoys a thriving career. But when I asked Dana what was her percentage of belief for Weight Mastery success, her number was 27 percent.

"I will never believe I'll be a success at Weight Mastery because I have failed so many times. There is a big part of me that knows I am going to be a failure again," she told me.

I asked Dana, "Are there other times in your life when things didn't go the way you wanted, but the setback ultimately created a breakthrough of some sort?"

Dana said, "My husband and I went through a very rough patch in our marriage after the birth of our second child. Our son was born with special medical needs. I spent most of my time caring for and paying attention to him. It wasn't intentional, but my husband and I grew apart and often argued. My husband seemed jealous of the attention I was giving my son. It was a very dark time in which we both were struggling with whether we wanted to stay married."

"So, what happened?" I asked.

She said, "We decided to get some help, and things really changed. Today our marriage is better than it ever was. We learned how to work together as a team. We also learned to have more empathy for each other and recognize how hard it is to parent a child with special needs. Our family life is so much happier because we went through that challenging time and were forced to shift our thinking."

"Dana, can you see how that dark time was really a part of your successful marriage story?" I asked.

Dana paused for a moment. You could read on her face the new perspective of her weight story that was forming in her mind. "So, you are saying that everything, all of my failures with my weight so far, are ultimately a part of my long-term Weight Mastery success story?"

I nodded. "At any time we want, we have the power to reframe the dark times that we have gone through during our weight struggle and reframe them from a different perspective as building blocks for our weight success story, allowing ourselves to believe with 100 percent that we can achieve weight mastery. So can you reframe your struggle and see it as part of your own successful Weight Mastery Journey, Dana?"

"Yes, I am now seeing that all of the diets I went on and all of the times I broke the diet and gained back the weight and all of the frustration I have felt with myself over the years has been preparing me to be finally figure things out for myself and release the weight once and for all." Dana smiled, "I feel like I have just released a 100-pound weight from my heart!"

....

"I am so relieved that no matter what happens on my journey, I will never fail again. I believe that 100 percent! 'Failure' is a word I have wiped from my mind for good." Dana C. (Released 70 pounds, maintaining for more than 2 years.)

....

WEIGHT MASTERY STORY EXERCISE

Are you ready? Now it is your turn to SHIFT your perceived failures of the past and use them to write your story of 100 percent belief. With the following exercise, we are going to use your past as building blocks for future success. How? By reinterpreting your Weight Struggle Story and reframing your conscious and unconscious beliefs.

I will show you how I shifted my Weight Struggle Story into my Weight Mastery Story as an example.

RITA'S WEIGHT MASTERY STORY

When did your Weight Mastery Story begin—how old were you? I was seven and in the second grade. I looked at my thighs hanging over the chair and noticed that no one else's thighs did that. It was the beginning of my journey around weight that brought mastery into my life.

(See how I shifted the beginning of my Weight Struggle Story to the beginning of my Weight Mastery Story?)

When you focused on weight loss in the past, what worked for you?

- Eating protein for breakfast keeps me feeling satisfied for many hours.

- I need a treat after dinner. If I give myself one, I won't overeat later at night.

- When I exercise four times a week, I want to eat healthfully.

- When I eat less than three servings of bread or starch I feel better, and I am less hungry.

- Eating salads and veggies are the best way for me to feel full for fewer calories.

- Support from friends and family helps me stay accountable and feel a part of something bigger than myself.

There are many things I found out from dieting and multiple weight loss attempts that I used as I began shifting from fat to thin thinking. I bet you, too, know many things that work for you from your past experiences. You can look upon these discoveries as part of your ladder to success.

What internal or external roadblocks in life have kept you from long-term success?

- Not planning ahead for the weekend.

- Thinking I was cured once I had lost weight.

- Celebrating weight-loss successes with food.

- Allowing myself cheat days.

- Emotional eating when on the phone with my parents.

- Coming home from work hungry.

Recognizing the habits and beliefs that held you back in the past will allow you to solve them in the future. This also makes them a part of your success story.

How was your weight struggle a journey of self-discovery and fodder

for your weight mastery? My weight struggle taught me that my health and my ability to show up for myself and be my own best friend are more important to me than overeating and eating decadent foods.

MY WEIGHT MASTERY STORY

Take another piece of loose paper or use a fresh page in your journal and write on the top: "My Weight Mastery Story." Take all the space you need to write your answers to each of questions below.

During this process, please work with an open mind and push past the resistance to fall back into limiting beliefs like "this won't work." I will be prompting you with questions to help your mind "see" yourself and your Weight Mastery Story differently than your Weight Struggle Story.

When did your Weight Mastery Story begin—how old were you? (This answer would be the same time as your Weight Struggle Story that you wrote down earlier.) It was the beginning of a powerful learning process of what works and doesn't work for you and weight mastery.

_____

When you released weight in the past, what worked for you? (List things you learned that you could apply now.)

_____

What internal or external roadblocks in life kept you from long-term success?

_____

How has your weight struggle been a journey of self-discovery and fodder for your weight mastery?

_____

Are you feeling lighter now that the struggles of the past are gone and that you are now aligned with your success story? Let's now officially turn up that dial to 100 percent!

Read the directions and close your eyes: Take a moment and imagine a dial with all the numbers on it from 0 percent to 100 percent. Imagine the dial arrow is pointed at the percent number that you began with at the beginning of this chapter. Now I would like you to imagine that you are turning up the dial from that number to 100 percent belief. Now, take a nice deep Shift Breath and lock that 100 percent belief in your mind!

Throw Away the Weight Struggle Exercise

This is one of my favorite exercises at the *Shift Weight Mastery Process* seminars. I have everyone take the piece of paper on which they have written their Weight Struggle Story, crumple it up, and throw it in the trash.

Doing this symbolically rids them of that heavy story. It was not serving them in any way and cluttered their precious brain space like a piece of trash!

Directions: Crush the paper on which you've told your Weight Struggle Story into a wad and THROW IT IN THE TRASH. You are now leaving that legacy behind you. You no longer need it, phew!

START THE JOURNEY REVIEW

Excellent work, Apprentice. You have completed the final Shift in your Start the Journey process.

Please confirm that you have:

- **Forgiven yourself** so that you can reconnect with yourself and love yourself down the scale.

- **Made the decision** that you are an Apprentice of Weight Mastery, leaving the struggler behind.

- **Created your mastery vision** and have stepped on the path to your ideal mastery weight and life.

- **Turned up your belief to 100 percent** so that you are moving toward long-term permanent weight release.

Great job. Give yourself acknowledgement for the SHIFT you have made so far. You are ready to move forward to your first hypnosis session—
START THE JOURNEY HYPNOSIS.

CHAPTER 19
HYPNOSIS SESSION #1

START THE JOURNEY HYPNOSIS

YOU ARE NOW READY TO begin the first hypnosis session in the *Shift Weight Mastery Process*. It is called Start the Journey. This hypnosis session is a wonderful end to the processing that you have done thus far. Hypnosis takes the work you completed in this section to a deep, subconscious level. I hope that you are excited!!

Remember, hypnosis is not mind control but a way of refocusing your mind and attention. Your conscious mind will still be present and acts as a filter for your subconscious so you cannot be made to do anything that is not aligned with your conscious desires.

INSTRUCTIONS

- Go to www.FromFatToThinThinking.com to access your Start the Journey hypnosis session.

- Listen to hypnosis only while you are in a relaxed position.

- Listen with an open mind that is expecting 100 percent success.

- DO NOT LISTEN TO ANY HYPNOSIS SESSION WHILE DRIVING OR OPERATING HEAVY OR COMPLEX MACHINERY.

- Expect to feel relaxed; don't expect to feel "hypnotized" in some out-of-body experience.

If you fall asleep, try the session in a less relaxed position next time (sitting more upright). However, hypnosis can make an impact even if you listen while you are asleep

Enjoy your hypnosis. When you finish the session, meet me at the next phase where we will find your guide—**YOUR INNER COACH.**

THE SHIFT
CREATING THE CONNECTION
TO YOUR INNER COACH

Tell me and I forget, teach me and I may
remember, involve me and I learn.

—*Benjamin Franklin*

CHAPTER 20
AT LAST, MY COACH HAS COME ALONG

MEET YOUR INNER COACH

W ELCOME BACK FROM YOUR FIRST hypnosis session! I hope you enjoyed the relaxed mind state and felt a shift starting to happen within you. Everyone's first experience with hypnosis varies, so whatever you experienced is perfect. After the first hypnosis session at *Shift Weight Mastery Process* seminar, a man once told me: "I heard everything you said during the session, but I am not sure I 'went there.' My mind was kind of all over the place."

I assured him that even when your conscious mind may wander during a session, your unconscious mind is listening and shifting. This man went on to release 50 pounds in the first year after the seminar. Thus far, he has maintained his weight release for five years. So even if you didn't think the first hypnosis session "worked," keep going and using this powerful mind tool. I assure you it makes a huge difference.

INSTRUCTIONS: MEET YOUR INNER COACH

- **Continue to have that pen and your journal handy.** You will be writing.

- **Go to the Online Resource Center at www.FromFatToThinThinking.com.** There you will find additional resources to augment your Meet your Inner Coach process. Head over there now to get started.

- **Download the Inner Coach hypnosis recording.** Listen to it at the end of this section. This recording will also be found at www.FromFatToThinThinking.com in the Online Resource Center.

MEETING YOUR INNER COACH

I bet you have no problem coaching, nurturing, or problem-solving for others and in certain areas of your own life where you are functioning well. But around the area of weight management, you probably are more accustomed to hearing your restrictive and condemning Inner Critic and your resistant and instant-gratification-seeking Inner Rebel.

This communication system has kept you riding the same un-merry-go-round of the Weight Struggle Cycle for years. Beginning at this moment, you are going to start a new dialogue between you and the wise, patient, rational, Weight Master within.

At first, the idea of working with an Inner Coach might seem like a stretch, but I assure you that not only will your coach's guiding voice become a part of you but also by the end of your *30-Day Thin Thinking Practice* this powerful way of communicating with yourself will become a natural and welcome part of your life. You will become hooked on the wonderful feeling you get from this special relationship with this aspect of yourself.

CASE STUDY: LEANNE TURNED THE NURTURING ON HERSELF

Leanne struggled with the same 20 pounds from her high school days through her thirties, losing and gaining it numerous times. Over a six-year time span, she had three children, gaining weight with each pregnancy. When she came to the *Shift Weight Mastery Process* seminar, Leanne was 50 pounds over her ideal weight. She hated how she looked and that she had been gradually going up in her clothing size. Her husband was also putting pressure on her to lose weight, which stressed her enormously. Not only did she have an Inner Critic but an outer one, too!

At the seminar she bravely raised her hand when I asked for a volunteer for the Meet Your Inner Coach exercise. She told the group, "I'm not sure about finding my Inner Coach. I think she has moved to the moon, but I will try."

"I know you might think that," I said, "but with three kids, you are coaching most of the time, right?"

"Yes, I guess that's true, but that doesn't involve me dealing with myself. I think differently when it comes to my kids. Their health and happiness is my priority," she said.

"Would you talk to your kids the way you talk to yourself about your eating challenges?" I asked.

"No, I am more cruel with myself than I would ever be with anyone in my life. I call myself 'lazy pig' and 'hopeless.'"

"Well, instead of being your worst enemy, you have a chance to be your own best friend. Are you game to bring your Inner Coach back from outer space?"

Leanne smiled and nodded.

"Okay good. Close your eyes and take a Shift Breath. Tell me about the vision you had of yourself in the long-term ideal weight exercise."

Leanne smiled and answered, "I see myself on vacation with my family in about five years. We're in the mountains where we go every summer. I'm slim and strong. I'm swimming off the dock in the lake with my kids. I'm not self-conscious in my bathing suit. In fact, I feel great, and my kids are proud of me for keeping the weight off and changing my life. We are a healthy family, and I am definitely leading the kids in feeling good about themselves and their bodies, too."

I asked Leanne to go further with this vision, and said, "This image of you is what I want you to cultivate as the image and essence of your Inner Coach. What does your Inner Coach sound like in this image? How do you imagine her sounding as she speaks to you?"

"She definitely has a reassuring, wise tone to her voice." Leanne's voice cracked with emotion. "I feel a little tug at my heart that something is going on inside of me that is warm and nurturing. It's like the ice is melting."

"Excellent, now take another Shift Breath and imagine stepping into the body of your Inner Coach and looking at the world through her eyes, hearing what she hears, feeling what she feels, and thinking the thoughts that she thinks. In other words, embody yourself at your long-term ideal weight and mastery mindset. Spend a moment acknowledging the you that is at your long-term ideal weight, the you that is confident, stronger, wiser, and skilled at Weight Mastery."

With Leanne in this imaginary place, I did the Meet Your Inner Coach Exercise (below) with her. (Doing this exercise will help you to meet and join with your own Inner Coach to create your own Weight Mastery team.)

When we finished the exercise, Leanne was smiling with tears streaming down her face. "Wow, I don't think I have spoken respectfully to myself like that in years!" she said. "I use this tender voice with my kids all the time but feeling myself as having belief in myself and inspiring myself is unbelievable. It's as if I am giving myself permission to be my own best friend for the first time in my life."

"I spent my life bullying myself around my weight. It never worked! The meaner I got, the more I ate. What a difference it is to work with my Inner Coach! Not only can my Inner Coach and I come up with great plans for keeping me on track so I am releasing weight steadily, I don't allow myself to get caught up in that "start over tomorrow" game that led to bingeing and then beating myself up even more. I now have confidence that whatever happens my Inner Coach and I can figure things out together." Leanne T. (Released 6 pounds in 30 days, 42 pounds overall. Her original goal was to release 50 pounds, but she liked the way she looked when she got to 42! She's been maintaining for 3 years.)

MEET YOUR INNER COACH EXERCISE

I would like to begin by introducing you to your Inner Coach. You will get to know your coach well on your journey to weight mastery. Grab your pen and journal. This involves some writing.

Directions: Close your eyes, take a Shift Breath, and bring to mind the vision of yourself at your long-term ideal weight. In your mind's eye, see an image of what you look like, where you are, and what you are doing. This is the image you want to cultivate as the visual representation of your own personal Inner Coach.

What does your Inner Coach look like? Describe in detail how they look, using the idea that they may look a lot like you will at your long-term loving and reasonable ideal weight.

What kind of voice does your Inner Coach have? (Gentle? Loving but firm?) If you can't imagine your coach-like voice, think of a friend or mentor and use that voice internally as you develop your own. The best voice is probably the one you use with loved ones when you are encouraging them.

Evoke your Inner Coach. Take another Shift breath and close your eyes again. Imagine stepping into the body of you at your ideal weight, seeing through your eyes, hearing what you hear, feeling what you feel, and thinking the thoughts they have. Spend a moment acknowledging yourself at your confident, long-term loving and reasonable ideal weight. It's still you, but this version of you is stronger, wiser, and more skilled at weight mastery than you are at the moment. You are evoking right now the emotional essence of your Inner Coach.

Inner Coach Directions: Ask your Inner Coach the questions that follow and respond to them as your Inner Coach.

Inner coach, what is the purpose of supporting (your name) in releasing weight? (It's most helpful for you both to want the same thing from this Weight Mastery Process. It may be health, energy, or feeling better.)

What is a higher goal that you want to achieve for (your name) other than health and weight release or whatever your original purpose (stated above) was? (Beneath your initial goal of releasing weight often lurks another goal that is more internal than external, such as confidence, self-esteem, or respect.)

What is an even a higher goal than the one you just wrote? (Really dig for this. Why lose weight? Why look great in clothes? Why get healthy? There are deeper core needs that your weight goals stem from. What is your core need? Is it security? Peace? Happiness?)

Without thinking about it, write whatever first comes to mind in answer to this question. What words of encouragement can you, as your Inner Coach, give to your apprentice as you begin this process? (For example, I believe in you or we can do this.)

Can you see that beneath your desire to release weight is the desire to be at peace and to love and respect yourself? How you communicate in the self-care area of your life is your experience of life. Can you see how changing the way you communicate with yourself on a daily basis supports your weight release and, more importantly, instills confidence, trust, and fortitude to release long-term? This is the mastery part of weight mastery, and it is the game changer!

CONNECT WITH YOUR INNER COACH

I remember being lost in a sea of inner criticism when I put myself on restrictive, highly disciplined regimes to control myself only to snap and go in the opposite direction. I was disconnecting and being rebellious and out of control. I swam around in those murky waters for years until all my frustration came to a head on that scale in my Santa Monica apartment.

That was when a small voice within me emerged and said, "Enough! No more diets and regimes. You are smart, you are better than this, I believe in you. You can make your own way forward. You can find a method that works for you. I can help you do that."

That was my first meeting with my Inner Coach. Finding that voice within me was like latching on to a life preserver in a sea of chaos. I held on and began paddling for my shore of weight mastery.

The voice within me literally saved my life. Without that inner resource, so unlike my Inner Critic or Inner Rebel, I would not have the amazing and fulfilling life I have today—free of the weight struggle and full of health, vibrancy, and purpose.

As my relationship with my Inner Coach developed, I realized that there were many roles that my Inner Coach was playing in my weight release and maintenance. Just like an athlete's coach performs many functions for them, my Inner Coach developed many skills to guide me. I learned to be both the coach and the learner. Now you can begin to do the same. Be patient with developing this aspect of yourself and your relationship to it...it will become stronger with time.

CONNECTING TO YOUR COACH WITH THE SHIFT BREATH

During the next section, the Nine Skills of Weight Mastery (Nine Skills), you, and you Inner Coach will learn strategies to release weight and keep it off. I invite you to begin practicing connecting with your Inner Coach by using your Shift Breath. Remember, your Shift Breath cuts through all the fat thinking chatter and makes an open space in your mind for your Inner Coach and thin thinking.

- Pause a moment.

- Take a Shift Breath.

- Say, "Hello, Inner Coach."

- Allow your Inner Coach to answer, "Hello I am here." (Remember if you don't have a voice for your coach, think of someone nurturing from your life or even the movies or television, and use his or her voice.)

- Allow your Inner Coach to say, "I am here to guide you. I believe in you and our journey to Weight Mastery."

- Take another Shift Breath. Feel connected to your Inner Coach.

THE S.H.I.F.T. FROM FAT TO THIN THINKING TECHNIQUE

I now want to quickly walk you through an important technique that you and your Inner Coach will use to break the habit of "starting over." It is called the S.H.I.F.T from Fat to Thin Thinking Technique.

During the Orientation, I walked you through both the Weight Struggle Cycle and the Weight Mastery Journey. The key to long-term weight mastery is consistently moving forward. You have learned though, when you are stuck in the Weight Struggle Cycle, you are often in the habit of getting off course and then disconnecting from yourself with the "I blew it, so screw it!" start-over-tomorrow mentality.

You know that moment I am talking about—you eat a brownie your friend offered you at a party, and in the next moment or even while eating the brownie, you begin to feel bad. You don't like feeling bad, and the urge to erase the bad feeling instantly with the "I'll start over tomorrow" fat thinking impulse comes up. The reason the "I blew it, so screw it" choice is so attractive at that moment is that it takes you from feeling bad to instantly feeling relieved. The problem is, often the decision to "start over" is followed by "...and since I'm starting over tomorrow, I may as well live it up tonight..." and you grab three more brownies and go and park yourself by the bowl of chips. You end up feeling like a failure the next day when the party is over. This "I blew it, so screw it" impulse is such a powerful force in the Weight Struggle Cycle.

The S.H.I.F.T from Fat to Thin Thinking Technique intercepts the impulse to "start over" and gives us a moment to pause for a quick time-out huddle with our Inner Coach, a moment to refocus, and get right back on track. When you use this technique often enough, you break the habit of starting over tomorrow and begin to live a life of consistently staying on track.

S.H.I.F.T. FROM FAT TO THINK THINKING TECHNIQUE

S—Shift Breath

Recognize the beginning of that "I blew it, so screw it!" impulse and intercept with a Shift Breath.

H—Harness your Inner Coach

Reach internally for your inner thin thinking guide.

I—Insert Thin Thinking

Rationally assess the situation. Instead of your Inner Critic judging you for eating the brownie ("You ate a brownie, that wasn't on your plan—you blew it!"), your Inner Coach can instead acknowledge what happened in a non-judgmental way. ("You ate a brownie, that wasn't on your plan, we can make it work though, let's think this through.")

This takes you from an emotionally charged, fat thinking reaction to a rational thin thinking mindset.

F—Forgive Yourself and Find a Solution.

You now know the importance of forgiveness, so forgive yourself for eating the brownie. This immediately removes the bad feelings and frees your mind to solve the challenge. "I forgive myself for eating the brownie."

Now, put you and your Inner Coach's heads together and solve the problem. The main solution will always be to get back on track immediately. In the Nine Skills section, you and your Inner Coach will learn many ways to get back on track. Often finding the solution will simply be giving yourself some choices as to how to move forward.

For example, you and your Inner Coach can work the challenge through. "That brownie wasn't the end of the world or my healthy eating lifestyle. It probably had about 225 calories, and if I keep on track for the rest of the party and adjust my intake the rest of the day, I can still be on track for releasing weight this week."

T—Take the Lesson and Move Forward to Mastery.

There is always a lesson to learn when things don't go as you wished. When you "start over," you lose the lesson. When you shift to thin thinking, you take a moment to learn how to avoid doing the same thing next time.

For example, you and your Inner Coach can observe "I mindlessly said 'yes' to that brownie when it was offered. That didn't work for me. What would work for me next time? Next time, before a party, I will practice saying 'No thank you' before leaving home, so it will feel natural and easy when my friend offers me things I don't really want or need."

S.H.I.F.T.
FROM FAT TO THIN THINKING TECHNIQUE

Shift Breath

Harness Your Inner Coach

Insert Thin Thinking

Forgive Yourself / Find a Solution

Take a Lesson / Move Forward to Mastery

Don't worry about "getting" this technique all right now. You will have many chances to review this during your *30-Day Thin Thinking Practice*.

CREATING THE CONNECTION TO YOUR INNER COACH SUM UP: MEET YOUR INNER COACH

The relationship between your apprentice and Inner Coach is the engine that will drive your journey to weight mastery.

- I have met my Inner Coach who will guide me to weight mastery.
- I understand that I can use my Shift Breath to pause and access my Inner Coach.
- I know the S.H.I.F.T. from Fat to Thin Thinking Technique that I can use with my Inner Coach to intercept the "start over" fat thinking and stay on track with thin thinking.

Excellent. I hope you are feeling stronger and more confident with your Inner Coach. You are never alone. You will always have someone who cares more about your freedom and health than eating a cupcake. It's time to connect you both on an even deeper level in your mind with the **INNER COACH** Hypnosis Session.

CHAPTER 21
HYPNOSIS SESSION
INNER COACH

YOU ARE NOW READY TO dive into the second hypnosis session in the *Shift Weight Mastery Process*. Listening to Inner Coach Hypnosis Session will help solidify your connection to your Inner Coach.

- Go to www.FromFatToThinThinking.com to access the hypnosis session.

- Listen only while you are in a relaxed position.

- Listen to the Inner Coach hypnosis session with an open mind that is expecting 100 percent success.

- DO NOT LISTEN TO ANY HYPNOSIS SESSION WHILE DRIVING OR OPERATING HEAVY OR COMPLEX MACHINERY.

- Expect to feel relaxed, don't expect to feel in a trance.

- If you fall asleep, try the session in a less relaxed position next time. However, hypnosis can make an impact while you are asleep.

Enjoy your hypnosis session, and then we will move to the Nine Skills where you and your Inner Coach begin laying the framework for your weight mastery.

THE SHIFT
THE NINE SKILLS OF WEIGHT MASTERY

The secret of change is to focus your energy, not on fighting the old, but on building the new.

—*Socrates*

CHAPTER 22

THE NINE SKILLS

TOOLS FOR WEIGHT RELEASE SUCCESS

Welcome to the next part of your journey. After listening to Inner Coach, the second hypnosis session, you can see that you have embarked on a way of managing your weight from the inside out.

We have now arrived at the point where you will begin using the Nine Skills of Weight Mastery to build your thin thinking mind. Remember these skills are based on over 200 studies of men and women who achieved long-term, permanent weight release.

Metaphors are powerful tools for learning. As you've noticed, I love using the mental construction of a Weight Mastery Home in the mind to convey how you will apply specific skills layer by layer to achieve weight mastery.

As I explained earlier, the Nine Skills of Weight Mastery can be thought of in three dimensions: Weight, Environment, and Mind. Thinking of them in these groups will also help you remember them.

Think of each group of skills as a new floor of your Weight Mastery Home. By the time you've completed the *Shift Weight Mastery Process*, you will have a three-story home of Nine Skills of Weight Mastery.

The First Floor: Weight Skills.
These are the most physical skills. They are the basic skills of releasing weight and form the foundation of your Weight Mastery Home.

Second Floor: Environmental Skills.
These lifestyle skills keep your weight release and maintenance consistent.

Top Floor: Mind Skills

These mental level skills manage your inner communication, the key to Weight Mastery success.

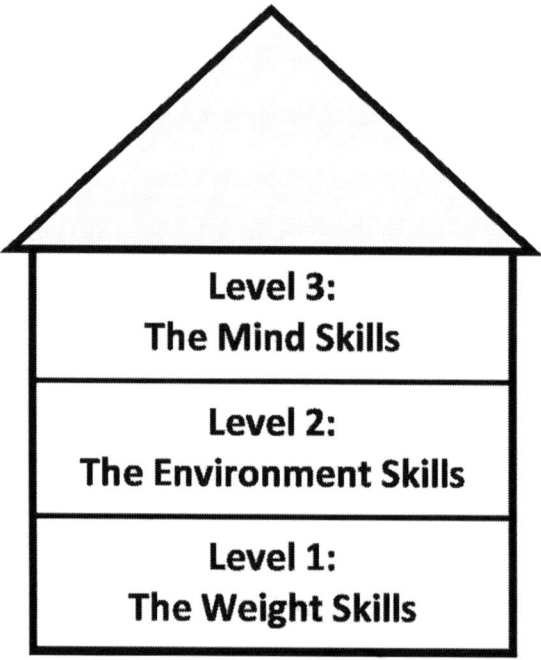

THE 9 SKILLS OF WEIGHT MASTERY

INSTRUCTIONS FOR THE NINE SKILLS OF WEIGHT MASTERY

Each chapter in this section will introduce you to a different skill and teach you how to begin mastering it.

1. **Read each skill chapter through completely.**

2. **Keep your Inner Coach with you at all times**. The skills are for you and your Inner Coach to use as a team. Read from the point of view of both aspects of yourself—the teacher and the learner. This back-and-forth, respectful, learning relationship within you is the heart of the *Shift Weight Mastery Process* success.

3. **Beware of fat thinking as you read.** Your Inner Critic and Inner Rebel may pop into your mind from time to time to say hello. As I warned at the beginning of this

book, beware of the harsh words and clever seductive lines these two characters might say to discourage or seduce you. Stay strong if one of them makes comments like these:

- **"I know this already."** Knowing something and embodying it are two different things. Remind yourself that you are open to learning on a deeper level.

- **"I did something like this before and it didn't work."** Being ready to change is key to success. You may not have been ready in the past, but I bet you are now.

- **"This is too hard." and "This will take too much time."** Remember these popular fat thinking refrains that we discussed before? Struggling with your weight and yourself takes more time and effort than learning to be confident and free. You are worth the investment!

4. **Complete the exercises:** Please complete the exercises in each of the chapters because they will help prepare you for your *30-Day Thin Thinking Practice*.

Okay, Apprentice, take a Shift Breath, harness your Inner Coach, and let's start building **THE THREE WEIGHT SKILLS**.

CHAPTER 23
THE FIRST LEVEL

THE THREE WEIGHT SKILLS

RE YOU READY TO RELEASE weight? These three skills are about the *weight* in weight mastery.

THE WEIGHT SKILLS

Skill 1 Living your Life within your Calorie Budget for Weight Release and Maintenance. You learn to live life within your Calorie Budget and release weight powerfully and consistently at a rate you decide.

Skill 2 Creating a Consistent Relationship with Exercise. You use exercise as a powerful tool to either speed your rate of weight release or eat more food as you are releasing. You see exercise as an essential part of your Weight Mastery lifestyle.

Skill 3 Creating a Masterful Relationship with Food. You hone the skills of being able to confidently use food to create a stable, balanced, nourishing way of eating that removes cravings and fake hunger and allows you to cultivate a way of eating that honors you and your life from the inside out.

First, before embarking upon your first set of skills, take a nice Shift Breath and set your mind for success. Since you are going to begin building your weight release home, you need some protective gear. Instead of a hard hat, though, I am handing you and your Inner Coach lab coats. Will you put them on, please? You are about to delve into the research.

The fat thinking side of our mind that is wired for weight struggle is full of pain, despair, and limiting beliefs. Our emotions run our fat thinking. That's why our good-or-bad, on-or-off-a-diet brain is as quick to leap on a diet as it is to fall off one.

Now, Apprentice, you are going to learn to use the more rational, thin thinking part of your mind to begin to release weight calmly in a straightforward, rational way, as if you are a scientist.

RESEARCH SHOWS THE BEST DIET IS "YOUR DIET"

The data from the National Weight Control Registry shows that although about half of Weight Masters may have released weight through diets or weight loss programs, their key to success wasn't a diet alone, but rather their ability to adapt any diet to their lives and make eating plans or programs their own.

The data also shows that no matter what diet the average Weight Master followed, his or her weight release was accomplished by reducing caloric intake, eating less fat, and consuming fruits and vegetables, as well as increasing physical activity. In other words, the key to long-term weight success wasn't any diet, per se, but establishing a healthy and active lifestyle. These same factors also helped sustain long term weight release.

My own weight breakthrough involved the shift from seeing weight management as the act of staying on a diet to aligning my beliefs and habits with living my life at 140 pounds instead of 180+ pounds. This took more than understanding about healthy eating; it took understanding how to release weight and keep it off.

Many of my clients know how to eat healthfully before they begin shifting with me. However, they discover when they begin working with me that they did not know how to use their minds to create a specific weight release outcome. I use calories and the physics of weight release to help clients release weight at a rate they decide and take back their power from fad diets.

I know there are diet programs that assume you can't handle counting calories. These programs may "dumb it down," using points, blocks, or color codes of what you can and cannot eat. Or some programs try to make it easy by requiring that you eat their special food and not much else. They don't show you how to use calories within the Weight Release Equation that will give you the ability to release weight on your own terms.

When you understand the Weight Release Equation and how to release weight at a rate you decide, you won't be stuck in the Weight Struggle Cycle. You will not fall victim to unrealistic goals and diets that cause you to throw in the towel before you've hardly started. Instead you will learn to live life within your Calorie Budget for Weight Release. You will also learn to partner with exercise and develop a masterful relationship with food so that you become the confident owner of your weight release journey and not some diet structure or set of rules that live outside of you.

"I chose to go slow, releasing one pound a week. I didn't want to be on another diet. I wanted a lifestyle I could live with and maintain a healthy weight the rest of my life." Mary S. (Released 35 pounds, maintaining for 8 years)

Okay, have you got your lab coat on? Onward to **Skill 1 Living your Life within your Calorie Budget for Weight Release and then Maintenance.**

CHAPTER 24
WEIGHT MASTERY SKILL 1

LIVING YOUR LIFE WITHIN YOUR CALORIE BUDGET

FOR WEIGHT RELEASE AND MAINTENANCE

SKILL 1: Living your Life within your Calorie Budget for Weight Release and Maintenance. The skill of creating a Daily Calorie Budget that will allow you to release weight (and then maintain) based at a rate you decide and then living your life within it.

FAT THINKING AND WEIGHT RELEASE

Fat thinking about weight loss runs deep and often keeps us a victim of our mind's distorted perceptions:

- I don't eat anything, and yet I am not losing weight!

- I work out so hard, but my weight stays the same!

- Losing weight is hard, and my body is broken. I don't think I have a metabolism!

When struggling with weight, the act of losing weight always carries with it the idea of having to pull it together, suffer through, and be deprived. This feeling doesn't usually start with you. The world is full of fat thinking images, beliefs, and stories that perpetuate the idea that losing weight is hard. This assumption strengthens your own belief system every time you try to release weight. We feel like we are serving a prison sentence.

If you are frustrated because you have been trying unsuccessfully to release weight, here are some weight release challenges you may not be conscious of:

- You don't understand the physics of weight release. You may eat healthfully and exercise regularly, but unless you have accurate data and know how to create specific results, success will elude you.

- You exercise regularly, but you are eating more calories than you burn. Often I have clients who are exercising but not aware of how many calories they are consuming. They are still eating more than they are burning, despite the exercise. I had a client who played tennis for an hour. Afterward he quenched his thirst with a high-calorie juice and refueled with a gluten-free muffin. The calories that he consumed were more than double the calories that he had burned on the court.

- Your perception of how much you are eating is more broken than your metabolism. Research shows that thin people underestimate the amounts of calories they eat by 25 percent. The typical Weight Struggler underestimates the amount of calories he consumes daily by 50 to 100 percent!

BROKEN METABOLISM OR BROKEN THINKING?

In the early 1990s, Steven B. Heymsfield, M.D., then deputy director of the New York Obesity Research Center at Columbia University, studied 17 people who felt they couldn't lose weight because of a faulty metabolism. Researchers monitored the volunteers food intake at intervals over four years. The volunteers recorded their meals over a three-day period in a food journal. Most entries came to about 1200 calories a day. However, when scientific methods were used to more accurately measure calories consumed over 14 days, the researchers found that actual calorie consumption was 2227 calories a day on average. The volunteers were underestimating their caloric intake by about 1200 calories a day! On metabolic tests, only one person was found to have a truly low metabolic rate, possibly due to medications she was taking.

Next, the volunteers were given controlled amounts of calories and closely monitored. The result of the controlled study? According to Dr. Heymsfield, "Obese subjects were placed into negative energy balance and were invariably shown to lose body weight as predicted by the first law of thermodynamics." In translation, when they were actually eating 1200 calories a day they released weight at a predictable rate.

I have in my office a machine that measures your resting metabolic rate. Now I know you are wondering "Why would a hypnotherapist have a machine like that?" The answer is simple. Truth dispels myth.

Many of my clients initially believe that years of dieting have ruined their metabolism, making them incapable of losing weight. They breathe into the Metacheck machine for ten minutes, and it gives us their resting metabolic rate so we know exactly how many calories their body is burning on an average day. Though some people have compromised metabolic rates, most peoples' metabolisms fall in the zone of what is normal for their weight. And I have measured the metabolisms of thousands of people! This often is a shock to many, but when we walk through what they have been eating on a daily basis, they very quickly begin to understand why they have been stuck on a plateau or have been gaining weight.

Then we go through the steps of how to actually release weight as per the laws of physics (as we are about to do for you), and people begin to get excited. The laws of physics finally begin to make sense. When clients learn to release weight according to the laws of physics, they see that they are perfectly capable of losing weight and can be in control without having to lean on diets, detoxes, or other methods. They take their power back from the weight loss industry. They let go of the old limiting beliefs that made them feel like their body was broken and become confident drivers of their own weight release.

I call this skill **Living Your Life within your Calorie Budget for Weight Release and Maintenance** because it's about learning to live your life within your natural energy needs to release and then maintain at your ideal weight. This skill is about thriving and not about depriving!

Don't worry, you don't need a metabolism machine to find out your metabolism. I will walk you through how to do that for yourself very shortly.

"When I learned how many calories my body burned each day and that I could decide how to feed myself within my calorie budget for weight release, it was an absolute game changer. I understood what to do for myself, and it felt so liberating and grown-up. I am the one in charge of what I do and how fast I release, not some diet guru or crazy combination of food. Let me just say that science works. Math works. Don't be afraid. Embrace weight-release science and see how empowering it can be." Tony G. (Released 38 pounds, maintaining at 2 years)

THE "C" WORD

"Is this a calorie counting program?" I'm asked frequently. Yes, I use calories to measure energy coming into your body as food and going out in activity. In my opinion, it's the only way to accurately, scientifically, and logically (and not haphazardly, emotionally, and irrationally) track weight release.

People associate the word "calorie" with the weight struggle. That poor word has come to mean restriction, obsession, deprivation, "white-knuckling it," etcetera. When you remove the emotional stigma that is stuck to the word "calorie" and define it accurately as "a unit of energy that is used for heat measurement," it's no longer a limiting belief.

For a moment, consider another unit of energy: money. When dealing with money, you wouldn't dream of saying, "Gosh. Let's not deal with dollars; let's use colors or blocks instead." If you did, how soon would it be before your bank account was out of whack? Measuring energy intake and output with calories is similar to dealing with money. It allows you to be exact and stay exact with the facts.

Food's energy values are measured universally in calories. Energy expenditures in activity, including exercise, are measured in calories. In order to truly embrace weight release, you need to embrace the word "calorie" in a positive light. So, if you are challenged by calorie counting, please pause and engage in the following Mind-Shifting Exercise. If you and calories are already cool together, just skip ahead.

SHIFTING "CALORIE"

Did you know that you keep things, people, and places that you associate negatively in your mind in a different place than your positive thoughts about these same things? Just for a moment think about someone you don't like. If it isn't someone from your life, maybe it's a politician or someone from history. Now, think about your best friend from school. You felt an internal shift take place as you moved your mind's focus from the person that you have negative associations with to the person you have positive associations with, didn't you?

Years of weight struggling have probably put the word "calorie" in your mind in the same place that you associate with other things you think of in a negative light. I would like to help you move that word from a disempowering file in your mind to an empowering file. It's kind of like dragging something from one folder on your desktop to another.

Here are directions for changing your mind about calories:

- Take a moment and imagine what a calorie looks like. Perhaps you see it as the word "calorie" or you see it as a little ball of fire or a radiator burning heat. Imagine it sprouting arms and legs. Imagine a head and face forming on it. It's the face of someone that you associate with good feelings, someone who is a big help to you and helps you achieve your goals. If you can't see it all, that's okay, do your best.

- Apprentice, I would like to introduce you to Calorie.

- Imagine that Calorie says, "Hi there, I am here to help you take your power back from your weight struggle. I am not here to bum you out or deprive you. I am here to give you freedom." Imagine Calorie extending a hand out to you to offer a warm greeting of friendship.

- Imagine extending your hand and saying, "Hello, Calorie, nice to meet you. I look forward to having a powerful experience achieving and then maintaining my ideal weight with you."

- Now in your mind, shift Calorie from the fat thinking Weight Struggle file to the thin thinking Weight Mastery file.

THIN THINKING AND WEIGHT RELEASE

Get ready to change your fat thinking once and for all. I want to introduce you to the idea that releasing weight as a Weight Master can be a journey of self-discovery that boosts your self-confidence and self-esteem.

You are now going to manipulate energy in the direction of releasing weight and then maintaining your loving and reasonable ideal weight. You are going to apply some science and simple math to retrain your brain. You are going to become aware of how the energy created by your body, exercise, and food work together to release and maintain weight or gain it.

Even if you were never good at math and science, never fear. You will get the basics quickly. The numbers in weight release sometimes freak out people, but avoiding the math keeps you in fat thinking. I know your thirst for knowledge will increase as you begin reaping its rewards. When you understand how to use your body's energy and leverage to release weight at your own speed, you engage the following thin thinking results:

You become more rational, because your release is based on facts and data, not dieting science fiction. Your rationality keeps you from that all-or-nothing fat thinking.

- You become more confident, because you are in charge of the results of your effort. You are no longer giving your power to some diet structure.

- Your belief system changes, because you don't see yourself as a failure. Rather you know you are quite capable and successful at releasing weight.

You are going to engage yourself and your Inner Coach in learning to:

1. Release weight at a rate you decide with the Weight Release Formula.

2. Calculate your Daily Calorie Budget for Weight Release to achieve your weekly weight goal.

1 – RELEASE WEIGHT AT A RATE YOU DECIDE

Apprentice, you and your Inner Coach are now ready to learn the strategy of how to release weight. I know you may understand weight loss basics, but you are going to construct the information in your Weight Mastery part of your mind versus where it is now in the Weight Struggle part. Please read the following with an apprentice's open attitude.

WEIGHT RELEASE BASICS 101

There are 3,500 calories in a pound of fat. In order to release one pound of weight off your body, 3,500 calories need to be burned. Your body burns food for fuel much like a car burns gas for fuel. Different cars require different amounts of fuel, depending on their sizes and makes. Each person's body burns fuel at a different rate, depending on many things, including his or her size, genetic makeup, age, and daily activity levels.

A big wide-body truck is going burn a lot more fuel each mile than a teeny gas-efficient hybrid car. Similarly, a 19-year-old, 6 '3," 290-pound linebacker who plays football 3 hours every day is going to burn a lot more fuel in a typical day than a 72-year-old, 5'1," 90-pound retired grandmother who sits in front of a television all day.

I call the number of calories that your body burns in a 24-hour period without exercise your fuel tank. The football player's fuel tank is going to be way bigger than Granny's fuel tank. (**Chart D**)

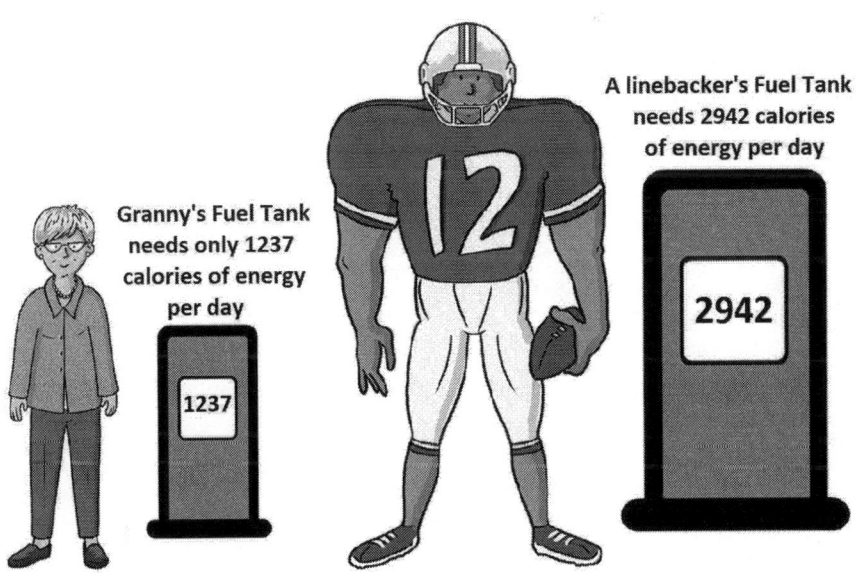

Chart D: Granny's Fuel Tank vs. Linebacker's Fuel Tank

The amount of calories that your body burns at rest in a 24-hour period is called your *resting metabolic rate (RMR)*. Even though it may not seem fair, the amount of calories of your RMR is out of your control for the most part, and there is little you can do to alter it. Adding a significant amount of muscle raises your resting metabolic rate a tiny bit but doesn't radically alter it. (Converting 12 pounds of fat to 12 pounds of muscle will only increase your resting metabolic rate by about 64 calories a day. That's not a lot!)

The only way you can significantly alter how many calories your body burns a day, other than unsafe diet pills, is with exercise. Research shows that exercise is one of the key skills for the long – term success of Weight Masters. (How to practice the exercise skill for weight release is the topic of the next chapter. For now, stay focused on weight release basics.)

THE WEIGHT RELEASE FORMULA

When I walk clients through the Weight Release Formula, which is based on physics and the first law of thermodynamics[3] they are amazed at the simplicity of it, especially since the term sounds so scientific and complicated!

In short, your body needs a consistent amount of energy on a daily basis to run itself. That energy has to come from fuel in the form of food or stored fat. When you burn more calories than you consume as food, you create an energy deficit. Your body then uses stored energy. That is when weight release occurs.

The law itself is simple. However, when applied to weight loss and all the emotions and fat thinking attached to it, that basic law can become confusing. Aren't you glad you have your lab coat on?

BASIC WEIGHT FORMULAS

Weight release. The amount of calories that your body burns at rest and in activity is greater than the amount of calories you consume.

Weight maintenance. The amount of calories that your body burns is the same as the amount of calories you consume. (Ultimately, this is the formula you will rely on to maintain your ideal weight.)

3 **FIRST LAW OF THERMODYNAMICS** is the total energy of an isolated system that is constant; energy can be transformed from one form to another but cannot be created or destroyed.

Weight gain. The amount of calories your body burns is fewer than the amount of calories you consume.

The calorie-based terms you will use in your Weight Release Formula are:

- **Daily Body Burn Calories.** The sum total of calories your body burns at rest and in sedentary activity over a 24-hour period.

- **Daily Weight Release Rate Calories.** The average amount of calories you need to burn daily in order to release weight at a rate you decide.

- **Daily Calorie Budget for Weight Release.** This is the amount of food calories you can consume daily and achieve the deficit necessary to achieve your weekly weight release goal.

DAILY BODY BURN CALORIES

Simply put, your Daily Body Burn Calories are the total amount of calories your body burns—not counting exercise—in a 24-hour period. Your Daily Body Burn Calories are the total of two energy sources: Your resting metabolic rate calories + your sedentary calories.

- **Resting metabolic rate (RMR).** The amount of energy (number of calories) that your body expends in a resting state over a 24-hour period. Your RMR is the sum total of how much energy your body uses to breathe, beat your heart, digest food, run your brain, and all the miraculous things your body does without getting out of bed. **(See Chart E)**

- **Sedentary calories.** The number of calories you burn performing daily, non-exercise-related activities. Assuming you get up at some point in 24 hours to live your life—make coffee, go to work, or read a book to your child. These sedentary activities take more energy than your resting body and burn so-called sedentary calories. **(See Chart F)**

- **Daily Body Burn calories.** The total number of calories the body burns during a 24-hour period (*resting metabolic rate + sedentary calories*). This number does not include calories used in exercise. **(See Chart G)**

Chart F

Your RMR calories	**Sedentary Calories**	**Daily Body Burn Calories**
The amount of calories your body burns at rest for 24 hours.	The amount of calories your body burns performing the tasks of everyday life.	**RMR + Sedentary Calories** The total number of calories burned by your body (without exercise) in 24 hours.
Chart E	**Chart F**	**Chart G**

Okay, Apprentice, you with me so far? You have a body and it burns energy (calories). You can use that energy burn to release weight. You will be calculating your specific Daily Body Burn numbers after you learn a few more things. Hang tight, that info is coming!

Now, for the next important part of the Weight Release Formula—your *Daily Weight Release Rate Calories*.

DAILY WEIGHT RELEASE RATE CALORIES

Some energy must be burned in the form of fat for weight release. As you learned, there are 3,500 calories in a pound of fat. If you want to release one pound a week, take 3,500 and divide it by the days of the week. That figure is your Daily Weight Release Rate Calories. **(Chart H)**

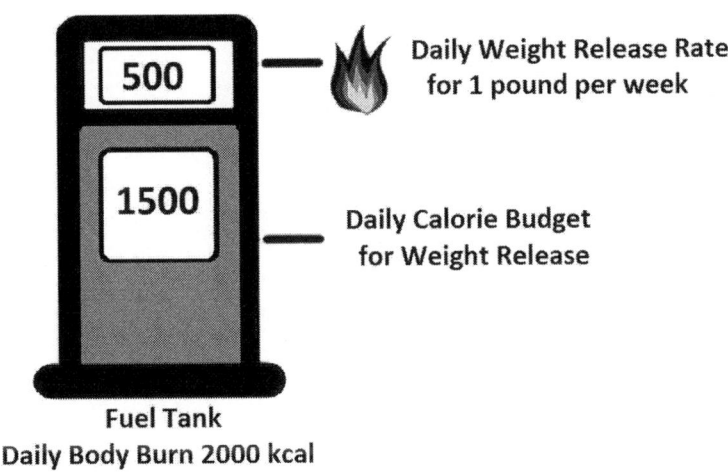

Daily Weight Release Rate for 1 pound per week

Daily Calorie Budget for Weight Release

Fuel Tank
Daily Body Burn 2000 kcal

CHART H: Daily Weight Release Rate Calories

In order to release one pound of weight a week, subtract 500 Daily Weight Release Rate Calories from your Daily Body Burn Calories. By the end of the seven days, you will have burned a full pound's worth of weight. 3,500 calories/7 days = 500 calories per day = Daily Weight Release Rate Calories for one pound, which is your Weekly Weight Release Rate Calories (**Chart I**).

500 calories **500 calories** **500 calories** **500 calories**

500 calories **500 calories** **500 calories** **3500 calories or 1 pound of fat**

CHART I: Weekly Weight Release Rate Calories for One Pound Weight Release for Week

Stick with me, we are almost there. Your body burns calories every day. When you use a defined amount of those calories to burn fat, you release weight at a rate you decide.

DAILY CALORIE BUDGET FOR WEIGHT RELEASE

What happens to the remaining calories from your Daily Body Burn after you take away the calories you are going to burn to release weight? You can eat the remaining calories in food. I call this your Daily Calorie Budget for Weight Release. It is the amount of calories you can eat each day and still release weight at a rate you decide. To determine your Daily Calorie Budget for Weight Release, subtract your Daily Weight Release Rate Calories from your Daily Body Burn Calories. Here's what the Weight Release Formula looks like:

Daily Body Burn Calories – Daily Weight Release Rate Calories = Daily Calorie Budget for Weight Release

CASE STUDY: BETTY THOMAS AND HER BROKEN METABOLISM

When Betty, a second-grade teacher in her late thirties, came to my office, she had almost given up on weight loss, thinking she might just be happy being "chubby." The problem was that she wasn't happy or just "chubby." Her health was failing: her cholesterol levels were up, and she had pre-diabetes.

"I just can't lose weight. I have tried everything. Last summer I was on the Paleo diet, the very low carb one. I did okay on the plan for a while and lost about 20 pounds. But then I stopped losing weight even though I had about 25 pounds more to go. I was doing everything perfectly, too. I wasn't eating any bread or white foods. Finally, I got so frustrated that I bought a loaf of bread, made ten pieces of toast with butter and jam, and ate them all. I didn't care anymore."

"Did you ever track calories to see how many you were eating daily on that Paleo plan?" I asked Betty.

She replied, "Calories? No, I hate counting calories. I would never do that. I choose diets that focus more on the food and not the calories."

"Well, Betty, my guess is that your body isn't broken, but the calories in the large amounts of bacon, almonds, and avocado you were eating added up and kept you from releasing more weight. I have many clients who came to me as overweight vegans, macrobiotic followers, raw foodies, Atkinites, Paleos, South Beachers, and Weight Watchers who all swear they are eating within their chosen system's guidelines.

"Unfortunately, they were just eating too many calories to have continued weight release. That is probably what happened for you. When these clients began using the Weight Release Formula, they released weight according to the laws of physics."

"I knew deep down I was kidding myself that I could eat all the bacon I wanted and keep losing weight." She sighed.

BETTY'S WEIGHT RELEASE FORMULA

Let's now take Betty through the Weight Release Formula.
Betty is 38, 5'5" tall, and weighs 198 pounds.
Betty's Daily Body Burn: 2,000 calories.

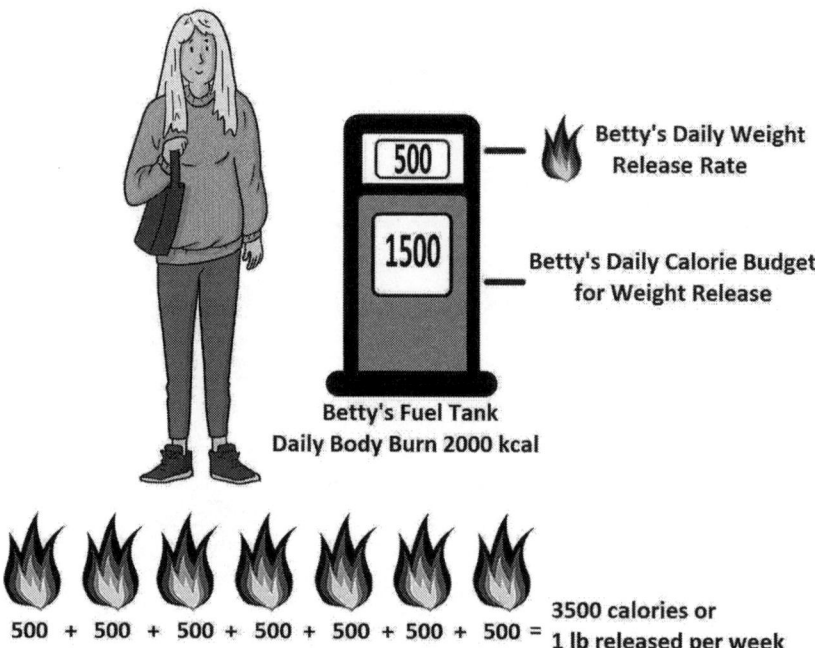

Betty's Daily Weight Release Rate

500

Betty's Daily Calorie Budget for Weight Release

1500

Betty's Fuel Tank
Daily Body Burn 2000 kcal

500 + 500 + 500 + 500 + 500 + 500 + 500 = 3500 calories or 1 lb released per week

CHART J: Betty's Weight Release Formula to Release One Pound per Week

Betty's Daily Body Burn Calories (2,000 calories) – Betty's Daily Weight Release Rate Calories (500 calories to release one pound per week) = Betty's Daily Calorie Budget for Weight Release (1,500 calories). **(See Chart J)**

Can you see that one way of releasing weight would be simply by reducing the amount of food that you consume to leverage your Daily Body Burn Calories to help you release weight at a specific rate? Betty can eat up to 1,500 calories a day and release a pound a week without adding any exercise.

THREE WEIGHT RELEASE STRATEGIES

Cutting back on the number of calories you consume is one of three ways you can release weight at a rate you decide. These three strategies are:

1. Releasing weight by reducing food intake only.

2. Releasing weight by increasing exercise only.

3. Releasing weight by reducing food intake and increasing exercise.

Releasing Weight by Reducing Food Intake Only

As we just learned **(See Chart J)**, Betty can lower her daily food intake to 500 calories below her 2,000 Daily Body Burn or "fuel tank" calories. That gives her a 1,500 calorie a day Calorie Budget for Weight Release, and now the remaining 500 calories (her Daily Weight Release Rate) are burned from her body. If her calorie intake stays at or below her 1,500 Calorie Budget for Weight Release each day for a week, she will burn enough stored fat to release a pound of weight.

Releasing Weight by Increasing Exercise Only

Instead of altering her food intake, Betty can decide to burn 500 calories a day in exercise. Those additional calories increase her Daily Body Burn from 2,000 to 2,500 calories a day.

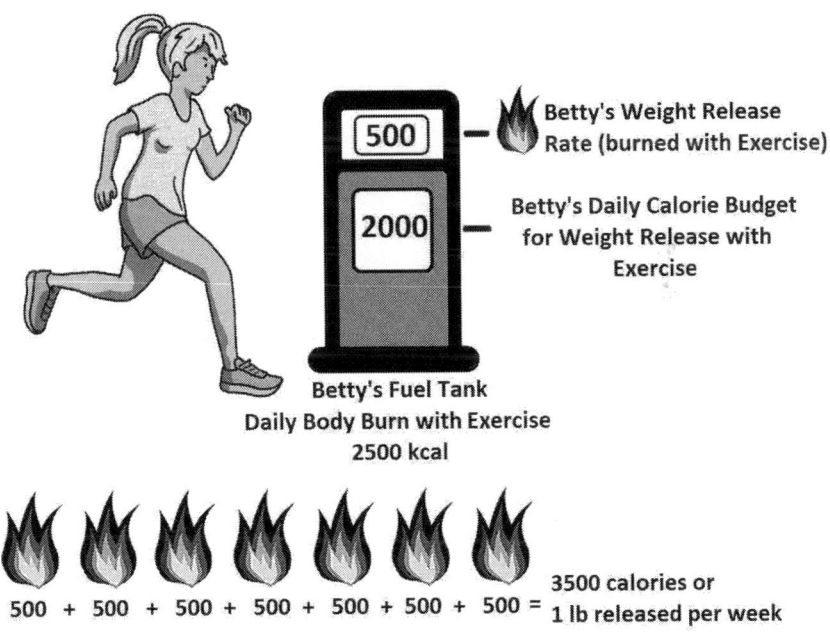

**CHART K: Betty Releases One Pound per Week
Through Increasing Exercise Only**

Using this technique, Betty's Daily Calorie Budget for Weight Release will be 2,000 calories, since she is burning the extra exercise calories.

When she is consistent with creating an overall burn of 3,500 calories in exercise a week and keeping her Daily Calorie Budget at 2,000 calories, she will release a pound a week. **(See Chart K)**

Releasing Weight by Reducing Food Intake and Increasing Exercise
What Betty will probably decide to do is a combination of consuming fewer calories and exercising more to create her 1-pound weight release per week. Most Weight Masters, research shows, release weight using this combination.

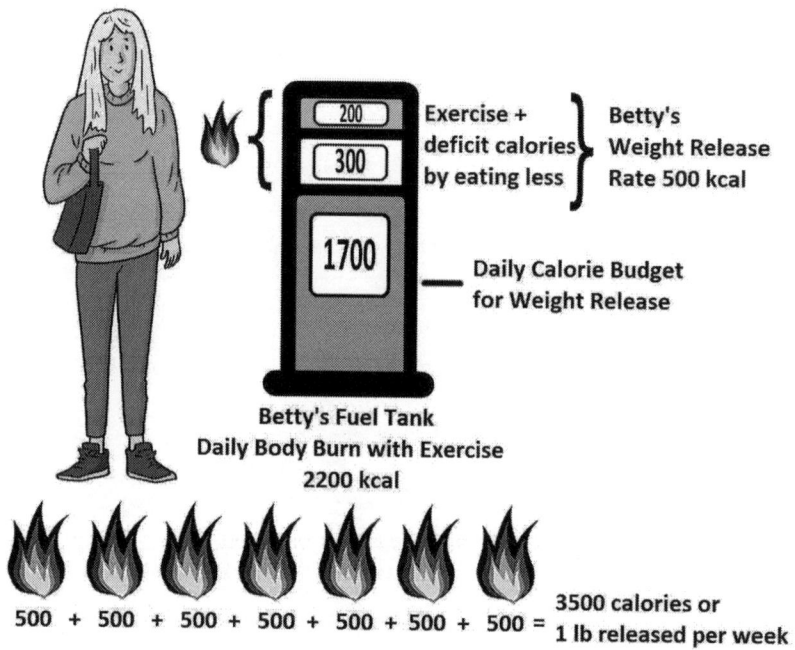

Chart L: Betty Releases One Pound per Week by Reducing Food Intake and Increasing Exercise

Let's say Betty burned 200 calories a day walking for 30 minutes. This increases her Daily Body Burn to 2,200. Now if she consumes 500 calories less (Her Daily Weight Release Rate) and consumes 1,700 calories as her Daily Calorie Budget, Betty would be creating a 500 calorie a day burn and, therefore, release a pound a week. **(See Chart L)**

CASE STUDY CONCLUSION

Betty decided to release a pound a week according to the formula described above with reducing food intake and adding exercise formula. She began tracking her food and exercise calories with an easy-to-use app so she could easily see how much she was consuming and stay within her Calorie Budget for Weight Release. (More on this in Skill 4.)

Betty felt in charge of her weight release for the first time in her life. She no longer had to stick to strict diet guidelines, but she did learn to stay within the boundaries of her own Calorie Budget for Weight Release. She had a choice and flexibility in planning her meals that she had never known before. She was happy with the way she was eating, because it fit her likes and lifestyle, allowing her to be consistent and release weight.

"There has been no more hoping for the magic wand outside of me. Once I was in the driver's seat, I could call the shots. That is very important for me. I am someone who likes to be in control, and for years this was the only part of my life that I felt that I had no control over. Now I do!" Betty T. (Released 45 pounds, maintaining at 2 years.)

Now, Apprentice, are you ready to learn to drive your own weight release?

2-Calculating Your Calorie Budget for Weight Release

Please pause and use the time to fill out the information in this section. Later you will revisit these pages and bring what you have worked out for yourself into your *30-Day Thin Thinking Practice*.

I am now going to walk you through two fairly accurate ways of figuring out your Daily Body Burn and your Calorie Budget for Weight Release:

- The Old-Fashioned Method of calculating your Calorie Budget for Weight Release yourself.

- The Newfangled Method of having the Online Resource Center's Weight Release Calculator determine your Calorie Budget for Weight Release.

THE OLD-FASHIONED METHOD: CALCULATING YOUR DAILY BODY BURN

This is the pre-digital age method of figuring out your Calorie Budget for Weight Release. I still teach this method to my seminar participants because walking through each step of the Weight Release Formula helps your brain understand the mechanics of weight release. So, play along with me even if you plan to go to the website and use the Weight Release Calculator.

In order to get your Daily Body Burn, you first determine your resting metabolic rate (RMR).

Calculate Your Resting Metabolic Rate

Get out a calculator and use the following Mifflin equation, which is the most scientifically accurate way of estimating your daily resting metabolic rate:

The Mifflin equation for RMR:

- For Men: $(4.5 \times w) + (15.88 \times h) - (5 \times a) + 5$
- For Women: $(4.5 \times w) + (15.88 \times h) - (5 \times a) - 161$

  w = weight in pounds

  h = height in inches

  a = age in years

  My RMR is_____

Calculate Your Daily Body Burn Calories

Now let's calculate your Daily Body Burn Calories, which include additional calories for a sedentary lifestyle. (Remember, those are the calories you burn by getting up and living life—driving to work, making meals, sitting at a desk, etc.)

Multiply your RMR x 1.2=Daily Body Burn Calories.

My Daily Body Burn is: _____

(Remember your Daily Body Burn Calories are your personal "fuel tank," the amount of energy that you need per 24 hours to live.)

CALCULATING YOUR WEIGHT RELEASE RATE CALORIES

Take a deep Shift Breath, and make sure you have your Inner Coach with you and your lab coats are on. This sometimes requires you wrapping your head around numbers. If you aren't a numbers person, it may take staying open-minded—plus, that is why we have the web-based calculator to do this all for you. Getting this is a big aha moment for many people. I know it was big for me personally. So, stick with me, Apprentice. Ready?

WEIGHT RELEASE RATE CALORIE TABLE

		Weekly	Daily
-.5 lb	=	(-1,750 calories)	(-250 calories)
-1 lb	=	(-3,500 calories)	(-500 calories)
-1.5 lbs	=	(-5,250 calories)	(-750 calories)
-2 lbs	=	(-7,000 calories)	(-1,000 calories)
-3 lbs	=	(-10,500 calories)	(-1,500 calories)

Chart M: Weight Release Rate Calories Table

The Weight Release Rate Calories Table (**Chart M**) shows how many calories need to be burned on both a daily and weekly basis to create the weight release outcome that you desire. Look at how much weight you wish to release each week and then the daily amount of calories that will need to be burned to achieve that desired outcome. Fill in your equation (Reminder: the calculator will figure this out for you but I want you to understand the mechanics. Knowledge is power!)

Calculate your Daily Calorie Budget for Weight Release

Your Daily Body Burn _____

Your Daily Weight Release Rate Calories (from Chart M) (-)_____

My Daily Calorie Budget (without exercise)   =_____

This will allow me to release _____lb/kg a week. (from Chart M)

THE NEWFANGLED DIGITAL METHOD

This is a web-based way to determine your Daily Calorie Burn for Weight Release.

ulate your Daily Calorie Budget for Weight Release Online

Go to the Shift Weight Release Calculator: www.FromFatToThinThinking.com

Enter your information into the calculator, and it will give you both your Daily Body Burn and your Daily Calorie Budget for Weight Release (without exercise). Record the results below or in your journal for reference.

My Daily Body Burn =_____ 1617

My Daily Calorie Budget (without exercise) = _____ 1307

This will allow me to release _____ lb/kg a week.

Do not proceed to Step 2 PLAN MY EXERCISE FOR THE WEEK. We will be using this in the next chapter.

NOTE: The numbers you got the old-fashioned way may vary a bit from the newfangled way. That is okay.

YOUR RATE OF WEIGHT RELEASE

I want to take a moment and address an issue that comes up when people set their weekly weight-release goals. There is a tendency to set a rapid weight-release rate (two pounds or more a week) in order to release weight as fast as possible. For many people, especially smaller women, this creates a very small Daily Calorie Budget for Weight Release.

You may have noticed from your own calculations that it is almost impossible (unless you weigh over 300 pounds) to realistically and comfortably release more than two pounds a week. Most experts do not recommend releasing more. I do not recommend it, and most research shows it is not a good idea.

I would like to recommend that you release weight slowly, at a rate of one to two pounds a week.

WHY? Releasing more than two pounds a week creates the following issues with your body:

- Toxins. Many of the environmental toxins you consume in food additives, pesticides, and water contaminants are stored in your fat. When fat is burned, it releases toxins into your bloodstream, and it takes a while for the body to rid the blood of these toxins. Slower weight release keeps you from poisoning yourself.

- Hunger. When weight is released too fast, your survival mechanisms trigger hunger hormones.

- Releasing Weight Quickly Sets You Up for Fat Thinking. If you are feeling fat, you likely have a big driving part of your mind screaming, "I have to lose the weight now. I don't have time to mess around with releasing 1 pound a week!" Your need to release quickly is coming from old fat thinking that you are not okay as you are. That is not true, and this process is as much about truly loving yourself down the scale so that you can cultivate a lifestyle that honors you. It's as important to be consistent over time as it is to release weight.

My advice would be to lower your rate of release to a place where your Daily Calorie Budget for Weight Release feels livable. Releasing weight slowly allows you to adjust your mind and body so that you will be ready for the thing that is as important as weight release, weight maintenance.

HOW TO SHIFT WITH A DAILY LOW-CALORIE BUDGET

Most weight experts say you shouldn't go below a 1,200 calorie a day budget. If your Daily Calorie Budget for releasing a pound a week falls below 1,200 calories, consider one of these options:

- You can lower your Daily/Weekly Weight Release Rate Calories. Doing so will increase your Daily Calorie Budget Calories.

- You can increase your exercise. This will allow you to release weight more quickly or allow you to add to your Daily Calorie Budget. (In the next chapter, you will learn how to add exercise calories burned to your Daily Calorie Budget.)

PERMISSION TO SCREAM

Hey, Apprentice, I want you to know you have gone through a lot of information! Your head may be swimming a bit and that's okay. I am just reminding you that change takes stretching, and we definitely stretched your mind a bit!

You have just created your Calorie Budget for Weight Release, and as powerful as that is, there is a bitter sweetness that comes with realizing there is no magic pill or detox that is going to create effortless weight release. It's similar to when you learned that the tooth fairy wasn't real. (You knew that, right?) The era of fairies and magical thinking with regards to weight is over for you.

It's at this point in my live *Shift Weight Mastery Process* that I get everyone to stand up, stretch, and then hold hands. I give everyone permission to stomp their feet and scream "It's not fair!" and get the feelings of injustice out of their systems. However large or small your Calorie Budget for Weight Release, as per your body's own energy burn, at least you have a realistic awareness of what it is. So, if you like, please take a moment to stand up and scream about it. Do it and get it all out...I will wait here for you.

Okay, good, feel better? After everyone in my workshops has a good scream and stomp, we acknowledge that we are stepping into a new and powerful era in our journey. We now get to be an adult and in charge of our own weight release.

So in leaving behind those old beliefs, you, too, get the benefits of adulthood and being in control and making your own decisions. Congratulations! Now you will discover what it is like to live life within your Calorie Budget for Weight Release and Maintenance and not look at it as if you are taking away something. You won't feel deprived, because you are getting to live life in a way you have designed, and you will THRIVE.

At this point in the process, we take a moment for everyone to jump up and down in excitement and cheer and applaud. Feel free to do the same. Again, I will wait for you...all done? Perfect.

Have faith, until you start your *30-Day Thin Thinking Practice* and track your food, you may have no idea of how much nourishing and stabilizing food you can eat and still stay within your Calorie Budget for Weight Release. In addition, many people are surprised how few calories they need when they start eating healthy vegetables, protein, and fiber. (Much more about this coming up in a bit, so hold on!)

WEIGHT MASTERY SKILL 1 SUM UP: BALANCING YOUR BODY'S ENERGY TO RELEASE WEIGHT

- Your *Daily Body Burn Calories* are the amount of calories, or energy, you burn each day being alive. You could call this your weight maintenance calories.

- In order to release weight, you need to consume less than your *Daily Body Burn Calories* or burn more calories with exercise or do both.

- Your *Daily Calorie Budget for Weight Release* is the number of calories you can consume each day and release weight at a rate you decide. This number may vary depending on how much you exercise and what your *Daily/Weekly Weight Release Rate* is.

- Understanding the physics of how your body releases weight sets you free from the fat thinking of dieting.

APPRENTICE PAUSE: Do you see how Skill 1 engages a deeper, more powerful part of your mind for releasing weight? Instead of relying upon diets and the latest fad, you are developing an understanding of how to create weight release for yourself. You are sitting in the driver's seat of your weight release, making change from the inside out. By the time you achieve your ideal weight, you will be in position to maintain it for good.

_____

Skill 1 is the first-floor framework for weight release. Next is **Skill 2, Building a Consistent Relationship with Exercise**.

CHAPTER 25
WEIGHT MASTERY SKILL 2

BUILDING A CONSISTENT

RELATIONSHIP WITH EXERCISE

SKILL 2: Building a Consistent Relationship with Exercise. The skill of uniting yourself with exercise to achieve your ideal weight and good health.

FAT THINKING AND EXERCISE

Doesn't it seem odd that we often resist something as powerful as exercise? Physical activity not only enhances well-being, it's also the only way to increase metabolism in a safe, consistent, and significant way. You can exercise to release weight faster or to consume more calories or both. Yet, when it comes to exercising, the Inner Rebel in you wants to throw a tantrum and say, "I'm not gonna!"

During the *Shift Weight Mastery Process*, I ask, "What is your fat thinking around exercise?" Of all the questions participants respond to during a seminar, this one receives the most negative and emotional answers.

- "I hate it!"

- "I don't have time."

- "Borrrrrrrrrrinnnnnnnnng!"

- "I do not like to sweat."

- "It hurts to move."

- "I hate the gym!"

- "I hate the people who go to the gym."

- "I hate the person who invented gyms!"

Fat thinking about exercise is simply any negative belief or habit that keeps you from consistent exercise. If you have been inconsistent with physical activity, these examples of fat thinking may be keeping you from building a consistent relationship with exercise:

- **You see exercise as a chore you have to do to release weight.** You see exercise as punishment for struggling with your weight. You think of it as something you have to suffer through to make the scale go down.

- **Your exercise goals are vague and not outcome-oriented.** "I am going to try to exercise this week" means absolutely nothing in your mind.

- **You are trying to fit exercise into your busy life**. Do you suffer from a chronic case of "I couldn't find time" or "I forgot to get to the gym?" Chances are you see exercise as low on your "to do" list and you don't see it as a regular part of your lifestyle.

Your fat thinking about exercise gives you little, if any, chance of creating a successful relationship with exercise. Yet when you shift a bit and begin to focus on your relationship to exercise with your thin thinking mind, you will start moving!

....

"I hadn't exercised in over five years. The Shift Weight Mastery Process seminar was being held at an athletic club in downtown Los Angeles. I remember that we did the section on exercise, and Rita finished with a hypnosis session just before lunch. I remember having the desire to just begin to walk around the track at that club during lunch. I walked that day and have kept on walking every day since." Brenda B. (Released 25 pounds, maintaining more than five years and still walking!)

....

THIN THINKING AND EXERCISE

Apprentice, please consider these thin thinking techniques that help shift a Weight Struggler to a Weight Master with exercise:

- **Use exercise with your weekly weight goals to create a specific outcome.** For example, tell yourself, "I am going to exercise for 30 minutes Monday, Wednesday, and Friday. The added calories burned will help me achieve my release of one pound this week." Your mind is motivated when you set a specific goal that has both a measurable outcome and a reward. Having exercise directly impact the results you see on your scale motivates you to follow through and keep working out.

- **Make exercise a priority in your weekly routine.** The mind loves structure. If exercise is built into the daily routine of your life, working out becomes a part of who you are and not just something that you do. Seeing yourself as an exerciser literally changes your perception of yourself and boosts positive feelings about yourself.

- **See exercise as a reward.** When you think of exercise as something you "get" to do not "have" to do, your mind becomes excited about it. You can become addicted to exercise, especially if you focus on the amazing feeling that exercise creates in you during and after your workout or fitness routine. Have you ever heard someone saying they regretted going for a walk or to the gym?

In this chapter, I explore some thin thinking strategies that will help you begin to wire a more powerful relationship with exercise into your Weight Mastery Home. These strategies will be helpful even if you already have a good relationship with exercise.

1. Setting clear weekly exercise goals

2. Creating your weekly exercise system

1 – SETTING CLEAR WEEKLY EXERCISE GOALS

In the last chapter, you created a Daily Calorie Budget for Weight Release without exercise based on your Weekly Weight Release Rate. Now, you and your Inner Coach are going to learn how to partner with exercise to further your weekly weight-release goals. Is that lab coat still on?

Why is setting a specific, weekly exercise goal so valuable? As you learned earlier in this book, vague goals do not create motivation or action in your mind. Notice the difference in brain engagement between:

- VAGUE GOAL. "I should try to exercise this week, because it will help me release weight."

- SPECIFIC GOAL. "When I burn 1,750 calories exercising this week, I can choose to burn –half a pound more in weight or eat 250 more calories a day."

By creating a specific outcome that your mind views as rewarding, you arouse your brain, focusing it on the actions needed to achieve your outcome. Here is how two sisters, with two totally different weight-release needs, used specific strategies to change their relationship to exercise.

CASE STUDY: A TALE OF TWO SISTERS

Tara and Gina signed up together for the *Shift Weight Mastery Process*. As the sisters entered my office, I noticed they couldn't be more different in appearance and personality! Tara was dark-haired, in her 50s, and was a quiet hospice nurse. Gina was gregarious and lighter than her sister in both her coloring and weight. She worked as a real estate agent in an affluent LA neighborhood.

At the consultation, Tara weighed nearly 300 pounds and was pre-diabetic. Carrying that weight was causing pain in her knees, so it was hard for her to move. When I asked her about exercise, she said, "I haven't ever exercised especially, and now with work and my long commute, there's no time. When I get home, it's already late. I eat the dinner my husband makes, watch TV for an hour, and then go to bed. I don't have time to exercise, and it hurts too much to try."

Gina didn't have a weight issue earlier in her life, but she had gained 20 pounds since menopause and weighed around 180 pounds. Her attempts to lose weight with exercise had been unsuccessful. "I don't get it. I was doing two yoga classes a week with my friends, and yet the scale didn't budge, so I gave up," she exclaimed. "I don't like this spare tire around my waist, and I can't fit into most of my expensive outfits. I thought the exercise was going to help, but it didn't."

What was missing for both sisters at this point was an Inner Coach that would work with them to create a powerful exercise vision. An Inner Coach would also be specific about how each of them could use exercise to create their specific health and weight goals.

I calculated their Daily Body Burns. Tara's Daily Body Burn was 2,450 calories. Gina's was 1,773 calories.

STRATEGY A: ADDING EXERCISE CALORIES TO INCREASE WEEKLY WEIGHT RELEASE

When you exercise, you add those exercise calories burned to your Daily Body Burn total for the day. Adding multiple exercise sessions over the week increases the overall total amount of calories that you burn for that week. The net effect is a larger weight release for the week. You decide how many exercise calories to burn in exercise to create the additional weight release you desire and work that specific amount of exercise into your week. This is what I did for Tara.

At 2,450 calories, Tara had a higher Daily Body Burn than her sister because it takes more energy to move 300 pounds than 180 pounds. First, we calculated Tara's Weekly/Daily Weight Release Rate goal (BEFORE figuring in exercise) for one and a half pounds per week, making her Daily Calorie Budget for Weight Release 1,700 calories a day.

2,450 Tara's Daily Body Burn

-750 Daily Weight Release Rate to release 1.5 pounds per week

=1,700 Tara's Daily Calorie Budget to release 1.5 pounds per week (without exercise)

Tara looked at the numbers. "Staying within 1,700 calories seems doable food-wise. I would like to release weight more quickly, but I don't think I can eat less at this point. It feels too restrictive. I am concerned about adding exercise, because, like I said, I don't have the time."

"I get it, Tara," I said, understanding her fear. "I think there is a happy medium for you. You will find that if you begin exercising a bit every day, you burn more calories, release more weight, and feel healthier. You may even reverse the pre-diabetes diagnosis."

"I would love to do that," she said, "but how much time are we talking about here and what kind of exercise? I ache too much to do anything too strenuous."

We figured out that at 300 pounds Tara burns about 500 calories an hour walking at a slow to moderate pace. If she walked 30 minutes a day, she could meet her goal of burning 250 calories. That added an additional 1,750 calories to her weekly calorie burn, increased her weight release by another half-pound, and allowed her to release a total of two pounds a week.

To demonstrate how this would work, I am going to introduce you to The Weekly Weight Release Planner. (**Chart N**) Use this tool during your *30-Day Thin Thinking Practice* to predictably track your rate of weight release and plan your exercise for the week.

	MO	TU	W	TH	FR	SA	SU	WEEKLY TOTALS
Daily Body Burn	2450	2450	2450	2450	2450	2450	2450	17150
+ Actual Exercise Calories (walking 30 min./day)	250	250	250	250	250	250	250	1750
= Total Daily Burn Calories	2700	2700	2700	2700	2700	2700	2700	18900
- (Less) Actual Food Calories	(1700)	(1700)	(1700)	(1700)	(1700)	(1700)	(1700)	(11900)
= Net Calories Burned	1000	1000	1000	1000	1000	1000	1000	7000
= Net Calories Running Total	1000	2000	3000	4000	5000	6000	7000	7000 = 2 lbs.

Grand Total

CHART N: Tara's Weekly Weight Release Increased with Added Exercise

By the end of the week, Tara will release two pounds by walking 30 minutes each day.

Tara was convinced but hesitant. "I am a little nervous. Thirty minutes seems like a lot of walking for me since I am starting at nothing," she said.

"You can start with less, Tara," I assured her. "As long as you stay within your 1,700 Daily Calorie Budget, you will be releasing at least a pound and a half a week. Then whatever you burn in exercise will be additional calories for more weight release. You can build up to 30 minutes over time."

"Sounds good. This makes sense to me. Having an exercise plan puts the power and choice in my hand. I like that."

Strategy B: Adding Exercise to bank extra calories for weekends, social events, and/or overages

Another strategy to shift your relationship with exercise is to bank calories burned exercising for times during the week when you go over your Daily Calorie Budget for weight release. Here is how Gina used this strategy to shift her relationship to exercise.

I calculated Gina's metabolism and found that she could release a pound a week without exercise by subtracting 500 calories a day from her body burn of 1,773 calories.

1,773 Gina's Daily Body Burn

-500 Daily Weight Release Rate to release one pound per week

=1,273 Gina's Daily Calorie Budget to release one pound per week (without exercise)

Gina looked at the number 1,273 and a light bulb went off. "No wonder I haven't been losing weight. I might have been losing weight during the week, because when I diet, I eat only about 1,200 calories a day. However, I like going out on the weekend and entertaining, so without knowing it I have been erasing whatever extra calories I burned during the week with extra food and drink on the weekend."

"If you exercise more, you can add the calories you burned to your weekend calorie budget," I said.

"I get it. It's kind of like a savings account?" Gina asked, the wheels in her mind turning. "How much does a yoga class burn?"

"About 300 calories for an hour-long class"

"Is that all? So my two yoga classes are burning only 600 calories for the week? That is why they didn't help much. I need to add more exercise, huh? " Gina asked.

"It all depends on how many more calories you want to bank for the weekend."

"Well, I probably need six hundred more each for Friday and Saturday. That's a glass of wine or two or a dessert. I want to be realistic. I am willing to work out more; I just needed to understand why and how. My friend wants me to come to her spin class once a week, how much does that burn?"

"Around 450 calories an hour," I answered.

"Okay," Gina said, determined, "so if I stay within my budget of 1,273 calories a day during the week with my food, add three yoga classes to burn 900 calories total, and add a 450-calorie spin class, that is another 1,350 calories I have for lunches out and weekends. I could handle that. In fact, I am kind of excited to try this out."

Here's how Gina's typical week played out without exercise. (**Chart O**)

	MO	TU	W	TH	FR	SA	SU	WEEKLY TOTALS
Daily Body Burn	1773	1773	1773	1773	1773	1773	1773	12411
+ Actual Exercise Calories	0	0	0	0	0	0	0	0
= Total Daily Burn Calories	1773	1773	1773	1773	1773	1773	1773	12411
- (Less) Actual Food Calories	(1200)	(1200)	(1980)	(1200)	(2640)	(1920)	(2211)	(12351)
= Net Calories Burned	573	573	(207)	573	(867)	(147)	(438)	60
= Net Calories Running Total	573	1146	939	1512	645	498	60	**60**

Grand Total

Chart O: Gina's Typical Week Without Exercise Creates a Weight Release Challenge

As you can see, with no exercise and adding socializing calories from lunch on Wednesday; a 3-course, restaurant dinner Friday with wine and dessert; wine on Saturday; and a Sunday brunch, Gina went over her calorie budget for weight release even though she stayed within that 1,200-calorie budget on the other days of the week. You can see why she was maintaining her weight and not releasing it, despite her calories being low three days out of seven.

Here is how she did when began shifting and burned a specific number of calories to create a bank of extra calories for her weekly splurges.

	MO	TU	W	TH	FR	SA	SU	WEEKLY TOTALS
Daily Body Burn	1773	1773	1773	1773	1773	1773	1773	12411
+ Actual Exercise Calories	0	300	300	0	300	450	300	1650
= Total Daily Burn Calories	1773	2073	2073	1773	2073	2223	2073	14061
- (Less) Actual Food Calories	(1273)	(1273)	(1500)	(1273)	(2000)	(1560)	(1600)	(10659)
= Net Calories Burned	500	800	493	500	73	662	473	3501
= Net Calories Running Total	500	1300	1793	2393	2466	3129	3501	3501

Grand Total

Chart P: Gina Uses Exercise to Bank Extra Calories for Her Social Life

Gina set her weekly exercise goals at three yoga classes (300 calories each), a 450-calorie spin class, and a Sunday walk (300 calories). She also lightened up a bit on those socializing calories. She hit her weekly weight release goals and still had fun and felt like she was splurging. (Chart P)

NOTE: If Gina had felt like 1,273 calories was too low a daily calorie budget, she could use her banked calories for overages during the week.

STRATEGY C: ADDING EXERCISE TO AVERAGE MORE CALORIES INTO YOUR DAILY CALORIE BUDGET

The last strategy is to use the exercise calories you burn over the course of a week to increase your Daily Calorie Budget for Weight Release. This is a great strategy, especially if you have a very low Daily Body Burn.

For example, let's say that Tara and Gina had a sister named Carmen who had a very low Calorie Budget for Weight Release.

1,559 Carmen's Daily Body Burn

-500 Daily Weight Release Rate to release one pound a week

=1,059 Carmen's Daily Calorie Budget to release one pound a week without exercise

For Carmen, 1,059 calories a day is a bit too low for comfort. Remember, Weight Mastery has to be sustainable and realistic.

Carmen could change her Weekly/Daily Weight Release Rate to half a pound a week (which would change the amount of calories she had to reduce daily to 250 instead of 500) and easily raise her Daily Calorie Budget for Weight Release to 1,309 (without added exercise), which would be much more reasonable. But what if she wanted that faster rate of a weight release of one pound a week?

Carmen could make these calculations:

1. Determine a Daily Calorie Budget that would be more comfortable, like 1,300 calories.

2. Figure out the difference between 1,300 and her Daily Calorie Budget for Weight Release of 1,059 calories. 1,300 – 1,059 = 241

3. Multiply that difference by seven for the seven days of the week. 241 x 7= 1,687.

4. Carmen would need to generate 1,687 more calories a week on average in exercise in order to keep her Calorie Budget for Weight Release at 1,300 per day and release a pound a week.

Carmen decides to take three Zumba classes (one hour each) at her local health club after work on Monday, Wednesday, and Friday. Each class burns 400 calories. She can burn an additional 487 calories with two brisk, 45-minute walks on the weekend.

	MO	TU	W	TH	FR	SA	SU	WEEKLY TOTALS
Daily Body Burn	1559	1559	1559	1559	1559	1559	1559	10913
+ Actual Exercise Calories	400	0	400	0	400	250	275	1700
= Total Daily Burn Calories	1959	1559	1959	1559	1959	1809	1834	12613
- (Less) Actual Food Calories	(1300)	(1300)	(1300)	(1300)	(1300)	(1300)	(1300)	(9100)
= Net Calories Burned	659	229	659	229	659	509	534	3478
= Net Calories Running Total	659	888	1547	1776	2435	2944	3478	3478 just shy of 1 lb.

Grand Total

Chart Q: Carmen Increases Her Daily Calorie Budget with Exercise

By adding exercise and averaging the energy burned by exercise for the week, Carmen is able to release one pound a week. She has a much more feasible Daily Calorie Budget for Weight Release than before. (**Chart Q**)

I hope that you are beginning to see the mechanics of using exercise for more of a daily calorie buffer or to speed your weight release. You and your Inner Coach can use exercise from the inside out, as a practical tool to create the change you want. The skill of having this more powerful relationship with exercise will not only allow for thin thinking but also thin living.

2 – CREATING YOUR WEEKLY EXERCISE SYSTEM

Setting up a weekly exercise system to suit your own needs is important for success. Companies run on systems, nature runs on systems, and so does Weight Mastery.

The first step toward consistency is to set up a flexible but solid system around exercise that you can repeat on a weekly basis. Having a system or plan is lacking in most Weight Struggler's relationships with exercise. Remember the research on Weight Masters and exercise? Most of those men and women exercise an hour a day, 6 days a week. You don't have to start there, but I invite you to see that long-term weight release takes commitment, and it takes a system to fulfill that commitment and keep it going.

RITA'S WEEKLY EXERCISE SYSTEM

I want to share with you how my weekly repeatable exercise system works. Like many of the Weight Masters mentioned earlier, I burn about 2,000 calories a week in exercise to maintain my weight of 140 pounds. As a woman in her early fifties, my metabolism is relatively low. My Daily Calorie Budget for Maintenance is 1,550 calories a day, so I bank my additional exercise calories (around 1,600-2,000) to use for social outings, entertaining, and days when I go over my budget.

RITA'S EXERCISE SYSTEM

My Weekly Exercise Calorie Burn Goal is: __2000__ calories.

Day	Time	Exercise Type	Minutes of Exercise	Calories Burned
Mon	8:30 am	Hi Intensity Interval Training	50 min.	550
Tue	7:30 pm	Spin	45 min.	300
Wed		Off		
Thu	5:30 pm	Boot Camp	55 min.	500
Fri	9:00 am	Spin	45 min.	300
Sat		Off		
Sun		Hike with family (or spin)	90 min.	400
			Total Weekly Calories Burned =	2050

Chart R: Rita's Weekly Exercise System

You may think that my Daily Calorie Budget is small and my exercise budget seems high. For me, it's perfect. I always feel well-fed and never deprived. After years of being an achy couch potato, I feel like a million dollars inside and out. I am not saying this to brag. I am saying this because I know you can have this, too.

I am currently burning about 2,000 calories a week with physical activity (**Chart R**). I get resistance training with light weights in my HIIT (High Intensity Interval Training) and Boot Camp classes, which helps tone my body. After age 40, men and women begin losing lean muscle mass every year. That muscle loss adds to the decline of metabolism. Doing some strength training, even if it is lifting soup cans while watching TV at night, will help slow this process. (Think of it as burning calories instead of consuming them in front of the TV.)

During my weekly planning huddle with my Inner Coach, I make sure my exercise sessions are set up within all the other appointments and events of my week. Planning in advance sets me up for success by creating a mental roadmap through my week and imagining how it will all play out. This helps me follow through on my plans about 90 percent more than if I just "hope" to exercise.

I carve out exercise times from my schedule. I make sure the workouts are on my calendar and honor those times as much as I would a client appointment, a birthday party, or a doctor's appointment. I put all those appointments in my weekly planner and keep them.

By planning ahead, you are making exercise a part of your life. This time is your time, and you and your body deserve to be a priority. After all, if you are not healthy, how can you be of service to those in your life who need you? Taking time to be healthy ahead of other things isn't selfish; it is selfless. Be a role model for others.

Now, let's get your exercise system set up.

SETTING UP YOUR EXERCISE SYSTEM

Now once again, you are going to lean on technology for help. You can go to www.FromFatToThinThinking.com and find the Shift Weekly Weight Release Planner-Calculator.

You can use the planner-calculator to figure out your Exercise System. It includes:

- What days you will exercise.

- What types of exercises you will engage in.

- How much time you will need to exercise to meet your weight release goal for the week.

The planner-calculator will help you see how your exercise plans align with your weight release goals for the week. The calculator will also help you decide your exercise strategy for the week. Remember, your exercise strategy defines how you are using exercise within your weight release goals. The calculator will demonstrate what those choices would look like to help you decide.

You can use exercise to:

- Increase your weekly weight release

- Bank calories for the weekend, social events, and/or daily overages

- Increase your Daily Calorie Budget for Weight Release

When you have planned out your week of exercise and decided upon your strategy, you can print your results. You can use this online planner every week during your *30-Day Thin Thinking Practice.* Or if you don't want to use this online resource, you can fill out the Exercise System Worksheet provided in the index along with the Exercise Calorie Per Hour Chart to plan out your exercise for the week.

EXERCISE SYSTEM WORKSHEET

My Weekly Exercise Calorie Burn Goal is: _____ calories.

Day	Time	Exercise Type	Minutes of Exercise	Calories Burned
Mon				
Tue				
Wed				
Thu				
Fri				
Sat				
Sun				
			Total Weekly Calories Burned =	

Chart S: Exercise System Worksheet

No Time? Break Up Exercise into Bite-Sized Chunks

When you have busy days that don't allow for an hour of exercise, break up your exercise into short segments and spread them out in mini sessions throughout your day.

For instance, Tara realized, as we were working out her thirty minutes of walking every day, that she could not do it at one time. She decided that first thing in the morning she could walk around her block for ten minutes. Lunchtime at work, she could walk around the floor of the hospital twice for ten more minutes. After dinner, she and her husband would walk around the block again for another ten minutes.

Tara found that dividing exercise into shorter sessions not only made achieving her goal doable, but she came to love the moments her walking gave her to refresh herself and think about her day. She also started pulling her friends Sue and Barbara along on her lunchtime walk. Soon they started the ten-minute club and made a social activity of it. Tara discovered a way to make exercising enjoyable and doable.

MARKET THE REWARD OF EXERCISE TO YOURSELF

Every time you think about exercise, practice thinking how good you are going to feel after your workout instead of how you feel leading up to it. Imagine yourself finishing the exercise and feeling:

- Strong in your body.

- Exhilarated in your mind.

- Your body and mind are connected as one.

- Proud of yourself for having exercised.

Here are some benefits to focus on. Exercise:

- Balances your hormones.

- Allows you to solve problems.

- Elevates your libido.

- Lowers your blood pressure.

- Helps regulate the hunger hormones leptin and ghrelin.

- Makes you feel good about yourself.

- Lifts your mood.

- Makes you smarter!

OVERCOME "I BLEW IT" FROM YOUR INNER CRITIC OR SEDUCTION FROM YOUR INNER REBEL

There are going to be times when exercise doesn't happen, perhaps for a good reason. If you decide that missing an exercise session Wednesday ruins your entire week and you'll start over with exercise on Monday, think again. Starting over is death to consistency. "Keep on going!" is the mantra of Weight Masters.

Do you sometimes talk yourself out of exercising? The Inner Rebel likes to resist exertion of any kind. I bet there are some distinct ways that your Inner Rebel knows how to talk you out of your exercise session, including:

- It's too warm in bed.

- You worked too hard today, so relax.

- You don't have time to exercise.

One way to overcome your Inner Rebel's resistance is to practice interacting with it. Create a good comeback for your Inner Rebel's seduction. If you practice this ahead of time, you will be ready and able to counteract the seduction when the time comes with a more positive exercise seduction. Market exercise to your Inner Rebel in a positive light.

Rebel Resistance. It's warm in bed…

Counteract. Think of how warm and invigorated I am going to feel when I am done with my morning walk!

Rebel Resistance. You worked so hard today…

Counteract. All the more reason to exercise and feel refreshed for later.

Rebel Resistance. You don't have the time to exercise…

Counteract. I can make the time to exercise and feel better, even if I have only a few minutes.

The more you focus on the positive outcome of exercising, the more you are engaging the reward neurotransmitters in your brain. Eventually your mind and body get hooked, and you begin craving that post-workout high. Let exercise become your drug of choice.

CASE STUDY: CONCLUSION

By the time Tara and Gina showed up at the *Shift Weight Mastery Process* seminar a month later, they had both released weight. Tara had released eight pounds as she had expected, shedding two pound a week for four weeks.

Gina had released a bit more than her expected four pounds. "I didn't have a very social month, so I banked calories for weight release," she said happily.

In the year since, Tara has released almost 95 pounds, her blood sugar levels have improved, and the pains in her knees only exist a tiny bit in the morning when she first wakes up.

Gina released 20 pounds, while keeping up with her social life. For the last eight months, she has been using exercise to maintain her loving and reasonable ideal weight.

....

"What I love is that I am the one in control. I don't feel so baffled about why the scale is or isn't doing what it is doing. I also love the fact that I can live in the real world and don't have to be a hermit, living alone and dieting with my carrot sticks." Gina G. (Released 20 lbs., maintaining at 1 year.)

....

....

"I am so proud of pushing myself past the negative beliefs that I could never exercise. Now I am someone who gets home, throws my running shoes on, and can't wait to get out the door. On my walk, I feel my heart pumping, my body working, and my mind is singing, enjoying feeling so alive and free.!" Tara R. (Released 93 pounds and...still releasing.)

....

WEIGHT MASTERY SKILL 2 SUM UP: MASTERING YOUR RELATIONSHIP WITH EXERCISE

When you use exercise as a partner to achieve your weight release goals, you create a relationship with exercise that you own.

You can use exercise to:

- Release weight at a faster rate.

- Bank exercise calories for extras, such as social events, eating out, and overages.

- Increase your Daily Calorie Budget for Weight Release, allowing you the flexibility to consume more food.

APPRENTICE PAUSE: Are you feeling like you have had a big mental workout? Good! We are here to stretch your mind past where it stops. I love Albert Einstein's quote "No problem can be solved from the same level of consciousness that created it." What you are learning is a new way of thinking about yourself and weight management. All of this will settle in and become familiar. For now, you are putting new wiring in your mind. Go with it, and be open to not having it all figured out yet.

It is now time to finish out our weight skills with the all-important **Skill 3, Creating a Powerful Relationship with Food.**

CHAPTER 26
WEIGHT MASTERY SKILL 3

CREATING A MASTERFUL
RELATIONSHIP WITH FOOD

SKILL 3: Creating a Masterful Relationship with Food. This skill focuses you on building a sustainable way of eating within your body's energy needs for weight release and maintenance. Honing this skill allows you to honor your tastes and lifestyle and feel satisfied and not deprived while you release and then maintain your ideal weight.

FAT THINKING AND FOOD

I hear the same story over and over from my clients. These phrases swirl and swirl around in their minds and pound the shores of their weight struggle like a hurricane that won't subside.

- "I hate food. I wish I didn't have to deal with it."

- "Brownies are bad. Kale is good."

- "I am a hopeless sugar addict."

- "I love food, but I hate what it does to me."

- "I don't know what to eat anymore."

When I struggled with my weight, I was confused by the conflicting information I heard and read. Like many of my clients, I had learned to fear food, often being not quite sure if what I was eating was "bad" and going to make me fat or if it was "good." This led me to distrust food and myself.

As we develop our struggle with weight, we tend to develop a fat thinking way of categorizing food as either "good" or "bad." In addition, we judge our eating mode as "being good" or "being bad" as well.

For instance, when we are "being good," we are eating the food that our weight loss plan, whatever it is, deems as good, and so we see ourselves as being good as well. Nothing is wrong about eating healthfully, but our distorted black-and-white, perfectionistic attitude about food sets us up for failure. That's because anything outside of the strict confines of "good" is "bad."

Once we fall from grace by eating a bad food, we tend to shift into eating "whatever" we want. After all, if we are going to be bad, we might as well be really bad, right?

Can you see how this good-or-bad attitude has been causing you to spin around in the Weight Struggle Cycle and has tarnished your relationship with food? This fat thinking mindset focuses your attention on an external structure (the diet, the detox, the plan) that when you are "good" about following it, you will lose weight. Your attention is focused outside of you on something that doesn't belong to you. There is no ownership in faithfully following a diet. You ultimately "fall off" not because you are a bad person or lack discipline but because you are focusing externally on "doing" something, rather than focused internally on "becoming" something—that is, being masterful with your own personal relationship with food.

THIN THINKING AND FOOD

One of the first relationships that all humans and animals establish is with food. I remember when the doctor put my newborn son on my belly. He nudged his way up to my breast to eat. How beautiful and amazing is the pure need to sustain ourselves in this world. As we grow up and are exposed to a world of food, both healthy and unhealthy, that relationship may become stained with pain, suffering, and limiting beliefs. We learn to fear food, hate it, and wish we didn't have to eat at all. We have distorted views of ourselves and our relationship to food.

My dear apprentice, this is going to be the longest skill chapter because our relationship with food is so layered and complex. Stick with me and know you will have a lot of time to master your relationship with food during our *30-Day Thin Thinking Practice*. With your lab coat on and your Inner Coach by your side, you're ready to begin wiring a new, positive relationship with food from the inside out.

IS A CALORIE A CALORIE?

You have already created your Daily Calorie Budget for Weight Release and know that when you stay within that daily parameter you can release weight at a rate you decide. Now let's begin to look at the calories themselves.

Are there good calories and bad calories when it comes to weight release? If your Calorie Budget for Weight Release is 1,200 calories a day and you eat 1,200 calories worth of French fries and ice cream, would you release the same pound of weight at the same rate as eating 1,200 calories of chicken and broccoli?

Well, luckily for us, Mark Haub, professor of nutrition at Kansas State University did a study on himself. For ten weeks, he ate a diet of mostly Twinkies and powdered doughnuts. Even though he was eating a junk food diet, he was also eating 1,000 calories less than his Daily Body Burn. Over the course of the 10-week study, he released nearly 27 pounds!

The truth is that a calorie is a calorie. When your calorie intake is less than your Daily Body Burn—no matter what you eat—you will release weight as per the laws of physics—just like Professor Haub. So if you eat a brownie, is it "bad?" Will it make you "fat" as you're often told? Will eating a brownie banish you from the heaven of good dieters and send you into the hell of brownie-eating sinners? The answer is no. The brownie itself is not fattening per se; our fat thinking around the brownie is. Generally, after eating the brownie, this thought comes to mind: "I blew it, I ate a brownie, and that was bad. Well, since I blew it, I may as well eat three more and start over tomorrow." The truth is: "Gee, I ate a brownie. It was probably about 300 calories, and I have about 500 calories left in my Calorie Budget for Weight Release for today. Let me move on, eat a healthy dinner, and get my body back in balance after the sugar and flour from the brownie and continue with my healthy lifestyle for the rest of the day."

THE FOOD STRUGGLE ZONE

With the revelation that calories are calories, why aren't most long-term Weight Masters eating a diet of French fries and Ben and Jerry's ice cream?

There are a few very important reasons:

- Refined foods are densely packed with calories. A small amount (1 ¾ cups of ice cream, which is 875 calories and a medium serving of French fries, which is 340 calories) is all you can eat in a day to stay within a 1,200 calorie per day range. And, no doubt, you would need to eat more than your Daily Calorie Budget to feel satisfied.

- Sugary and starchy refined foods eaten on an empty stomach spike your blood sugar and cause an insulin imbalance. If you kept eating this way over time, you would become resistant to insulin and the satiety hormone leptin. This would lead you to suffer from what I call a constant feeling of fake hunger—feeling hungry even though you have just eaten.

- Also, the sugar, fat, and salt in refined food stimulates the dopamine neurotransmitters in your brain creating cravings for more refined food.

In short, by eating a majority of the calories within your Calorie Budget for Weight Release in refined foods—especially those "white foods" containing sugar and flour—you awaken what I call the Carb Zombie, a deprived feeling and a food-obsessed, always hungry, and nonstop thinking about food state. In that mode, your mind is hijacked by the excessive priming of your neuropathways with refined carbohydrates. The Carb Zombie makes you:

- Think obsessively about food.

- Feel hungry even though you may have recently eaten.

- More prone to overeat, binge eat, and have the impulse to eat any refined food that crosses your path.

This Carb Zombie ultimately pulls you into what I call your Food Struggle Zone by reigniting your old fat thinking wiring—the eating habits and food cravings that caused you to struggle with weight in the first place. So even though a calorie is a calorie and there are no "good" or "bad" calories, when you are consistently overeating certain foods, your body and mind revert into a state of imbalance and instability that leads you back to struggling.

THE FOOD MASTERY ZONE

So, my dear apprentice, instead of relying on some outside structure: a diet book, a meal plan, or a ketogenic app to tell you when you are being good or bad, I am proposing a revolutionary inner structure that has nothing to do with outside rules, regulations, or dogma. Rather this is a structure you create, and you will take back all the power you have given away over the years. You are going to shift the focus and learn to use food to create internal states of:

- **Stability.** The state of satiety, a feeling of being fed, comforted, and even-keeled in body and mind.

- **Nourishment.** The state of vibrancy that comes from eating foods with vitamins, minerals, antioxidants, and other nutrients the body needs for optimal health. Also a state of mental nourishment that comes from self-care and seeking pleasure in things other than food.

- **Balance.** The state of confidence that comes from being able to find pleasure in healthy whole foods and use them as the foundation of our Calorie Budget for Weight Release, while allowing for a small Buffer Zone of calories that allow for treats, desserts, and other foods that were once seen as "bad." This allows that wonderful feeling of being able to live in the real world and yet stay out of fake hunger and cravings and the grasp of the Carb Zombie.

These internal states form what I call the Food Mastery Zone. Learning to live in this zone allows you to develop a way of eating that honors you, your lifestyle, and your Calorie Budget for Weight Release and then Maintenance.

In this chapter, I am going to guide you and your Inner Coach through:

- The 85-15 Percent Food Mastery Zone Eating Strategy

- Living in Your Food Mastery Zone: Guidelines for Success

The 85-15 Percent Food Mastery Zone Eating St

When I started mastering my relationship with food, I realized that instead of focusing on what I couldn't have and feeling deprived, I could figure out how to spend my Calorie Budget for Weight Release wisely and create a wonderful way of eating that I enjoyed.

I learned that with my Calorie Budget for Weight Release, like my money budget, I could spend a certain percentage on food that allowed me to feel healthy and nourished and keep my blood sugar on an even keel. These foods took up most of my daily calories. I might call them my living expenses. The more I ate lean proteins, vegetables and fruits, and healthy fats, the more I liked them, even craved them. If I spent my budget well with these healthy wholesome foods, I would have some extra calories for foods that were maybe not so healthy, like a small dessert, a glass of wine, or some dark chocolate. (Think of these foods as nonessential luxury items.) The calories remaining after I created a stable foundation with healthy, whole foods allowed me a Buffer Zone of calories that let me live in the real world and not in a rigid "good food, bad food" diet prison.

I learned what many Weight Masters learn along the way to mastery— that is, to eat mostly healthy, nourishing foods and allow some wiggle room for small servings of snacks, desserts, or treats. It's the 85-15 Percent Food Mastery Zone Eating Strategy. Each day your focus is on eating approximately:

- 85 percent (to 100 percent, depending on the day) of calories from foods that allow you to achieve a nourished, stabilized, and balanced state in both your body and mind. These calories include protein, healthy fats, vegetables, fruits, some complex carbohydrates, and water.

- 15 percent (from 0 percent to 15 percent, depending on the day) of calories from less nutritious foods that offer value in other ways—sociability, flexibility, and pleasure. Desserts, bread, chocolate, and alcohol are examples.

....

"It was funny, once I started working those old 'prohibited' foods into my diet and they were no longer "off limits," they suddenly lost their appeal. When the guilt

and thrill of eating "bad" foods was removed, and I actually began tasting them, I realized I didn't even like many of them! I also learned that I was perfectly capable of being moderate with pleasure foods. I like my healthy, grown-up relationship with food." Susan J. (Released 5 pounds in 30 days, maintaining a 20-pound release for 10 years)

85 PERCENT NOURISHING AND STABILIZING FOODS

Below are groups of foods that, when you eat them consistently, will allow you to feel nourished and stabilized—free of fake hunger and Carb Zombie-driven cravings. These nourishing and stabilizing foods aren't "good" per se; they simply provide a positive value for your body. You want to strive, therefore, to make them the largest portion of your Calorie Budget for Weight Release. Feeling nourished and stabilized is a great way to love and care for yourself. It also feels amazing!

Please don't look at the following section as a lesson in nutrition. The information listed is primarily to aid you to begin tuning into your mind and body and experience for yourself how different food groups offer value to your body and mind. If you need additional resources with more nutritional specifics, please visit the Online Resource Center at www.FromFatToThinThinking.com.

Protein

It's satisfying in any form. The body is made up of more than 50,000 different proteins. Nothing hits your system and immediately stabilizes you the way protein does. This food source delivers and stays by your side, keeping you satisfied for long periods of time. Protein nourishes and stabilizes you by:

- Stabilizing your blood sugar.

- Satisfying you with the fewest calories of any of the food groups.

- Allowing you to stay satisfied longer than any of the other food groups.

- Helping you maintain lean muscle mass, which burns more calories than fat.

How much protein do you need?

Most adults should shoot for 72 to 80 grams of protein per day (That's about four 3-ounce servings or three 4-ounce servings.) while you are reducing calories and if your Calorie Budget for Weight Release is 1,600 calories or less. If your Daily Calorie Budget is above 1,600, you can follow this formula: Multiply your current weight in pounds by 0.5 to get the minimum grams of protein to eat per day. (Make sure to disperse protein throughout the day.)

When you eat too little protein and too many refined carbohydrates, the brain develops an amino acid deficiency, resulting in emotional imbalances that lead you to crave sugary and starchy carbohydrates.

NOTE: Keep fatty cuts and processed meats to a minimum. Overconsumption of these foods is linked to heart disease and cancer. Choose lean, lower-fat cuts of meat, poultry, fish, and low-fat dairy products. They're also lower in calories!

SOURCES OF PROTEIN

Seafood (50 to 80 calories and 7 to 10 grams of protein per ounce): Halibut, cod, salmon, shellfish, tuna, and snapper.

Low-Fat/Fat-Free Dairy (50 to 120 calories and 3 to 7 grams of protein per ounce): Fat-free (or low-fat yogurt, cheese, milk, and cottage cheese.

Poultry, Eggs, Wild Meats (70 to 90 calories and 8 to 10 grams of protein per ounce): Chicken, turkey, buffalo (bison), elk, and ostrich.

Red Meat (90 to 130 calories and 7 to 9 grams of protein per ounce): Steak, ground beef, pork, sausage, veal, ham, etc. Look for super lean cuts and reduced-fat bacon or sausage.

Vegetarian Sources (50 to 120 calories and 2 to 6 grams of protein per ounce): Tofu and tempeh. Vegetarian versions of bacon and sausage that taste almost like the real McCoy are lower in calories and contain no saturated fat.

Beans (120 calories, 5 grams of protein, and 18 grams of carbohydrates per ½ cup): Red kidney beans, chickpeas, pinto beans, cannellini beans, lentils, black-eyed peas, and black beans.

Vegetables and Fruit

What tempted Adam? Was it a bowl of macaroni and cheese? No! It was an apple. Its crisp, clean taste is tart with a sweet edge. Try a crunchy Romaine lettuce leaf or a hot and spicy bite of a radish. Allow yourself to be seduced by fruits and vegetables. It will be worth it, I assure you.

These two food groups nourish and stabilize you in two ways:

- They offer the highest percentage of nutrients and antioxidants per calorie of any food group.

- The fiber and water in fruits and vegetables fill you up with a minimum of calories.

Are you eating enough vegetables and fruits?

If there were a drug that reduced your risk of cancer by 20 percent, would you take it? The American Cancer Institute for Cancer Research and The World Cancer Research Fund combined their efforts and evaluated over 4,500 diet and cancer studies. This comprehensive report—The Food, Nutrition, and the Prevention of Cancer: A Global Perspective—claims that if people were to eat five servings of fruits and vegetables each day, cancer rates would drop by 20 percent.

Recommended daily minimum of vegetable and fruits:

- Women: five or more ½-cup servings a day

- Men: eight or more ½-cup servings a day

SOURCES OF VEGETABLES AND FRUITS

Low Carbohydrate Vegetables are the most nutritious foods for you. Romaine and other lettuces, kale, collards, spinach, Swiss chard, artichokes, asparagus, Bok choy, broccoli, Brussels sprouts, cabbage, celery, cucumber, okra, peppers, snow peas, string beans, zucchini, eggplant, mushrooms, onions, tomatoes, yellow and red peppers, bamboo shoots, and cauliflower. (Approximately 25 to 40 calories and 5 to 11 grams of carbohydrates per ½ cup of veggies or one cup of lettuce or spinach.)

Fruits are higher in calories than vegetables but highly nutritious. Apples, apricots, bananas, blackberries, blueberries, cantaloupe, grapefruit, grapes, mangoes, pears, pineapples, plums, raspberries, strawberries, tangerines, and melons. (Approximately 50 to 90 calories and 7 to 17 grams of carbohydrates per ½-cup serving.)

Starchy Vegetables have nutrients but are also higher in carbohydrates. Potatoes, sweet potatoes, butternut squash, peas, acorn squash, winter squash, parsnips, pumpkins, beets, turnips, corn, carrots, and chestnuts. (Potatoes are on this list but not in the form of a French fries.) (Approximately 60 calories and 10 to 23 grams of carbohydrates per ½-cup serving.)

NOTE: Research shows that Weight Masters consume 7 to 11 servings of vegetables and fruits a day. It may seem like a daunting task to eat that much, but a large salad contains about four to 6 vegetable servings.

Even if you are not a fan of fruits and vegetables, there are usually a few that you like. You don't have to like them all. Know what you do like and go for it. I have seen people completely change their minds about fruits and vegetables once they recognize their value as a powerful tool for feeling full and nourished.

Healthy Fats

Healthy fats are awesome, delivering satisfying taste to your tongue and giving you a feeling of being loved. There's a reason why high fat foods, like mac and cheese, are called comfort foods! Eat just enough healthy fats to make life worth living. Use them in cooking, for infusing food with flavor, or on their own, like nuts and olives.. Healthy fats nourish and stabilize you in three ways:

- They provide flavor.

- They help you feel satisfied.

- They regulate blood sugar and mood.

Recommended daily healthy fat serving:

- Make sure you are getting 600-1000 milligrams of omega-3 fatty acids a day by taking a supplement and/or eating at least three servings of omega-3-rich fish (salmon, sardines, trout) a week.

- While releasing weight, keep healthy fat to a minimum, about three teaspoons a day or a small handful of nuts.

SOURCES OF HEALTHY FATS

Raw nuts and seeds (Almonds, cashews, filberts, macadamias, pecans, pine nuts, pistachios, pumpkin seeds, sunflower seeds,) olives, avocado, olive oil, nut oils, and nut butters. (180 to 220 calories an ounce)

NOTE: Watch the amount of healthy fat you eat or cook with daily, since fat is high in calories. Any food ceases to be healthy when you consume more than your body needs in a day. Any food that takes you over your calorie needs for the day becomes an unhealthy food. Also, AVOID trans fats and polyunsaturated fats in such foods as margarine, shortening, and most processed foods.

Whole Grains

Whole grains nourish and stabilize you in two ways:

- They are rich in fiber.

- They contain phyto-chemicals and vitamins.

Recommended daily minimum of whole grain servings:

- Zero to two ½-cup servings per day (this will depend on your "Carb Sensitivity," which you'll determine soon)

There is no official minimum of whole grains, but there is a maximum on the overall carbohydrate range you should stay within to be within your Weight Mastery Zone of about around 75 to 150 grams per day. You can enjoy a few servings a day of grains by using them as a condiment and not as a main part of your meal—one that covers the plate and you heap other things on. This rule of thumb changes if you are a vegetarian and need to balance grains with beans to form a complete protein.

SOURCES OF WHOLE GRAINS

Barley, buckwheat, millet, oats, brown rice, wild rice, quinoa, whole grain breads, whole grain pasta, whole grain cereals, etc. (Approximately 120 calories and 19 to 27 grams of carbohydrates per ½-cup serving of cooked grains.)

NOTE: 95 percent of the grain products Americans eat are refined grains, such as white flour and white rice. We need to shift our focus to eating whole grains as part of our balanced way of life. The refined grains are the 15 percent of the 85-15 Percent Food Mastery Zone Eating Strategy.

Water

It's an essential part of life and weight mastery. Our bodies are composed of 50 to 60 percent water by weight. Thirst is often mistaken for hunger, so being well hydrated is a step toward managing hunger and health. Water brings value to the body in these ways:

- Transports nutrients to cells and carries waste away.

- Too little water saps energy and mental alertness.

- Dilutes waste products filtered by the kidneys.

- Some studies have shown water drinkers consume up to 200 fewer calories per day than non-water drinkers.

Recommended daily minimum of water servings:

- Eight 8 oz. glasses a day. More when exercising.

SOURCES OF WATER

Water, mineral water, herbal teas, and flavored waters count as long as they don't contain caffeine, which is dehydrating, or sugar.

Okay, Apprentice, if your head is spinning in a nutritional whirlwind, don't worry, it will all settle in your mind. Take a moment to take a Shift Breath. Let me remind you that over your *30-Day Thin Thinking Practice* you will have time to get used to feeding yourself within the 85-15 Percent Food Mastery Zone Eating Strategy. The good news is that nature presents us with many tasty and healthy ways to nourish ourselves. The more you eat of these foods, the more you will enjoy them and even desire them for the way they make you feel in your body and mind.

Now let's look at Buffer Zone foods.

15 PERCENT BUFFER ZONE FOODS

Life in the real world presents you with food choices galore. You're not a nun or monk in a cloistered monastery, nor are you living in prehistoric times and existing on bugs and ferns. You are living in the modern world that is filled with modern food.

As a Weight Master, you have the flexibility to work some of these sometimes not-so-healthy Buffer Zone foods into your Calorie Budget for Weight Release, while still being consistent within your nourishing and stabilized Mastery Zone. You can be sociable, eat at parties and restaurants, and enjoy not having to rigidly stick to a diet. Once you have the ability to stay within your Buffer Zone calories, you have flexibility in food choices. That flexibility allows you to live in the real world.

SOURCES OF NON-NOURISHING PLEASURE FOODS

Refined grains and starches and baked goods. White-flour breads, pasta, bagels, tortillas, flatbreads, English muffins, chips, pretzels, French fries, doughnuts, cakes, cookies, croissants, muffins, pastries, and pies. (Approximately 80 to 150 calories and 7 to 20 grams of carbohydrates per ounce.)

Full-fat dairy. High-fat cheese, whipping cream, etc. (Approximately 80 to 220 calories an ounce.)

Refined sweets. Chocolate, hard candy, chewy candy, lollipops, and sugary gum. (100 to 300 calories an ounce.)

Condiments. Ketchup (America's second favorite vegetable after French fries!), syrup, BBQ sauce, etc. (25 to 120 calories a tablespoon.)

Other. (Calories vary enormously.) Alcohol, sugary juice, sodas, coffee beverages, sweetened iced tea, fried foods, sugary blended fruit shakes, frozen yogurt...and on and on and so forth!)

NOTE: The best time to eat Buffer Zone foods is with a meal or within an hour of eating. Why? Because when you eat refined foods on a stomach that is already stabilized with protein and whole foods, the mental and physical effects of the refined food have less of an impact on your body and mind.

I invite you to think of your Buffer Zone as the percentage of your daily Calorie Budget for Weight Release that allows you to share a dessert with a friend or have a glass of wine with dinner or a not-so-healthy "something" without feeling bad or guilty. It allows you the breathing room to create a way of eating that honors your life. No longer do you live just in the world of super clean "good" foods or super naughty "bad" foods, but there is an area where you can create some gray that allows you to feel, to quote Goldilocks, "just right."

The important thing to remember is that while a small amount of these Buffer Zone foods are manageable for long-term weight release and maintenance, too many refined sugary and white foods stimulate ard center in your brain, causing an imbalance in your body and awakening the Carb Zombie which then makes you feel hungry (even when you have eaten) and crave even more of these foods.

The recommended 15 percent daily maximum of Buffer Zone food servings for weight release looks like this:

- 1,200-calorie budget = 180 Buffer Zone calories

- 1,400-calorie budget = 210 Buffer Zone calories

- 1,600-calorie budget = 240 Buffer Zone calories

- 2,000-calorie budget = 300 Buffer Zone calories

There are many ways you can use your Buffer Zone calories. Here are some tools for using your Buffer Zone calories that have been tried and tested over many years by myself, my clients, and *Shift Weight Mastery Process* participants:

The three-bite tool for decadent, stimulating foods.
According to a study in *The Journal of the American Dietetic Association*, the mouth's sensory experience of a food diminishes from 90 to about 20 percent after three bites. Many Weight Masters use this three-bite tool to taste desserts and other dense-calorie foods and find they can easily skip eating a whole portion. Really! Try it out. Many of my clients are surprised when they realize that after the sensation of the first few bites, the food is less about pleasure and more an unconscious shoveling of calories down their gullets.

My client Jane said that when she went to a local fish and chips restaurant with her husband, which was a family ritual, she always ate an entire order of fish and chips. Once she started eating within her 85-15 Percent Food Mastery Zone Eating Strategy she realized that if she just took three bites of her husband's deep-fried fish and a few fries and ordered the lower-calorie non-fried fish dish, she was completely satisfied.

The three-bite tool is especially useful when dining at a restaurant or at social events. You will be surprised how easily three bites will satisfy you.
NOTE: Three average bites or sips of the following equals 100 calories: Chocolate, most pies, muffins, cinnamon rolls, cake, brownies, cookies, milkshakes, candy bars, deluxe cheeseburgers, thick and gooey pizza, garlic bread, onion rings, and loaded ice cream.

Enjoy an end of day "treat."
The Oxford Study, a cognitive behavioral weight loss study, found that

participants were less likely to treat themselves during the day when th , knew they had an after-dinner treat planned.

I've noticed similar results when my clients have their 15 percent Buffer Zone calories as a treat at the end of the day. Nourish and stabilize yourself, though, before you have that treat. After dinner (not before on an empty stomach) is the best time. Have wine with dinner and not before for the same reason; the impact it will have on your mind and body will be lessened when you have some healthy food in your stomach as a buffer.

KEEP YOUR TRIGGER FOODS OUT OF THE BUFFER ZONE

Everyone, even thin people, has trigger foods that when they eat them create *hyper-eating*, that out-of-control way of eating that will not stop until the bag or the box or the carton is empty. Everyone's trigger foods are different but the effect is the same. If we eat a bite of our trigger food, our Carb Zombie awakens, and we are going to eat much more than we intended. You probably have an idea of what your trigger foods are now. Were you thinking that you might be able to have that food within your Buffer Zone and manage it? The answer is, for the most part, no. We will go into trigger foods more with Skill 7 Stimulus Control. Sorry, don't blame the messenger; blame the trigger food. There are plenty of other foods you can enjoy in your Buffer Zone that don't trigger you.

0-15 PERCENT SHADES OF GRAY

Don't get the wrong idea—you don't have to eat 15 percent refined foods every day. You can and, probably will, choose to fill your 15 percent Buffer Zone some days with even more of the 85 percent nourished, stabilized, and Balanced Zone foods. Or you may only eat five percent Buffer Zone Foods, or ten percent—depending on how you feel and what is going on in your life. You can see this is sort of an art form of feeding yourself that you are now beginning to master.

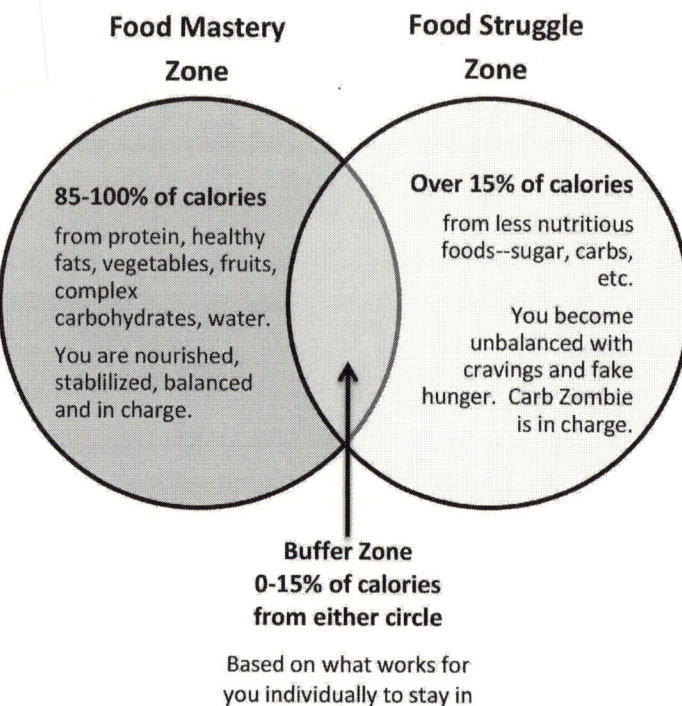

Food Mastery Zone

Food Struggle Zone

85-100% of calories
from protein, healthy fats, vegetables, fruits, complex carbohydrates, water.

You are nourished, stablilized, balanced and in charge.

Over 15% of calories
from less nutritious foods--sugar, carbs, etc.

You become unbalanced with cravings and fake hunger. Carb Zombie is in charge.

Buffer Zone
0-15% of calories
from either circle

Based on what works for you individually to stay in the Mastery Zone.

Chart T: 85/15 Food Mastery Zone Eating Strategy

Living Within Your Food Mastery Zone: Guidelines for Success

Now that you have your 85-15 Percent Food Mastery Zone Eating Strategy, I'll walk you through setting up your own Food Mastery Zone Eating Structure, and then give you some guidelines for living in your Food Mastery Zone. That's right, guidelines. What I am going to share with you are tools—not rules.

GROWING UP YOUR RELATIONSHIP WITH FOOD

These guidelines are going to build upon the 85-15 Percent Food Mastery Zone Eating Strategy that you just learned. I want you to understand that none of this is a diet or dogma. The idea is that you can take what I am teaching you and learn to evolve a way of eating for yourself based on the foods you like and what works for you—your body, mind, and lifestyle.

You cannot fail here, only learn and improve—even by making mistakes—what works best for you. Rena Wing, a professor of psychiatry and human behavior at Brown University, who has headed the National Weight Control Registry, said that the biggest takeaway from the research of all the Weight Masters to date (over 10,000 of them) is that no two people released their weight in the exact same way. You need to create and own what works for you in the long run.

I know some of you might be reading this and feel that not having a rigid structure to hold on to is a little odd. If you are feeling nervous with the idea of being in charge for yourself, I understand. When we struggle with our weight, we give our power away to structures outside of us and become dependent on something to "save us" from ourselves. We feel like we need a strict regime to whip us into shape because we are so naughty, so addicted, and so incapable of being in charge of ourselves and our relationship to food. Those days are over.

You are now here to begin growing up your relationship to food. You are here to put you in charge and let you be an adult and make your own decisions about what you feed yourself based on how those allow you to feel stabilized, nourished, and balanced.

STARTING WHERE YOU ARE

I deal with a variety of clients who start from different places with their relationship to food:

1. **Already Food Mastery Zoners:** I have clients who come to me and are already eating a very healthy diet. They might be following a low-carbohydrate Paleo Plan, Ketogenic diet, or some other "clean and healthy" popular plan, or they may be vegetarian or vegan. The weight challenge most of these people have is that they are just eating too much food! Even super "clean" diets with super organic and nutrient-dense food become unhealthy and fattening when we are eating more than our body needs for weight release.

   Their Journey to Weight Mastery: As these people begin tracking their calories (as we will learn in the next chapter) and become clear on how to live within their body's Calorie Budget for Weight Release, they release weight consistently and fairly easily because their bodies are already in a nourished and stabilized state.

2. **The Good-Bad, On and Off-ers:** This is the most common of my clients. They eat a healthy diet most of the time. The problem is they are rigidly eating "good," and when they eat something "bad," they "go off" at the drop of a hat. They may be happily eating the 85 percent Food Mastery Zone healthy foods Monday through Thursday, and even burning the calories to release weight; however, the problem is once they go off their healthy eating plan, they consume far more than the 15 percent Buffer Zone calories and become a victim of their Carb Zombie. By the time they pull themselves out of their Struggle Zone, they have filled in any calorie deficit they may have created and so their weight remains plateaued or is slowly creeping up.

Their Journey to Weight Mastery: When the Good-Bad, On and Off-ers begin to live life in the Food Mastery Zone and start using the Buffer Zone as a way to keep their mind flexible (there is no "bad" food) and their life flexible, they can live in the real world and enjoy being consistent. Instead of relying upon being "good," they now focus on feeding themselves within their 85-15 Percent Food Mastery Eating Zone while staying in balance within their Calorie Budget for Weight Release. They can release weight while enjoying the flexibility of the Buffer Zone foods without awakening their Carb Zombie. They begin to feel in charge and confident from the inside out.

3. **Stuck in the Food Struggle Zoner:** This group feels totally addicted to refined foods and spends most of their time struggling with their relationship to them, especially those foods that contain sugar and flour. They want to eat healthfully, but because their body is out of balance with fake hunger and their Carb Zombie is controlling their mind always looking for the next fix, they feel a need for refined foods just to feel "normal."

Their Journey to Weight Mastery: In order to break free from the tyranny of the Carb Zombie and get back into the Food Mastery Zone, the Food Struggle Zoner needs to spend some time resetting their mind and body from the spell of too many refined sugars and carbs. When someone is in this Food Struggle Zone, I usually have them begin by what I call Hibernating the Carb Zombie by eating in mostly the 85 percent part of the Food Mastery Zone for three days to a week. What they begin to notice within a few days is that their mind is released from the food fog, and they begin to lose the crazy fake hunger. They begin to desire eating foods that allow them to feel even-keeled and sane. Again, this focus isn't on being "good." The focus is on "healing" the body into a state of balance. Once this is achieved, they can begin to explore more variety in the 15 percent Buffer Zone. However, I find that some people are much more carb sensitive than others and must continue to be extremely moderate with their relationship with foods containing sugar and flour.

You may find yourself in one of the client groups I have described above or maybe somewhere in between. Wherever you are is perfect and will change as time goes on. My journey to weight mastery evolved as I learned to tune into my body, self-correcting along the way and becoming more masterful as I went.

MY MASTERY ZONE EVOLUTION

I know for me when I was 40 pounds overweight I was living in my Food Struggle Zone—overeating sugary foods and refined carbs. Even when I was dieting, it seemed like most of the diet foods that I ate contained abundant amounts of refined ingredients. Some days 90 percent of what I ate was composed of refined carbs and carby-fatty foods. As I started my journey and began eating more nourishing and stabilizing foods, I felt better and less addicted. I released weight and felt like I had it down.

As I began tuning in even more to when and what I was eating, I became more aware of the foods that "took my mind away" and started to avoid them. There were still lots of great foods I could eat, but I no longer desired foods that controlled me rather than me controlling them. As I evolved more, I became more stabilized with food. I learned to focus on my calorie budget and became aware of the caloric content of foods. I had that idea of a budget: What was the food going to buy me? If I knew a food would stabilize me and keep me feeling even-keeled, it became more attractive to me, especially if the food kept me within my calorie budget. I quickly found myself being the person who could say no to a doughnut, not because I had to (because I was on a diet) but because I didn't want the wasted calories from a food that gave my body a blood sugar spike and then crash and also might arouse my Carb Zombie. It was during this stage that I reached my ideal weight.

Nowadays I eat in a way I love where I eat healthfully with wiggle room in my Buffer Zone for living my full and social life. Sure, there are times when I tickle my Carb Zombie here and there and need to go through steps to put her back into hibernation. Now, though, I do that quickly and swiftly without self-recrimination or remorse. I understand how my mind and body work with food—I respect food and it respects me.

Now that you understand the mechanics of living within your Food Mastery Zone, let's look at how you create your own Food Mastery Zone Eating Structure.

BUILD YOUR FOOD MASTERY ZONE EATING STRUCTURE

I am going to walk you through the three steps of setting up your Food Mastery Zone Eating Structure. Research shows that having a repeating daily meal structure with food helps with consistency because it becomes ingrained over time and removes a lot of the decision-making that pulls at our limited resource—willpower. We are going to get you started here and then review these steps before you head into your *30-Day Thin Thinking Practice*. You will then have the support during your 30 Days to begin implementing your new structure. The structure that you create is going to be unique to you and will evolve as you go along. I want you just to get into the spirit of experimenting and thinking about food in a thin thinking way. Please don't worry about getting it perfect.

> **Make sure your Calorie Budget for Weight Release honors you and your life.** We discussed this earlier, but I will repeat it because it is so important: Be careful to make sure your weight release goal allows you a Calorie Budget for Weight Release that is not so restrictive that you feel deprived. Yes, you can feel full and satisfied on 1,200 calories when you are eating

quality foods, but lowering your calorie budget any further may defeat the purpose of finding a way of eating that you can live with long-term.

Divide your Daily Calories into meals and snacks. Start with where you need the most calories first. I advise clients planning their daily structure to ask themselves how much fuel (calories) they want for their biggest meal of the day. Then, they can figure out the number of calories to allot to snacks and other meals that stay within their Daily Calorie Budget for Weight Release.

Here is how a few of my clients figured out their Food Mastery Zone Meal Structures:

Example 1: Robert has a Daily Calorie Budget for Weight Release of 1,900 calories.

He works hard physically most days in his construction job, and he likes a big dinner.

- Robert allocates 850 calories for his dinner. Within those 850 calories are a light beer.

- Next Robert thinks about breakfast and how it needs to last until lunch, so he has 450 calories at breakfast.

- Finally, with 600 calories left, he decides to allot 400 for lunch and 200 for an after-dinner treat of dark chocolate.

Robert's Weight-Release Eating Structure
Breakfast 450 calories
Lunch 400 calories
Dinner 850 calories
Treat 200 calories
Total 1,900 calories

Example 2: Jody works in sales and does much of her business over lunch with clients. Jody's Calorie Budget for Weight Release is 1,250 calories a day. For her, lunch is the largest meal of the day. Keeping things light at dinner works for her because when she comes home, she's exhausted and doesn't like to cook.

- Jody puts aside 550 calories for lunch, which includes sharing a dessert (She uses the three-bite tool I mentioned.)

- She has a 200-calorie protein shake at breakfast.

- Jody has a 150-calorie protein-based snack before going to the gym after work.

- She has 350 calories for dinner, so she plans to have something light, such as yogurt and fruit or soup with some raw vegetables with hummus or guacamole.

Jody's Weight-Release Eating Structure
Breakfast 200 calories
Lunch 550 calories
Snack 150 calories
<u>Dinner 350 calories</u>
Total 1,250 calories

Do you see how each of these clients sat down with their Inner Coach and thought about their lifestyle to figure out what works best? This is how you create a way of eating that is going to support you and be sustainable in your life.

Of course, calories and what you eat vary from day to day, and the weekends might look entirely different. Having a structure gives your mind a daily roadmap with caloric milestones. Knowing that by staying fairly close to these parameters, you will be below your Calorie Budget for Weight Release gives you confidence, too.

EXERCISE: Build your Food Mastery Zone Eating Structure:
Take out your journal, or use the Build your Food Mastery Zone worksheet in the Index and work out these steps on paper to begin to get an idea of what your daily eating structure might look like.

FOOD MASTERY ZONE EATING STRUCTURE

Breakfast	_0_	calories
Lunch	_500_	calories
Snack	_300_	calories
Dinner	_600_	calories
Treat	_100_	calories
TOTAL	_1500_	**calories**

NOTE: You may choose to leave out the snack or treat or even one of the meals. You may even choose not to use the terms breakfast, lunch or dinner. For instance, I often combine lunch and dinner and eat this larger meal around 4:30 or 5:00 p.m., and I call this meal linner. The point is to use the calories where they serve you best and remember this is a flexible structure. Try to make sure you don't go more than four hours during the day without a little bit of stabilizing protein unless you can go longer without it jeopardizing your feeling of stability.

STEP 3: Use the 5-4-3-2-1 Servings Guideline as a way to get the minimum (and maximum) amounts of foods that will keep you nourished, stabilized, and balanced. The 5-4-3-2-1 Servings Guideline is an easy way to keep in mind the minimum and maximum amounts of all the food groups you need to stay nourished, stabilized, and balanced within approximately 1,200 calories. Those with larger Calorie Budgets for Weight Release can increase the protein, healthy fats, and vegetable servings accordingly. Your 15 percent Buffer Zone Calories would be a larger amount too, as we discussed in the previous section.

5-4-3-2-1 Servings Guideline

- **Five ½-cup servings (or more) of vegetables and fruits** to get the nutrients and fiber you need. Vegetables are the easiest way to fill up at meals if you need a large volume of food to feel satisfied.

- **Four 3-ounce servings (or more) of protein** to stabilize you and manage your hunger. Clients who start becoming imbalanced and are eating too many carbs usually are not getting adequate protein. Shoot for 72 grams or four 3-ounce servings—one protein at every meal and one for a snack. (You can eat more ounces of protein at one meal and less at another. This is a tool not a rule.)

- **Three 1-teaspoon servings of healthy fats** will help you with satiety and add flavor. Again, three servings are a minimum amount based on consuming 1,200 calories a day. Eat some healthy fats at each meal because it will create satiety. If you choose not to eat grains, you can use those additional calories in healthy forms of fat. If you choose to eat more, be careful in the weight release phase because fat calories can add up fast!

- **Two ½-cup servings (or less) of whole grains and tubers** can add fiber and bulk to meals. Some people are sensitive to whole grains and may find that eating too many creates imbalance and prompts cravings. This is something you can tune into over your *30-Day Thin Thinking Practice* and adjust for you.

- **One small serving Buffer Zone food and no more than 15 percent of your daily calories** can be used for many things over the course of your weight mastery. Three bites here and there of decadent foods, a small dessert, or a glass of wine is likely to be enough. Enjoy the freedom of having a less rigid dogmatic food plan that you can "fall off" of, but be mindful not to give your freedom away to the Carb Zombie by eating too much!

5-4-3-2-1 Servings Guideline
(example for 1200 calories)

5	Vegetables or Fruits	4 x ½ cup vegetable 1 x ½ cup fruit	100 calories 50 calories
4	Protein 72 gram min.	4 x 3 oz. servings	620 calories
3	Healthy Fats	3 x 1 teaspoon servings	120 calories
2	Whole Grains	1 x ½ cup serving	130 calories
1	Buffer Zone Foods	15% of calories 15% of 1200	180 calories
			1200 calories

CHART U: 5-4-3-2-1 Servings Guideline
within 1,200-Calorie Budget

In Chart U, I show you how the 5-4-3-2-1 Servings Guideline can stay within a daily calorie budget of 1,200 calories. The calories are approximations. Please understand that every day will look different and will not align perfectly with this chart, and some of you may choose (as we discuss in a moment) to leave out the two servings of whole grains or the single Buffer Zone serving here and there or altogether. The main point of 5-4-3-2-1 is to give you a simple way to remember the minimum servings of the 85 percent foods that will create a consistent foundation of feeling fed and even-keeled.

In the next chapter, Skill 4 Self-Monitoring, I will explain calorie tracking which will allow you to make sure that your daily food choices allow you to stay within your Caloric Budget for Weight Release. What we have just walked through are the tools to make sure you are getting enough of the nourishing and stabilizing foods you need to stay in the Food Mastery Zone.

Guidelines for your Food Mastery Zone Eating Structure

Now I want to walk you through three sets of guidelines for mastering hunger, cravings, and the Carb Zombie that will give you and your Inner Coach additional tools (not rules) to keep eating happily within the 85-15 Percent Food Mastery Zone Eating Strategy.

Master Your Hunger Guidelines

Hunger is a powerful sensation and a powerful word. When your mind hears "hunger," you likely equate it with starvation or "not enough." A true hunger signal is the body's way of saying "Hey, I need a little nourishment here!" In addition to real hunger, there is also fake hunger that is created not by the need for food (Fake hunger might happen right after you eat a meal.) but by either fat thinking beliefs or imbalances in your body. I want to take a moment to look at tools to manage both types of hunger.

Manage your real hunger by protecting your "0."
Many Weight Strugglers go way too long without food, hit "0," and then experience profound overeating. When clients need my help with portion control or night eating and claim "I cannot stop eating once I start," I know that eight times out of ten they are waiting too long to eat, sabotaging their success.

If you share this problem, two things may be at fault. One, when your blood sugar is low and you begin to eat, your body doesn't register "full" soon enough, and you eat too much. Two, when you are seriously hungry, you're likely to reach for anything that is easy, quick, and convenient. Usually that is fast and refined, high-calorie foods. This state of hunger is what I call "hitting 0," meaning your gas tank is empty. Don't let this happen!! Here's how to avoid it:

- **Plan your meals ahead for the day**. Weight Strugglers are notorious for forgetting about their need to stabilize themselves during the day or they hoard their calories in order to eat a lot at night. Both of these strategies end up with overeating at night. By planning ahead, you can make sure you keep yourself fed enough through the day but leave some room for a nice meal at night.

- **Stabilize yourself with four 3-ounce servings of protein**

(aproximatley 72 to 80 grams) a day or more. People struggling with weight are often undereating protein and overeating sugar and/or refined flour products. Eating that way keeps them victims of the Carb Zombie. If your Calorie Budget for Weight Release is above 1,600 calories per day, use the following equation to figure out how much protein to eat per day: 0.5 x your weight in pounds = minimum grams of protein intake per day.

- **Don't eat refined foods, including snacks, or fruit on an empty stomach.** If you do, your blood sugar will spike and then crash. Result: you feel even hungrier than before and so you continue eating. Plus, the sugar and fat hit the brain's pleasure center, waking up your inner Carb Zombie.

- **Include protein in your snacks.** It's especially tempting to eat a sugary or otherwise high-carb snack at 4:00 p.m. when you are starting to get hungry. Having a refined, processed snack may only increase your hunger and leads you to eating more later. Beware, too, of food supplement bars. Many of them contain large amounts of refined carbohydrates, including sugar, and little protein.

- **Steer clear of refined carbohydrates for breakfast.** Toast, processed cereal, pancakes, and waffles may initially fill you up, but chances are you will feel hungrier sooner in the day and be more prone to cravings. If you do want toast, have protein with it like an egg, vegetarian sausage, or some almond butter to stabilize the meal's effects on your body and mind.

- **Eat protein and veggies at each meal.** Consider a carbohydrate an optional condiment.

- **Look at menus carefully when you dine out.** Choose foods that nourish and stabilize you with a few hundred calories. Think in terms of having a serving of protein (three to four ounces, which is typically the size of the palm of your hand), one or two servings of vegetables or a salad, and, if you like carbs, a small amount of a whole grain or bread as a condiment.

Manage your fake hunger by shifting your mind and stabilizing your body.

Here are a few tools to combat the sneaky fake hunger that takes away your power and sabotages your weight.

- **Avoid being a victim of feeling deprived.** You've heard people say the glass is half empty or half full, right? The same goes with our perceptions of how much is enough on our plate as well. If you have been eating over your Calorie Budget for Weight Release and then begin eating within it, it may seem like you are taking food out of your mouth and you may feel victimized. If this resonates for you, shift your mindset. You want to look at the fact that you have powerfully made the decision to adapt to living within your body's energy needs to melt away the excess fat and live life at a lighter weight. The food you eat within your calorie budget is enough when you:

  - **Have a calorie budget that honors you,,** and doesn't make you feel deprived (1200 calories a day or more).

  - Use the 5-4-3 guideline of five servings of vegetables and fruits, four 3-ounce servings of protein and three healthy fat servings as a minimum foundation to keep you nourished and stabilized and your plate full for few calories.

  - Keep refined food calories under 15 percent, within your Buffer Zone.

- **Recognize blood sugar dips, re-regulation, and leptin resistance not as real hunger but for what they are.** If you have been eating in an imbalanced way and begin eating in the Food Mastery Zone you may experience pangs and feelings of your body re-regulating your insulin levels. If you have been out of balance with your eating and then begin eating healthfully, it will take a few days for your body to get your insulin in a more manageable place. It also takes time for your mind to begin recognizing the satiety hormone leptin and letting you know when you are full again. So, if you feel these pangs, just say to yourself "Oh, there's my mind and body healing itself back into balance—cool!" Learn to love those feelings instead of fearing them and trying to feed them. After a few days in your Food Mastery Zone, the feelings of fake hunger will diminish, and you will start feeling great.

MASTERY CRAVING GUIDELINES

Cravings happen when the mind associates an internal or external cue (an emotion, a place, time, or visual cue) with a need for food as a comfort, reward, or pastime. The "craving" you experience might feel like it's coming from your body but usually it is the reward neurotransmitter dopamine agitating you (aka Carb Zombie) for a treat. Often the craving won't let up until you give it what it wants. During your *30-Day Thin Thinking Practice* we will use daily meditation and hypnosis to combat cravings, but here are some other ways to refocus your mind and master cravings:

- **Focus on a new reward.** When you believe you are "doing without," an old fat thinking food reward, the craving doesn't go away. It becomes stronger. Focus on a new treat and reward, breaking your mind's focus on the old one.

    -Take a walk and focus on the reward of feeling refreshed afterward.

    -Take a catnap or meditate for ten minutes and focus on the reward of resetting your mind.

    -Eat a healthy snack and focus on feeling light and stabilized instead of imbalanced.

- **Plan meals the night before.** Focus on what you can have, not what you can't. By making these decisions ahead of time, you create impulse control without relying on your willpower reserves.

- **"Fast" in between meals and snacks and from dinner until the next morning.** When you are "trying not to eat," you feel deprived and crave the food you cannot have. By cultivating the process of "fasting," which implies creating an absence of eating, in order to rest the digestive system and promote health and longevity, you'll see yourself as doing something powerful and positive. You feel good about resting from eating and quieting the part of the mind that "expects something."

- **Get curious and look deeper than the food cue.** Cravings are often the plea for deeper self-care in disguise. The call for a cookie might really be a need for self-nurturing. The desire for wine, cheese, and crackers might really be a signal that you need to find a healthier way to let your hair down at the end of the day. When you are feeling a craving that you know isn't hunger, ask yourself this question: "What do I really need right now that is hiding under the idea of food? Do I need a break? Do I need more fun in my life? Do I need to give myself some empathy?" The more you dig and begin giving yourself deeper self-care, the more the surface cravings begin to vanish.

- **Use sauces or condiments for flavor and pleasure.** Flavorful sauces and condiments add pleasurable flavor to a meal for a limited number of calories. When putting a meal together, I think in terms of the type of protein I want, what vegetable to serve with it, and what flavor can I use to add personality and sizzle.

Here are some sauces and condiments that elevate protein and vegetables into enjoyable, mouth-satisfying, craving-busting meals. These flavor add-ons are low in calories (no more than 60 calories a serving) but provide huge flavor, making the difference between a boring, skimpy meal and a sensuous feast!

- Marinara sauce
- Curry simmer sauces
- Asian-themed sauces
- Thai green curry sauce
- Salsas
- Hot sauce
- Chicken stock packets (It's amazing sprinkled over vegetables.)
- A tiny bit of olive oil, sesame oil, or even butter over vegetables

MASTER YOUR CARB ZOMBIE GUIDELINES

I would like to dive a bit deeper into how you can learn to balance enjoying your Buffer Zone foods while steering clear of waking that powerful force within, the Carb Zombie. I want to walk through some tools with you to get that Carb Zombie back in hibernation should you tickle the pleasure center in your brain and throw your body out of balance.

Anyone who has struggled with weight knows the feeling of being "possessed" by this monster that seems to drive him or her to eat even when they rationally do not want to. The Carb Zombie mechanism doesn't care about your weight goals, your need to be healthy, or even your happiness. The Carb Zombie just wants to be fed refined foods at any cost. Research studies have shown rats willing to experience electrical shocks in order to eat refined foods. In other studies, rats continued to drink sugar water, stimulating the reward centers in their brains until their stomachs exploded.

By staying within your Food Mastery Zone, you keep the Carb Zombie in hibernation and out of our Weight Struggle Zone and avoid the fate of those poor rats. Mastering this state of balance will mean tuning in to your body and noticing the effects that various foods have on you. Here are some guidelines as to how:

- **"Hibernate your Carb Zombie" with three days of eating 5-4-3 foods without the grains or 15 percent Buffer Zone foods.** If you have been eating a diet riddled with refined foods, you may need to balance your body out for three days or so by eating primarily foods from the 85 percent part of the Mastery Zone and staying away from the 15 percent entirely until you feel stabilized and nourished. Once your Carb Zombie is in hibernation, you can slowly experiment with adding in some foods in the Buffer Zone.

- **Once your Carb Zombie is hibernating, keep her hibernated by using your Mastery Zone Eating Strategy and staying below your "carb ceiling."** After years of maintaining my weight and helping others manage their weight, I have come to appreciate how important it is to get 72 to 80 grams of protein a day (the four 3-ounce servings) and limit carbohydrates below what I call "the carb ceiling" of 75 to 150 grams. (That amount is equivalent to five or six servings of complex vegetables and one or two fruit servings plus a whole grain serving and small, refined carb serving. See the Carbohydrate Comparison Chart to get a sense of this). Eating this way creates a hunger-free state—the Food Mastery Zone. The more time you spend in this place, the easier it is to release weight. You become more confident and peaceful, too, because you—not the refined foods—are in control.

- **Become Carb Aware as you begin eating within your Food Mastery Zone and read labels and use your tracking app to know how many grams of carbohydrates are in various foods you consume.** Educating yourself about the foods you eat and how different foods help you feel when in your body will allow you to make educated choices with your Inner Coach. These choices will be based on how various carbohydrate foods either allow you to feel stable or trigger fake hunger and cravings. Understand that even foods that are seen as healthy, like brown rice, dried fruit, and certain fruits that contain higher levels of natural sugar like pineapple and mango, could trigger your fake hunger. If a food does that, steer clear of it. By becoming aware and tuned in, you become an educated, rational consumer of what you put into your body.

CARBOHYDRATE COMPARISON

Don't worry, 100 to 150 grams of carbohydrates is far from low carbohydrate. For example, here are some foods and their carbohydrate content a serving:

Food	Calories	Grams of carbs
Broccoli (½ cup)	15	3
Strawberries (1 cup)	49	12
Kale (1 cup)	22	7
Soda (8 oz.)	97	27
Bagel	289	56
Cupcake	186	28
Candy bar	250	16.5

Healthier complex carbs are lower in carbohydrate content than their refined counterparts. If you have four servings of vegetables, a couple of fruits, a serving of whole grains, and even a couple of squares of dark chocolate, you should be within your carb ceiling for a day.

- **Don't fret about having to count carbohydrates.** You will quickly learn the amounts in the servings of foods you usually eat from recording your food on the tracking applications that I recommend. They track protein and carbohydrate intake for you.

- **Keep your trigger foods out of your Food Mastery Zone Eating Strategy.** Remember your trigger foods are the ones that take your power away even after you eat a small serving.

- **If you start to awaken the Carb Zombie—put him back to sleep ASAP.** One of the mistakes people often make when they eat a refined food is to say "I'll start over tomorrow" and eat more refined food. Would you pour gasoline on a fire once it's started? That is what the effect of eating more refined food does. It pulls you deeper into your Food Struggle Zone—the lair of the Carb Zombie. Instead—if you feel yourself being pulled in by the Carb Zombie—hit the fire with water by stabilizing yourself immediately with a serving of protein and pulling back from complex or refined carbohydrates for the rest of the day— bringing yourself back into balance.

- **If you get pulled into the Carb Zombie's Weight Struggle lair, get out by following the steps to force the monster into hibernation.** If you find yourself in the Food Struggle Zone from a few days of overeating refined carbs, follow the steps to hibernate your Carb Zombie by eating only in the 85 percent 5-4-3 foods from the Food Mastery Zone for about three days. This should bring you back into balance.

- **Tune in and learn your "balance" when you eat foods within the 15 percent.** In the first few months you will have to be very mindful when eating within your 15 percent Buffer Zone. Tune in to how various Buffer Zone foods make you feel while you are eating them, ten minutes after, an hour after, three hours after and so on. You will learn quickly what foods work best for you within your Buffer Zone. Use this type of food forensics and adapt to foods that work best for you and keep you free from feeling imbalanced, fake hungry, or craving.

- **If you are sensitive to sugar or flour or both, avoid foods containing these ingredients and eat low-carbohydrate treats instead.** There are many Weight Strugglers who have a genetic vulnerability to sugar and flour. You will know this if even a tiny bit of sugar or a flour-based product starts your Carb Zombie rumbling. If this is true for you—do not despair—there are many great foods you can enjoy in your Buffer Zone that do not contain sugar or flour. See the Resources section for some low-carb treat ideas.

- **If you drink alcohol, focus on 5-4-3 eating the following day.** Drinking alcohol can be managed when you keep the servings within your 15 percent and you have a foundation of being nourished and stabilized. However, be careful because alcohol may tickle your Carb Zombie and leave you feeling hungrier the next day. This is the fake hunger triggered when the alcohol creates an imbalance in your system. Make sure to eat a protein-based breakfast and lunch the days following an evening when you drank alcohol. It is also best to keep alcohol intake to a minimum, especially while in weight-release mode. That's not only because of the calories but also for the way it diminishes your impulse control.

• **Notice the sweeteners that work for you and those that don't and use those sparingly.** Ahhh, the whole sweetener or artificial sweetener debate. Again, dear apprentice, you will need to make some decisions for yourself. There are many theories and studies that have been dismantled over the years with various sweeteners. You are now the adult in charge, and I invite you to do your own research in the world and on yourself and make your own decisions. I know many Weight Masters who use (not abuse) sweeteners like sucralose (Splenda, etc.) who feel fine about using it. There are studies that support having a low-calorie sweetener; since it allows you to keep your calories down, it can be a tool in your weight release. There are also more natural and low-calorie sweeteners like xylitol and Erythritol that work well in baking and for sweetening drinks. There are others who prefer to train themselves off the taste of sweet altogether. I have seen many people use brown sugar or agave as the healthy alternative to white sugar, not knowing that these more natural sweeteners can wake up the Carb Zombie as easily as white sugar for many people.

WHAT 1,200 CALORIES LOOK LIKE

Okay, Apprentice, now that I have walked you through setting up your Food Mastery Zone Eating Structure and the guidelines to master hunger, cravings, and your Carb Zombie, I would like you to see menus of a few days of eating in the Food Mastery Zone.

Here is a filling and nourishing example of Calorie Budget for Weight Release of 1,200 calories. **(Chart V).** Notice that the refined foods add up to 180 calories over the course of the day and that I honored the 5-4-3-2-1 servings. Notice, too, that I include more protein than the four 3-ounce servings. I've included the grams of carbs and protein so that you can see how this day is balanced.

If you are on a higher calorie budget, you can add bigger servings or another snack.

1,200 Calorie Daily Budget

	F/V*	PROTEIN	CARBS	CALORIES
Greek 0% yogurt (1 cup)		17 gm	6 gm	120
Strawberries (1 cup)	2	1 gm	12 gm	46
Granola (2 Tblsp) *15% buffer		1 gm	4 gm	40
Water,coffee, tea, etc.				0
				206
Turkey Slices – 4 x 1 oz. rolled				
around cucumber wedges	1	9 gm	3 gm	130
Chicken Veg. soup (1.5cup)	3	4 gm	19 gm	150
Lo-carb tortilla with wedge				
Laughing Cow cheese				
+ no sugar jam (1 tsp)		7 gm	14 gm	110
				390
Small apple	1		14 gm	60
10 almonds		3 gm	3 gm	70
				130
Cauliflower – steamed (1cup)	2	2 gm	5 gm	50
Chicken – pre-cooked (4 oz)		35 gm	35 gm	180
tossed w/ curry sauce (.5 cup)			6 gm	70
Over sautéed spinach (2 cups)	2	4 gm	5 gm	50
Skinny Cow ice cream				
Sandwich *15% buffer zone		4 gm	30 gm	140
				490
Total	11	87 gm	126 gm	**1206**

* Servings of Fruits / Vegetables

CHART V: 1,200 Calorie Daily Budget

Here is a Food Mastery Zone day of fast food meals that you can eat and still come in on a 1,200 – calorie budget within a low carbohydrate range and keeping the protein servings at the meals to provide stability. The 15 percent Buffer Zone choice was within the 180-calorie range. (**Chart W**)

1,200 Calorie Daily Budget with Fast Foods

	F/V*	PROTEIN	CARBS	CALORIES
Starbucks turkey bacon				
Sandwich/whole wheat				
(remove top bun)		14 gm	27 gm	270
Fruit cup	2	2 gm	12 gm	45
Coffee w/ 1/4 cup milk		2 gm	3 gm	30
				345
Subway club salad				
With extra chicken(4 ounce)	5	35 gm	12 gm	**200**
10 almonds		3 gm	3 gm	70
2 Baja Fresh fish tacos				
(remove outer tortilla)		12 gm	24 gm	310
Salsa	1		2 gm	10
McDonald's ice cream cone*				
(15% buffer zone)		5 gm	27 gm	150
Total	8	73 gm	110 gm	**1085**

* Servings of Fruits / Vegetables

CHART W: 1,200 Calorie Daily Budget with Fast Food Meals

CASE STUDY: BARBARA CREATED HER OWN WAY OF EATING

My client Barbara released 20 pounds in three months with the *Shift Weight Mastery Process*. She was never obese, but because she didn't have a good relationship with food, she was overweight.

"I hated dieting, but I was afraid of not being on a diet. I needed the structure of a diet. When I wasn't on a diet, I went crazy, eating everything that wasn't nailed down and feeling sick afterwards. I was convinced that I was out of control with food.

"When I started my journey to weight mastery, I began to trust myself and my instincts. I was able to feed myself mostly healthy, nourishing foods that I enjoyed. I loosened my restrictive grip and started allowing for treats in my day: some chocolate, some wine, and popcorn. If I was on a strict diet, I would have considered those treats bad foods, but I had room for them with the 85-15 Percent Food Mastery Zone Eating Strategy and a realistic Calorie Budget for Weight Release.

"With my loving Inner Coach, I figured out the best time of day for me to eat food with the most staying power, such as protein and vegetables. And, I noted the times that were best for giving myself treats. For a treat, I ate a few bites of cake. I didn't need the whole thing."

"I let go of the fear of food and saw I could be in charge and nourish my body and soul. I created my own structure that worked for me. It was a very freeing process. Now I feel masterful and in charge of how I feed myself." Barbara B. (Released 20 pounds, maintaining for 3 years)

WEIGHT MASTERY SKILL 3 SUM UP: MASTERING YOUR RELATIONSHIP WITH FOOD

- Instead of deeming food as "good" or "bad," you can develop a healthy way of eating where all food serves you well, giving you one or more of the following:

    - Nourishment

    - Stabilization

    - Balance

- By using the 85-15 Percent Food Mastery Zone Eating Strategy, you live life on your terms within your Calorie Budget for Weight Release. You choose from a wide variety of food and have meals and snacks that honor your lifestyle and personal taste preferences. Using this Weight Mastery Skill helps you to be consistent and release weight over time.

- Staying within your Food Mastery Zone avoids false hunger and prevents cravings that might lead to overeating and bingeing.

  - Get at least four 3-ounce servings (72 to 80 grams) of protein a day.

  - Stay under 75 to 150 grams of carbohydrates per day, including complex carbs-vegetables, fruits, a minimum of whole grain, and 15 percent Buffer Zone foods. Your carb ceiling will depend on many things: how carb sensitive you are, how many refined foods you eat, and how stabilized and balanced your body is.

APPRENTICE PAUSE: Are you feeling full...of information, that is? You have learned the first three skills of weight mastery. These skills engage you in the creative art of balancing energy in different ways, depending on who you are and the way you live. During this process, you are starting to become the artistic master of your weight destiny. Finally, the power is in your hands!

Congratulations! You have finished building the first floor of your home of Weight Mastery with the three weight skills! Now proceed to the next level—**THE ENVIRONMENT SKILLS**—to continue building.

CHAPTER 27
THE SECOND LEVEL
THE THREE ENVIRONMENT SKILLS

PEOPLE WHO PRACTICE THE THREE environment skills consistently are the ones who have released weight and kept it off the longest, according to the research from the National Weight Control Registry (NWCR). Now you are going to learn to build the next level of your Weight Mastery Home. The second level consists of these three powerful skills.

THE ENVIRONMENT SKILLS

Skill 4 Self-Monitoring. You track your food intake, some nutritional values, and your exercise. You monitor your weight to check your progress and stay on track.

Skill 5 Stimulus Control. You keep your environment set up for success.

Skill 6 Building a Powerful Support Team. You surround yourself with people who are advocates for your journey to weight release.

I am sure you have wished, as I did when I struggled, that you could live on an island far away from all the temptations of everyday life in order to release weight. But unless you are enrolling in a popular weight loss reality show where you will be sheltered at "The Ranch" or have a lot of money to check yourself into a health spa for a few months, chances are you are going to be releasing weight in the real world.

When I struggled with my weight, I always gave my attention to the diet aspect of losing weight and not my environment. With hindsight, I see that I wasn't a failure at releasing weight, but my environment was set up to fail me and sabotage my best efforts.

- I kept no accurate data on my progress, so distorted thinking and emotions sabotaged me.

- My house, car, and work were booby trapped with trigger foods that I spent much of my time trying to resist and then giving in to.

- The people in my life didn't support me because I hid the fact I was even trying to lose weight.

When I began honing my environment skills, I not only changed my world, I also changed how I saw myself. I realized I could take a stand for my own health and success. I'm looking forward to you making this shift for yourself.

....

"I avoided the scale and what I was eating for years. I thought the scale was my enemy and that tracking my food would make me obsessed about it. So I struggled, wondering why I wasn't progressing with my attempts at weight release. I was thinking about food all of the time. Learning the environment skills was the key to being free of my food obsession and to focus instead on success." Mandy F. (Released 31 pounds, maintaining 28 months.)

....

Step up to the second level of your home of weight mastery and begin building with **Skill 4 Self-Monitoring.**

CHAPTER 28
WEIGHT MASTERY SKILL 4

SELF-MONITORING

SKILL 4: Self-Monitoring. The skill of using your personal data (food intake, nutrient intake, exercise, weight) to stay on track for weight release, mentally and physically.

There is mounting evidence that aligns the practice of self-monitoring with long-term weight success. Over 74 percent of Weight Masters tracked their food, exercise, and weight as they released weight. Fifty percent of them continued tracking their food and weight as they maintained the release.

A lot of the pain of the weight struggle is the frustration that arises from not being able to correlate the effort you give to weight release with the results you see on the scale.

Self-monitoring allows you to release weight from a rational place rather than an emotional one.

You are now going to be free from:

- Guessing. "Did I eat too much?"

- Distortion. "I blew it!"

- Emotional Assumptions. "I was bad." "I hardly ate anything, so why did I gain weight?" "I must have pigged out."

We are now going to look at self-monitoring data in two key areas of weight mastery.

1-Tracking your food and exercise each day.

2-Tracking your weight at least once a week.

1-Self-Monitoring: Tracking Your Daily Food and Exercise

FAT THINKING AND TRACKING FOOD AND EXERCISE

Here are some comments that my clients express when I bring up tracking for the first time.

- "Tracking food takes too much time."

- "I hate counting calories. It's soooo diet-y!"

- "Thin people don't have to track their food. Why can't I be like them?"

- "Tracking makes me think too much about food."

Maybe you share some of these sentiments? That's okay, because whatever experience you have had with tracking has been as a Weight Struggler. Many of my clients discover that tracking becomes their favorite part of Weight Mastery. Self-monitoring their food and exercise helps them make decisions based on fact and not emotions or distorted thinking.

THIN THINKING AND TRACKING FOOD AND EXERCISE

Here are five important reasons why tracking your food and exercise helps you shift from fat to thin thinking:

1. **You know how much energy you are eating and burning over the week, so you can predict your weekly weight release.** Unless you have a clear goal and track to achieve it, your mind can easily distort your behaviors and thwart your expectations of the scale. That leads to frustration, disappointment, and giving up. (Coming up, you'll learn the role of the scale in tracking.)

2. **You are free of distorted, all-or-nothing thinking.** Instead you concentrate on fact-based, problem-solving thin thinking.

3. **You won't underestimate how much you eat and exercise.** Most people underestimate how much they eat. Research shows non-dieters underestimate their food consumption by 20 to 30 percent and dieters underestimate by 50 to 100 percent. If

you think you are eating only 1,200 calories a day, you may be eating 2,000 or more calories. **(See Chart X)**

Recording your food keeps you on track with facts. The difference between the "I Blew It" day and the "I Only Had" day illustrates why.

"I Only Had" day		**"I Blew It" day**	
Bagel w/cream cheese	600	2 Egg whites	40
California roll + 3 pieces of sushi	950	Canadian bacon	20
2 handfuls almonds	400	Low carb tortilla	60
Half a Chili's cheeseburger	600	Apple	50
A few French fries	150	Subway club salad	150
One Margarita	500	Banana	80
Total	**3,200**	1.5 oz. choc. chip cookie	200
		McDonald's cheeseburger	310
		Side salad	30
		15 French fries	150
		1 Ice cream cone	150
		Total	**1,240**

The person who didn't track food on "I Blew It" day felt like he had overeaten, whereas the "I Only Had" person, who also didn't track, thought she had eaten lightly.

CHART X: But I Only Ate

4. **You make better choices and build better habits based on what works.** If you don't have the facts, you are never clear about what works for you and what doesn't when you try to change your behavior. For instance, if you mindlessly reach for sugar every afternoon when you lose energy at 3:00 p.m. you can spot this trend in your food records. Once you are aware

that the sugary snack is taking you over your Daily Calorie Budget for Weight Release, you can figure out a solution like bringing in a healthier snack for that time.

5. **You avoid the anxiety of not knowing whether or not what you are eating is causing you to gain weight.** When you don't know the energy value of what you eat, it is easy to fall prey to estimating and judging what you eat and then worrying about the impact of the food on your weight release.

    Many people won't count calories because they think it makes them think too much about food. I find the more you know how many calories a food has and fit it into your budget, the more it releases you from anxiety, and you are free to truly enjoy the food.

"With the Shift Weight Mastery Process, I finally understand tracking calories from a powerful place. It's not about being "good" on a diet and restricting myself. It's about getting clear, getting the facts, and making adjustments so that I can release weight without mystery or drama. Self-monitoring is a skill that I now appreciate from a whole new perspective." Josh K. (Released 27 pounds, maintaining for 1 year.)

CASE STUDY: NO WAY, I AM NOT DOING THAAAAAAAAT!

Nancy owned a company that helped save big corporations from going under. She had a brilliant business mind, and, let me tell you, this woman was tough. When she sat down in my office, she got right to business and didn't mince words. She said, "I want you to know that you probably aren't going to be able to help me. No one has helped me to date."

Nancy quickly got to the heart of the matter. "No matter what I do, I cannot shake this weight. I have tried trainers and diet programs. I was checked out medically, and I know I am healthy. I am in control of every aspect of my life except my weight, and I can't stand it!" she said.

I told Nancy that I could guide her to help herself and that all of her skills in coaching high-level CEO's in business could help her create her own Inner Coach. Nancy loved the Inner Coach concept. As we talked, she began to relax and even lighten up a bit. That is, until I mentioned that she would be tracking her food and exercise calories.

Her face darkened. "I am not going to do that. It's ridiculous! I don't have time to write down my food! Even if I did, isn't that going to make me think about food all of the time? I did that in other diet programs, and I hated it. Can't you just hypnotize me to hate food, so I can leave and never think about food again?" she asked.

I could clearly see Nancy's anger, agitation, and impatience. She looked ready to hop up and leave my office, never to return. I took a deep Shift Breath and said calmly, "Nancy, I have a question for you, if you went to a big corporation and sat down with the CEO who needed your help to save his company, what would be the first thing that you'd ask of him?"

Nancy replied immediately, "Well I would want to see that company's monthly profit and loss and financial statements, of course. I would want to see where they were losing money, what they were spending too much on, and where was the company failing to generate revenue."

I asked, "What if the CEO told you 'I'm sorry, we don't bother with bookkeeping. We found it too annoying and time consuming. We just go by how we feel the company is doing."

Nancy narrowed her eyes at me. "I would tell that CEO that he was a fool and didn't know how to run a business. There is no way I can solve the problems of his company unless I know what the problems are. Where was the money going and how much did the company make and lose each month. There is no way to assess a company's performance without accurate recordkeeping." As she listened to herself, she chuckled and relaxed into her chair as she realized my point. "Oh, I get it. I am that CEO. I am the fool ruining my weight loss?"

I told her, "Nancy, writing down your food and tracking may seem like a 'diet,' but consider tracking through the eyes of the CEO of your weight release. Tracking is the only way to accurately assess why you might not be losing weight. Tracking also gives your brain the tools and incentive to perform better."

"I get it," she said. "People who monitor results accurately are able to improve based on their desired outcome. You are right. There is no way I could SHIFT the needle on my weight without tracking my food intake of calories and calories burned in exercise and metabolism. I am excited now. How do I start?"

DAILY TRACKING

I am going to insist you try tracking your food and exercise calories during the *30-Day Thin Thinking Practice* to see the power and benefits of this skill. You will be convinced, I am sure! You can track manually in your own journal or on the printable worksheets provided online or you can try an app like *Lose It!* or *My Fitness Pal*.

Here is an example of an "on track" day in recordkeeping for Nancy. According to her Calorie Budget for Weight Release of 1,550 calories, she would release a pound a week. (**Chart Y**)

TIME	ACTUAL FOOD	CALORIES
8a	Whole wheat toast – 1pc.	80
	Cottage cheese (1/2 cup)	80
	Strawberries (1 cup)	40
	10 almonds	80
		280
12:30p	Grilled steak (4 oz)	300
	Salad greens (2 cups)	40
	1 tablespoon dressing	80
		420
3p	Greek yogurt (6 ounces)	110
	Small apple	60
		170
6:30p	Stir fried chicken (4 ounces)	250
	Asian vegetable mix (1 cup)	120
	Brown rice (1/2 cup)	120
		490
	Glass red wine	120
	Dark chocolate square	80
Actual Food Grand Totals:		1560

CHART Y: Nancy "On Track" Day

Here's an example of a day when Nancy had birthday cake at an office party. **(Chart Z)** Oops! But see, by recordkeeping, she didn't go into "I blew it!" mode. Instead she ate lightly at the end of the day. She was able to stay within her Calorie Budget for Weight Release. If she wasn't tracking her food, chances are she would have said, "I blew it." Then she would have eaten too much that day and possibly for the rest of the week.

TIME	ACTUAL FOOD	CALORIES
8a	Whole wheat toast - 1pc.	80
	Almond Butter (1 Tablespoon)	120
	Medium Banana	110
		310
12:30p	Chicken Ceaser Salad (4 oz)	400
	Salad Dressing	80
		480
4 p	Birthday Cake (1 piece)	250
6:30p	Turkey chili (1/2 cup)	330
	Over steamed zucchini (1 cup)	40
		370
8p	Small apple	60
Actual Food Grand Totals:		1520

CHART Z: Nancy Office Party Day

WEEKLY TRACKING

If you keep tabs on your weekly calorie burn levels and not just daily ones, you avoid being pulled into the "I blew it today" cycle.

During your *30-Day Thin Thinking Practice*, you will keep an ongoing record of what you eat and how you exercise. Using this weekly system for the 30 days of the process with a food and exercise app or journal you gain insight on how to problem-solve and stay consistent with weight release.

	MO	TU	W	TH	FR	SA	SU	WEEKLY TOTALS
Daily Body Burn	2050	2050	2050	2050	2050	2050	2050	14350
+ Actual Exercise Calories	0	0	0	0	0	300	300	600
= Total Daily Burn Calories	2050	2050	2050	2050	2050	2350	2350	14950
- (Less) Actual Food Calories	(1550	(1550)	**(2200)**	**(2250)**	(1250)	(1200)	(1450)	(11450)
= Net Calories Burned	500	500	(150)	(200)	800	1150	900	3500
= Net Calories Running Total	500	1000	850	650	1450	2600	3500	3500

Grand Total

Chart AA: Nancy's Stressful Week Weight Release Planner

Here is a week (**Chart AA**) where Nancy had a stressful two days (see bold numbers) at the office. She ate too much pizza Wednesday night with her team (Wednesday). The next night (Thursday) she celebrated and ate steak and drank wine. But because she was tracking, she could monitor her calorie intake, make adjustments, get back on course, and still release weight that week. Nancy was happy to feel in charge of her weight release during a stressful time.

The advantage of staying connected to yourself with tracking your food and exercise is that it keeps you in a powerful, problem-solving dialogue with your Inner Coach. When things don't go as planned, you and your Inner Coach can decide how to solve the challenge instead of saying "I blew it!" You can learn to be okay with going over budget occasionally. When you overeat one day, you can adjust on other days and keep the total calories for the week within your Calorie Budget for Weight Release. It's the going "off" your budget, day after day, that creates caloric damage and leads to weight gain.

WEIGHING AND MEASURING YOUR PORTIONS

When you first begin tracking your daily food intake, you will need to be clear on portion sizes. Food products have nutritional labels that tell you exactly how big a serving is and how many calories is in the portion. Some foods even come pre-packaged in single servings. This makes it very easy to know how many calories you are consuming. Nevertheless, you may have to measure portions, especially at first, so that you are clear on what a food's specific portion size is.

Remember there is a tendency to underestimate the amount of calories you eat. You may think of something as "just a hundred calories" when it's two or three hundred. These incorrect estimates add up quickly and cause frustration. You expect to have released weight, and the scale says you haven't. It could be that the scale isn't broken, but your eyeballs are.

There are two ways to train your eyes to know portions:

- Use a food scale and measuring cups for accurate portion sizes.
- Use everyday objects to estimate the size of a serving.

Use a Food Scale and Measuring Cups and Spoons for accurate portion sizes. When you begin tracking food, it helps to weigh and measure everything you eat so you know what an appropriate portion size is. Many people think they know what three ounces of fish looks like, but they are overestimating or underestimating. And what about the creamer you put in your coffee? What may seem like a tablespoon might actually be three tablespoons. The best way to know is to use measuring cups and spoons and a digital food scale. I assure you it is worth the effort and can be incredibly enlightening.

THE "BIG" APPLE

I often bring my scale to *Shift Weight Mastery Process* seminars to show how easy it is to be off in visual estimates. My Kitrics™ scale is great, because you put the food item on it and punch in a code number for the food. The scale will then tell you exactly how many calories are in the food on the scale.

I demonstrate by taking small, medium, and large apples, and asking the participants for calorie estimates before I weigh each apple. The small apple is around 60 calories, the medium is around 125 calories, and the large apple (The one I would always choose when any diet said "an apple.") can be as much as 250 calories. Yes, for one apple! Participants are often amazed and amused at the difference in calories between a small and large apple.

If you picked up a big apple and said to yourself, "it's an apple and around 80 calories." You could be consuming over 150 extra calories and not even know it. This is what I mean about distortion. Even after years of shifting, I still put certain foods on a scale to retrain my eyes at least once a month.

Use everyday objects to estimate the size of a portion. If you don't have your scale handy, you can eyeball portions. Here are some ideas for estimating portion size.

- 1 cup of cereal = baseball
- 2 tablespoons coffee creamer = shot glass
- 1 ounce of nuts = fits into the cup of your palm
- 1ounce of cheese = 3 small game dice
- ½ cup mashed potatoes = small ice cream scoop
- 1 tablespoon peanut butter = 2 Scrabble tiles
- ½ cup pasta = golf ball
- 3 oz. meat or fish = bar of soap

Many of my clients clear up what they think is their "slow metabolism problem" by getting out their measuring devices and accurately determining how many calories they are eating.

NANCY TOOK CONTROL OF HER RECORDS AND EXCELLED

Nancy began tracking, measuring her food, and listening to hypnosis. She immediately began releasing weight, because she finally saw how many calories she was mindlessly eating. She also realized that what she thought was eating healthfully was in excess of her body's daily calorie needs.

Nancy released 25 pounds in six months and felt on top of the world. More importantly she gained mastery in an area of life that had eluded her—managing her weight.

"The hypnosis made a huge difference to my overall shift, but I have to say that tracking my food and exercise helped me so much by changing my perceptions, calming me down, and giving me insights into behaviors I needed to change. I don't think I would have been this successful without tracking my food and exercise and weighing myself every week." Nancy C. (Released 25 pounds, maintaining at 2 years)

2-Self-Monitoring: Tracking Your Weight Release

The other important strategy that goes hand in hand with tracking your food and exercise is weighing yourself daily or weekly. Why? Without tracking your weight along with your weekly food and exercise records, it's difficult to:

- Know whether your food and exercise recordkeeping is accurate and allowing you to release weight at your desired rate.

- Recognize and target issues and problem-solve when your weight release slows.

- Stay in your thin thinking mind, guided by facts and not emotions.

FAT THINKING AND WEIGHING OURSELVES

Now, I understand that weighing oneself is a heated subject for many. The challenge with the scale isn't the device itself. It's the mind's distorted fat thinking that happens around and on the scale. For years you may have been weighing yourself as a dieter. Now you are going to weigh yourself powerfully like a Weight Master. The difference is not on the scale; it's in your head. Maybe you have fallen into one of these groups that struggle with the scale:

- **You weigh yourself regularly hoping the scale will be down.** Since you haven't been keeping food and exercise records, you have no idea what the number on the scale should be. So, you often are disappointed when you get on the scale and it's not the news you want.

- **You weigh yourself obsessively while you are trying to lose weight.** The problem with running to the scale to see if there

246

is any action is that you are now putting the focus only on the numbers and not on creating long-lasting changes in your thinking and habits.

- **You have thrown away your scale and go by the fit of your clothes.** This tactic may seem sound, but clothes are unreliable and inaccurate, since they stretch and shrink with washing and dry cleaning. By not weighing yourself, you are still giving power to the scale.

THIN THINKING AND WEIGHING YOURSELF

According to the National Weight Control Registry, 75 percent of Weight Masters weighed themselves once a day or once a week, while releasing weight.

Numbers help you to be accurate. Numbers help you set goals. Numbers help you problem solve. Numbers do not define you. You are not the number on the scale. When you begin thin thinking, you stop letting the number on the scale take your power. You are going to use the scale to gather data and, along with your Inner Coach, you're going to assess the numbers in a way that helps you track your progress and make changes if needed—that is all!

When you make the sole point of your weight release journey about the numbers on the scale, you lose its purpose. The focus should be on your internal journey and mastering the thinking that allows the scale to go down and remain down. Your attention needs to be on learning to nourish yourself within your Calorie Budget for Weight Release. When you attend to that, the scale will go down.

Remember, when you achieve your ideal weight, it is just a number too. That number isn't the magic. The journey you took and how you changed your thinking and life to achieve your ideal weight is the real magic. Take the power back from numbers and the scale, and begin weighing like a master.

HOW TO TRACK YOUR WEIGHT LIKE A MASTER

Here is the step-by-step process of weighing in masterfully:

- Weigh yourself daily in the morning before eating, without clothes, and after using the bathroom. If you choose to weigh weekly, I recommend you do so on Thursday or Friday morning when your weight tends to be lightest. Weighing on Monday after the weekend's extra food indulgences may include water weight and will be inaccurate.

- Take a breath before you get on the scale. Remind yourself you are going to love yourself no matter what the number is.

- Step on the scale, get the number, and get off. In other words, be like a scientist—collect data not drama.

- Record the number on your app (all apps I mention have the ability to record your weight on a digital graph) or the weight chart (provided online at www.FromFatToThinkThinking.com). This gives you an important visual guide for assessing your weight trend over time and not just day to day.

Assess data as a loving scientist to see if the number on the scale is in line with your recordkeeping.

If the number isn't what you expected, take a moment to figure out whether your recordkeeping is 100 percent accurate. Inaccurate food and exercise records are usually responsible for weight errors.

But weight gain on the scale may be due to something beyond your control. For instance, water retention may be responsible for a gain. If the scale reads a pound up from the day before, ask yourself "Did I eat 3,500 calories more than my Daily Body Burn yesterday?" Probably not, and chances are one of these culprits is to blame:

- Estrogen fluctuations in women (PMS, ovulation, menopause)
- Excess sodium intake
- Humidity
- Dehydration
- Altitude
- Post-travel water retention
- Illness or infection

Another possibility is that you are experiencing the "water weight plateau." You can expect this to occur during the first six weeks of any weight loss. You can avoid the freak outs and cognitive distortion when this happens by using this next strategy—Avoid the Water-Weight Plateau Trap.

AVOID THE WATER-WEIGHT PLATEAU TRAP

Have you ever dieted with great weight release results for the first few weeks and then it stops for no good reason? And did that weight plateau seems to last forever? Did it cause you to get discouraged and give up? Does it lead you to make assumptions, such as "I have no metabolism" or "That diet was good at the beginning but then stopped working."

Chances are that you were experiencing the water-weight plateau trap. Your interpretation of what was happening on the scale caused fat thinking and put you back into the Weight Struggle Cycle.

I would like to walk you through how the water-weight plateau works and a strategy to help you and your Inner Coach be powerful during the plateau.

Water Weight 101

Before you started staying within the limits of your Calorie Budget for Weight Release, you were feeding your body more calories than it needed. Many of those excess calories probably came from carbohydrates. Your body took that extra carbohydrate and converted it to glycogen molecules, which were stored in your muscles and liver. These glycogen molecules are bonded to water molecules, resulting in about three to four grams of water for every gram of glycogen.

When you begin any weight loss plan, cleanse, or detox, you are cutting calories, including those from carbohydrates. When you're eating less food, your body still needs to function, so it pulls those glycogen molecules from your muscles and liver to make up for the calorie deficit and releases the water molecules for excretion from your body.

This water loss is where all the fat thinking begins. Let's say your weekly weight release goal is one pound. You eat less and exercise more to burn that 3,500 calories. Your body releases one pound, but chances are the scale will tell you that you released more, sometimes much more.

You step on the scale, see a dramatic weight loss, and say "Wow I've lost four pounds this week!" You actually haven't lost four pounds; you released one pound as per the laws of physics, and the rest was water!

The first three weeks you stay within your Calorie Budget for Weight Release, the scale could be down as much as ten pounds or more, but according to the laws of physics you have only really burned three pounds, the rest is water weight. Usually, around week three or four, the tide begins to turn, so your weight appears to plateau according to the scale. The plateau represents the fact that the water stores are gone, and you are catching up to the scale with your weight release.

The Ecstasy and the Agony of Water Weight

The initial water weight that causes "illusionary" weight loss is how a lot of fad diets, low-carb plans, cleanses, and bad-science, weight-loss programs hook you with dramatic weight loss claims. Don't fall for them! I know it's wonderful to think that you are losing all this weight so quickly in the beginning, but the weight release inevitably comes to a screeching halt and you don't know why. You blame yourself and your body. You give up, feel like a failure, and fall deeper into the Weight Struggle Cycle.

This "catching up with the scale" plateau is tricky mentally. This is where Weight Masters look to their recordkeeping for assurance. Like them, you will find you are still releasing weight, even through the plateau, because you are still burning 3,500 calories a week. In a few weeks, you will catch up with the scale and see a weight release that is more consistent with your weight release goal.

Here is how you and your Inner Coach can stay rational during a water-weight plateau:

- Keep food, exercise, and weight records.

- Expect the water-weight release up front and don't get conned into believing that it's fat loss.

- Look at your records frequently in the first few weeks to see how many calories you have burned, and whether you have stayed within your Calorie Budget for Weight Release.

- You can also calculate how much actual weight you have released by looking at the overall amount of calories you have burned since beginning and dividing that number by 3500. When the plateau begins, keep reminding yourself that you will catch up with the scale, and the plateau will end.

- Keep your weight records on an app, such as *Lose It!* or *My Fitness Pal*, or on a graph in a paper notebook.

Once you start building the skill of keeping records, you will experience a real sense of confidence in your ability to truly be able to create your own weight release and not fall prey to fad diets or get discouraged on the scale. You and your Inner Coach will now be savvy weight releasers who use recordkeeping to accurately move forward on your journey to weight release.

CASE STUDY: JENNIFER MASTERED THE SCALE

My client Jennifer thought her body was broken. For years she was caught in the frustration of the water-weight trap. Invariably, she gave up when she stopped losing weight in the first few weeks of whatever diet she tried. She came to me and got the facts about how to release weight at a rate she decided using her Calorie Budget for Weight Release. She learned how to track her food and exercise and let her Inner Coach guide her through the expected plateau.

"I reminded myself that I was releasing weight even when it didn't show up on the scale. My recordkeeping helped me confirm that I was burning calories with exercise. I spoke calmly to myself about paying attention to things that made me feel good other than the numbers on the scale."

Jennifer managed to stay within her Daily Calorie Budget for Weight Release (1,400 calories) for one pound to be released a week, even while eating things like waffles and the occasional hamburger. Over the course of the year, she tracked her weight release on a piece of graph paper she kept by her scale. She would come and show me the graph as she consistently stayed within her budget for weight release.

Some months later, her weight went down quickly, but there were other times when Jennifer experienced a plateau for four weeks. Then the weight on the scale dropped, and realigned with her recordkeeping. I assured her all the while that this is normal in a weight release journey. There are so many internal and external variables with fluctuations in water weight that the scale won't always show results day to day.

At the end of the year, 52 weeks later, Jennifer came in beaming and showed me her graph paper. Sure enough, she had released 50.8 pounds.

"The laws of physics work!" she said. "My scale and my body work just fine."

....

"Understanding how to weigh myself on the scale not only gave me the mental tools I needed to push past long plateaus during my process, but the knowledge also helped me pay attention to more important things than the numbers going up and down. Since I realized my body wasn't broken after all, I began to truly love my body. I became more patient with learning how to care for it. By nurturing myself, I finally began to feel I had a nice relationship with myself—on and off the scale. That's worth my weight in gold!" she said. Jennifer R, (Released 51 pounds, maintaining 4 years)

....

WEIGHT MASTERY SKILL 4 SUM UP: SELF-MONITORING

- Monitoring your food, exercise, and weight allows you to consistently stay within your Calorie Budget for Weight Release and keep moving forward.

- Monitoring your food, exercise, and weight gives you and your Inner Coach data needed to adjust things quickly if you get off track.

- By tracking daily, you are able to spot challenging times and foods and make adjustments—continuing to improve your healthy eating and exercise systems.

- Weighing yourself consistently yields data that lets you know if the actions you are taking are allowing you to release weight at a rate you decide.

- Tracking your weight on a graph is a clear picture of the pace with which you are releasing weight. This rational viewpoint keeps you out of that "this isn't working" head that tempts you to give up.

APPRENTICE PAUSE: I hope you are beginning to see how self-monitoring helps you interface with the weight skills and understand the synergy between the Nine Skills. Self-monitoring is the skill that many clients initially question the most. Eventually, though, they say they gain the most value from it. I still track my food and exercise to this day. Over the years I have come to see it as one of the loving ways I tune into myself over the course of my day.

_____

Okay, let's get off the scale and look at another skill that impacts the scale but in a different way—**SKILL 5, Stimulus Control**.

CHAPTER 29
WEIGHT MASTERY SKILL 5
STIMULUS CONTROL

SKILL 5: Stimulus Control. The skill of keeping your environments stocked with healthy food choices and cleared of trigger foods that create temptation.

For millions of years, man spent a good part of his life chasing down food to eat. Today in a world overloaded with food choices, food is now chasing us, and it's winning.

FAT THINKING AND STIMULUS CONTROL

I always ask *Shift Weight Mastery Process* participants to list the environments, times of day, and trigger foods they reach for. Most of their lists aren't long, but they are powerful!

- Cheese when I come home from work—with wine!

- Crackers or chips in front of the TV.

- My boss's candy jar in the afternoon when I'm stressed.

- Leftover birthday cake in the staff room.

Nine times out of ten, when a client has had had a slip and regained a few pounds, it is because a tempting food or a particular set of foods has come into one of his or her environments. Never underestimate the power that food—especially a stimulating trigger food—has on your brain and your ability to control it.

Trigger foods are foods that you can't eat just a little of. They tend to be a food that turns on your brain's need to eat more and more until the bag, box, or bowl is empty. Trigger foods also tend to be highly refined foods that contain big mouth and brain pleasers, such as sugar, fat, and salt. There are exceptions to this rule. Some people go for peanut butter, dried fruits, cheeses, or high-fat dairy. Any food you find yourself circling back for or thinking about constantly can pose a "stimulus" issue.

According to Brian Wansink, PhD, author of *Mindless Eating*, when adults are put into a state of perpetually having to decide whether or not to give in to food temptations, they get worn down and eventually give in. That is why relying on your ability to be strong and exert willpower in the presence of your favorite, fattening trigger food is a form of fat thinking. It just doesn't work.

THIN THINKING AND STIMULUS CONTROL

Weight Masters adopt a proactive attitude with their environments rather than a defensive one. They use their minds to think on a different level—protection. You can cultivate thin thinking by choosing foods that are going to be best for you in your environments and avoiding foods that challenge your weight release and maintenance.

Here are two thin thinking strategies that will make a huge difference to your long-term weight release success:

1. Stimulus-proof your environments, such as your home, work, gym, car, or any place where you spend time and/or are prone to eat your trigger foods.

2. Create loving boundaries with your trigger foods.

1-Stimulus-Proof Your Environments

This three-part stimulus control strategy is incredibly easy in theory. Your challenge is to make it a practice.

Keep Healthy Snacks Available

You walk in your front door after spending the last 45 minutes in traffic, and your blood sugar level is dropping as you head into the kitchen. You have to start dinner, but as you open the fridge to pull out the salmon and salad fixings, the first things your eyes fall on are three leftover pieces of pizza. How much willpower do you have to assert in order not to stand there and eat at least a few bites of that pizza, if not all three slices?

What if the pizza was in the back of the fridge in a covered container, and the first thing you saw was the salmon and green beans you're going to prepare for dinner and a container of pea pods and cucumber slices to munch on while you cook. Because you wouldn't see the pizza, your mind isn't engaged to think about it and doesn't have to exert energy to resist it. Out of sight, out of mind, and out of mouth!

Make a point when you shop to have healthy snacks to reach for at work and at home and in all of your environments. If you keep the healthier options up front and easily available, your mind will stay tuned to nourishing yourself.

If a Food is Challenging You, Move It or Get Rid of It

There are a few ways to do this:

- **Keep challenging food out of sight.** Creating a visual barrier between you and the food sometimes is enough. I had a client who created a visual barrier between her and the corn chips on the table at Mexican restaurants by putting the napkin holder and glasses between her and the chips. Put trigger foods in cupboards or drawers or in the back of the pantry so they aren't in view.

- **Freeze the trigger food.** This works great for bagels, bread, cookies, and baked goods. It removes the urge to pop some into your mouth impulsively.

- **Dispose of the food.** If the previous tactics still don't work, put the food in the garbage, and if you continue thinking about it, put the food in the garbage on the street. That, my dear apprentice, is stimulus control. The garbage disposal works well too. Remember, it's not a waste of money if it saves you from pain and suffering. Avoiding the few hours of feeling bad about yourself is worth the price of disposing some trigger foods.

Stimulus-Proof Your Shopping

Millions of dollars are spent getting you to walk zombie-like down grocery aisles, putting the pretty packages in your cart and getting them through checkout without thinking about the later consequences to your body and your weight struggle. Don't be a pawn in their numbers game! Take back your power at the store.

We often undermine our weight management by buying things for other people at the grocery store. Parents often use the excuse that "it's for the kids." Two more common excuses are "what if friends come over" and "it's on sale." Shift your mind and stay focused on what you need from the grocery store. Walk by anything that you know will be calling your name later that night. Make a shopping list and stick to it!

If your Inner Rebel says "I have to buy ice cream for the kids," but it's you who ends up eating it, pass on the ice cream. How? Take a deep Shift Breath, connect with your thin thinking Inner Coach, and ask yourself:

- If I buy this ice cream, what will really happen to it?

- Is that ice cream going to be calling my name all night?

- Is that ice cream going to be for the kids or the guests? Will I end up looking at the bottom of the empty carton and cursing myself for falling for the old "it's for the kids" con again?

Love yourself enough in the moment to say "no" to the impulse. You are doing yourself a huge favor by setting yourself free from the cravings, the food-sneaking behavior, and the guilt after you eat it. Just walk on by. Have you passed the ice cream aisle yet? Phew!

....

"Whenever I am in the grocery store and I see something tempting, I now hear that song ,"Walk on By" and take a Shift Breath and keep walking. I never regret not purchasing those things I have the impulse to grab off the shelf. The more I walk on by, the easier it is to do again and again." Reema Y. (Released 16 pounds, maintaining for 18 months.)

....

Stimulus-proofing your environments is a very powerful strategy. You will be amazed at how much easier weight management is when your environments are free of the trigger foods that cause you problems.

I am not saying that you have to remove all the unhealthy foods or treats from your house. I am sure there are many foods that do not hook you. I know that I can have bags of potato chips sitting in my cupboard for months, and I couldn't care less. Chips don't do it for me, so they don't need to leave my house. However, it's a different issue altogether when you are talking candy corn and gumdrops! Those sugary candies are a trigger food for me. I know if I have one, I have to eat the whole bag. So guess what? They don't come in my house. If they do, my family is under orders not to let me know. What my mind doesn't know about won't stimulate it.

2-Creating Loving Boundaries with Your Trigger Foods

Life is long, and there will be times when you want to indulge in a pleasurable treat, including your trigger foods. How do you set your mind up for success when having that treat? Make a rule with your Inner Coach ahead of time about when and how much of a treat you are going to enjoy. That treat is not an option at any other time. I call this strategy "creating a loving boundary."

Alain Dagher, PhD, a neurologist at Montreal's Neurological Institute, conducted a study on expectation and brain activity with regard to smoking. He measured the brain activity of smokers who were kept from smoking for four hours. One group was told that after four hours they could smoke; the other group was told they needed to continue to abstain from smoking for six more hours. The smokers who expected the cigarette after four hours began to show high levels of arousal, the closer their time to smoke came.

The others smokers, who did not expect a cigarette, showed no arousal. When the brain knows that a reward or treat will not be forthcoming, it puts its attention elsewhere. Once you make a decision about something, and you are clear about that boundary, it helps your mind say "no" easily.

Here's how to do it step by step.

- **Identify the trigger food.** This should be easy; it's the one you can't stop eating!

- **Think of what a single serving would be both in amount and calories.** Make sure it allows you to stay within your Calorie Budget for Weight Release.

- **Think of an environment in which it might be safe to eat a single serving**. This environment is one that you have not had a stimulus control issue in.

- **Create a limit on how often you might enjoy you trigger food**

in this setting. Creating a limit keeps you from overindulging or abusing the boundary.

For example, say your trigger food is ice cream. If you can't stop eating the ice cream until the carton is empty, our stimulus control strategy would be to keep ice cream out of your house. But what if you want to be able to enjoy its creamy goodness every once in a while? You can create a new loving boundary with ice cream.

For example, a loving boundary for ice cream might be "Once a week I can have a scoop of my favorite at the ice cream parlor."

You are giving yourself something you enjoy but in a moderate and measured way outside your environment. You can even look up the ice cream calories online and see that one scoop of rocky road is 170 calories. You can make it work calorically for you on the day you're having it, too. You have the ice cream but still remain within your Calorie Budget for Weight Release.

MY LOVING CAKE BOUNDARY

Frosting was my drug of choice when I struggled with my weight. At one wedding, I went back for five pieces of wedding cake. Of course, I had to keep face. I didn't want the server to think that I was an out-of-control cake fiend. I told him that I was bringing the extra slices to others at my table. Little did he know that the others at my table were my Inner Rebel and her wild friends partying on cake deep inside of me!

As I began my journey to weight mastery, I created a powerful loving boundary around cake that works for me still. I tell myself "Cake and frosting for me is not an option unless it's my birthday or the birthday of anyone in my immediate family."

This inner rule around cake is a perfect fit for me. For each family member's birthday I will make a cake and have a wonderful piece with extra icing. In my inner rule system, cake is not an option unless it's my birthday or my husband's and children's birthdays.

CREATE YOUR TRIGGER FOOD LOVING BOUNDARY EXERCISE

Take a moment to fill in your trigger foods and create a loving boundary.

Trigger Foods to "Put in a Box"	When to Take "Out of the Box"
Example: Cake with frosting	On my birthday and family members' birthdays.

WEIGHT MASTERY SKILL 5 SUM UP: STIMULUS CONTROL

- Stimulus-proof your environments by removing the trigger foods that tempt you and having healthy choices available. When you are not falling victim to high-calorie foods in your environment, it is much easier to stay consistently on track with weight release.

- Bringing healthy food into your environments and having them on hand for meals and snacks is another way to ensure your environment is set up to help you succeed.

- Create loving mental boundaries around your favorite trigger foods so that you can have them in your life occasionally but in a controlled way. Knowing your trigger foods and creating a masterful relationship with them puts you in charge.

- Stimulus control is an important skill not only for releasing weight but also for long-term weight management.

APPRENTICE PAUSE: Have you ever felt protective of someone or something? Perhaps you have cared for a small child or a pet? It is quite an intense feeling, right? Why is it that when it comes to your own self-care and weight, you don't step in to protect yourself? Now that you understand the skill of stimulus control, you can be your own protector, bringing a new level of self-protection to your life in the way you take care of yourself and the environments you live in.

_____

Let's move on to the skill that will allow you to not only deal with the foods in your environment but those living, breathing beings that you share your environments with—**Skill 6, Creating and Maintaining Your Weight Mastery Support Team.**

CHAPTER 30
WEIGHT MASTERY SKILL 6

CREATING AND MAINTAINING YOUR
WEIGHT MASTERY SUPPORT TEAM

SKILL 6: Creating Your Weight Mastery Support Team. This is the artful skill of recruiting the people in your life to be cheerleaders, coaches, and advocates for you during your journey to weight mastery.

When you read a weight loss success story, you never hear the person say "I did it alone. No one helped me!" Weight Masters say just the opposite. They acknowledge a coach, mentor, friend, group and/or family member who walked with them, helped them to eat more healthfully, and/or encouraged them along the way.

FAT THINKING AND SUPPORT

Research shows that people with support double their chances of success. However, many Weight Strugglers have the limiting belief that people can't, won't, or don't support them in their attempts to lose weight. In addition, many Weight Strugglers are hesitant to seek support because of past failures.

- I don't want to draw attention to myself.

- I hate to fail publicly.

- Nobody will help me. My friends and family think I'm a lost cause.

- My friends will try to sabotage me.

I agree. It's demoralizing to announce to everyone that "I am going on a diet so you better not tempt me and bring your fattening food around me!" and then go off the diet. However, the kind of support I am speaking about involves recruiting the people in your life to play an ongoing part in your journey to Weight Mastery. The more people you have on your team, the better your chances for long-term weight release success.

THIN THINKING AND SUPPORT

Every person in your life plays a role in your weight mastery. There are three ways that people influence your efforts:

1. Some will SUPPORT you and have a positive influence.

2. Some will SABOTAGE you and have a negative (intentional or unintentional) influence.

3. Some will be NEUTRAL and have neither a positive or negative influence.

As a Weight Master, you want to have as many people on the side of supporting you as possible. How do you recruit your team? I find the best way to recruit people is to ask. But don't assume they are going to know what to do. Teach people how to support you and share your visions and goals. When most people feel included as part of an "improvement" project, they feel excited and happy to help.

JANICE SHIFTED HER OFFICE WITH SUPPORT

My client Janice slowly got her whole office recruited in her weight release.

- First, just by keeping candies and cookies out of her sight.

- Then, by making healthy choices when they ordered lunch.

- Finally, she got four coworkers to walk with her at lunchtime.

Janice's entire office has been transformed. She released about 80 pounds in 24 months. Some of her coworkers released significant weight as well.

....

"Once I made the decision I was going to master my weight, I also decided to ask for others to help. In the past, I would hide the fact I was on a diet, but I

figured, hey, if this is going to last, I have to train my coworkers how to treat me like my future slimmer self. People are happy to help, and it all ended up being a great group project." Janice J. (80 pounds, maintaining for 1 year)

Your team can support you by:

- Keeping food out of sight.
- Walking or exercising with you.
- Buying food when you don't have time.
- Eating healthy meals with you.
- Sharing recipes and ideas for menus.
- Bringing fruits and veggies into the office or home.
- Choosing restaurants that have healthy options on the menu.

BUILDING YOUR SUPPORT TEAM

Get out your pen and journal; it's time to brainstorm and make this important list. The good news is that the person who was usually the most resistant to support you in the past with weight mastery is now already on your team. That person is YOU.

It is quite possible, almost probable, that you got a big, stinking "F" when it came to being a support for yourself in the past. Weight Strugglers are not in the habit of making themselves a priority. When stressed or overwhelmed, their healthy resolve diminishes. Have you heard yourself say "My boss needed me, so I couldn't take a walk on my break." Or maybe it was "I felt guilty about exercising when I should be spending time in the afternoon with my kids."

It's time to put you on the top of your support team list. Remember, the boss, the kids, and everyone else suffers when you are unhealthy, feel bad about yourself, and run yourself ragged to meet their needs. Make time for what is most important. Get used to the idea that you are on the top of that list and love it. On the top of the list below, write your name first.

MY SUPPORT TEAM EXERCISE

Give your Inner Coach a moment to think through other key players who can fulfill your team. On the left-hand side of your journal page, create a list called "Support Team Member." Under it write the people in your life that you want to recruit for your team—starting with your name! To the right of each name, write the specific role you will ask them to play.

SUPPORT TEAM MEMBER (Friends, Family, Co-workers)	SUPPORT ROLE (Exercise partner, help shop, keep foods out of sight)
1. Your name	
2.	
3.	
4.	

Keep going......

SOME SUPPORT TEAM DO'S AND DON'TS

DO make sure your supporters are reinforcing the Nine Skills you are building rather than pointing to what you are not doing. "Wow, you exercised every day during the week!" versus "I didn't see you drinking enough water."

DON'T focus your supporters on your weight change. Sure, an occasional comment is okay, but you want them to help you be healthy and masterful not "skinny."

DO keep asking for encouragement. Remind your supporters from the start that you want their continual support with the new skills. Often once you release the weight, people believe "you are okay now." They don't realize that being a Weight Master is an ongoing pursuit. The early stage of maintenance is not a time for them to bring all the junk back into the house or start offering you cookies, saying "You look great! Have a cookie!" You can even write a list of positive things they can give you compliments about achieving, such as drinking water, avoiding TV or Internet eating, or consuming more vegetables.

I have been maintaining my weight for years, but I still ask my husband and kids to keep certain foods out of sight. Or I ask them for support in helping me have time to exercise. They are happy to do it, because they see it makes such a difference to me.

CASE STUDY: GENEROUS BOB AND HIS DOUGHNUTS

Carla had a difficult situation at work. Bob brought in doughnuts every day and left them out for the staff at the small insurance company where she worked. The problem was that her desk was by the side counter where Bob left the doughnuts. Carla had asked Bob in the past to not buy doughnuts, and Bob said, "But everyone here loves the doughnuts. Just don't eat them!"

When that attempt failed, Carla asked Bob to keep the doughnuts in his office. "No one can see them in there," Bob scoffed. "Like I said, practice a little self-control." But as Carla knew, willpower doesn't go very far, especially when faced with glazed doughnuts from morning until afternoon, right outside her cubicle.

When Carla began her *Shift Weight Mastery Process*, she decided to ask Bob for support. She sat down with him in his office and gave him a card. Pleased, he read it. "Thank you for your generosity," it read.

Carla went on to thank Bob for being such a generous person and told him how nice he was for thinking to bring doughnuts as a way for people to enjoy the day. She went on to explain that she needed his help. The doughnuts really were a distraction for her. She knew he was a generous person and wouldn't want her to feel distracted, so she had come up with a great idea to honor his generosity even more. She pulled out a nice sign that she had made that read "Bob's doughnut cupboard. Please enjoy a doughnut from the cupboard below."

Carla walked Bob out and showed him how the doughnuts went nicely in the cupboard below the counter. People would know they were there because of the sign, but the doughnuts would not be a distraction for her. Bob loved the sign. It gave him credit for his generosity but allowed Carla to overcome her challenge. Many people went on to quietly thank Carla for ridding the office of the tempting doughnuts by keeping them out of sight and out of mind.

....

"It is so helpful to have a tool to ask people for change in a way that we can both win. In the past, I would eat the resentment I would feel towards people who made me feel powerless. I now feel like I have a voice and am doing much more asking instead of eating!" Carla U. (Released 48 pounds, maintaining for 3 years.)

....

WEIGHT MASTERY SKILL 6 SUM UP: BUILDING YOUR SUPPORT TEAM

- By creating a support team you are creating an external set of motivators and helpers that are committed to your Weight Mastery goals.

- Make yourself the leader of your cheerleading squad.

- Give others specific roles they can play in supporting you.

- Keep reminding your team to support you, and work on shifting the weight saboteurs onto your team as well.

APPRENTICE PAUSE: By engaging the environment skills, you are spreading your scope of mastery not only with your weight but into your outer world as well. When your world is lined up for your success not only does our weight and health benefit but so does the rest of your life. Are you beginning to see that weight mastery is really life mastery?

_____

Good job, and now let's move on to the **Mind Skills.**

CHAPTER 31
THE THIRD LEVEL

THE THREE MIND SKILLS

Y OU HAVE COME SO FAR and are almost done with all Nine Skills! These last three skills will finish construction of your Weight Mastery Home. In many ways, the Mind Skills are the most important of all.

THE MIND SKILLS

Skill 7 Communicating With your Inner Coach. You cultivate a powerful relationship with the wise goal-setting, planning, solution-seeking, Weight-Mastery-committed part of you with specific daily and weekly huddle sessions designed to help you reach and maintain your ideal weight.

Skill 8 Managing your Inner Critic. You manage your Inner Critic and shift out of limiting beliefs and negative self-talk.

Skill 9 Managing Your Inner Rebel. You use strategies that make you immune to the seductive voice of your Inner Rebel, the one that wants to sabotage your best efforts.

Most of the challenges you have had with consistency in eating or exercise or any other aspect of weight management started in your mind:

- With a critical thought: "I blew it, so screw it."

- A lack of thought: "Gee, I forgot to exercise."

- A limiting belief: "It's too hard."

- A mindless habit, such as eating in front of the TV.

Up until now, the negative wiring in your mind has dominated your ability to manage your weight long-term. Next you are going to construct the powerful thinking skills that will free you of those beliefs and habits.

The Mind Skills give you a powerful communication system within yourself that keeps you focused on your goals, managing your thoughts and emotions, and keeps you motivated to keep releasing weight and then ultimately maintaining your weight. These skills put the "mastery" in weight mastery.

"Every day I used to wake up into a living nightmare of self-criticism about my body, about my out-of-control eating, and my out-of-control life. I now wake up to a different inner voice that feels more like the real me. This voice helps me plan for a winning day and makes me feel great about myself and my life." Grant G. (Released 11 pounds in 30 days, maintaining for 2 years.)

Let's get started with **Skill 7, Communicating with Your Inner Coach.**

CHAPTER 32
WEIGHT MASTERY SKILL 7

COMMUNICATING WITH YOUR INNER COACH

> **SKILL 7: Communicating with Your Inner Coach.** This skill involves powerfully interacting with your Inner Coach to keep you thin thinking and moving steadily forward toward your ideal weight and weight mastery.

Welcome to my favorite skill of all! I hope that you will love the skill of Communicating with your Inner Coach as much as I do. Yes, the other skills are so powerful and open the door to steady weight release, but I am convinced this is the skill that allows you to soar into long-term weight mastery.

Fat Thinking And Communicating With your Inner Coach

What is missing from most Weight Strugglers' thinking are the habits of planning, strategizing, and problem-solving. These communication habits are the cornerstone of thin thinking. Many of my clients know how to eat healthfully and work exercise into their days. But the long-term challenge for everyone is consistency—that is, sticking with healthy food choices and exercise over time.

"I am able to be good for a while, but then I get bored."

"I always give in on the weekend."

"When I travel, my discipline and I go to different destinations."

"I am a victim of my cravings!"

"I forget to eat, and then I overeat."

"I just forget...period."

Often this lack of attention, continuity, and willpower doesn't come from a lack of discipline or a character flaw but rather because Weight Strugglers have never had a consistent motivating, strategizing, and problem-solving voice in their heads. They haven't had a voice continually communicating with them, driving them toward their Weight Mastery destination.

THIN THINKING AND COMMUNICATING WITH YOUR INNER COACH

Research says adults check their digital devices 79 times a day on average. But how often do you check in with yourself? Weight Strugglers tend to spend most of their days directing attention outward and neglect tuning into their own needs. Put down that device and start checking in with your Inner Coach over the course of your day!

I will now begin guiding you through two types of communication that you and your Inner Coach can have with each other:

1. **Proactive Communications.** Thin thinking communications designed to move you toward your ideal weight goal/vision.

2. **Defensive Communications.** Thin Thinking communications designed to intercept fat thinking and move you immediately back on track toward your goal/vision.

1-Proactive Communications

Right now, you have begun your journey to weight mastery and your mind is shifting to thin thinking. The next step will be for you to begin to build specific times into your life—weekly and daily—for you to communicate with your Inner Coach in order to stay on the path of weight release and mastery. You and your Inner Coach will create:

- Clear weekly weight release visions.

- Specific weight release goals.

- Plan exercise sessions and healthy meals.

- Think through stimulus control, support, tracking, and troubleshooting challenges

By focusing the brain in this way at key times, you will not only leverage willpower from your conscious mind but add the creative power of your subconscious to it. This will help you have more:

- Focused motivation and drive.

- Consistent healthy actions to meet your goals.

- Confidence in yourself and your abilities to release weight.

Sound good? It should. These "huddles" with your Inner Coach can be life transforming and are at the heart of lasting change. During your *30-Day Thin Thinking Practice,* these huddles will become a habitual part of your new Weight Mastery lifestyle.

THE FIVE KEY INNER COACH HUDDLES

There are five main proactive huddles that you and your Inner Coach can begin practicing daily and weekly:

1. The Weekly Planning Huddle
2. The Morning Meditation Huddle
3. The Shift Breath Huddle
4. The Afternoon Refocus Huddle
5. The Evening Planning Huddle

The Weekly Planning Huddle

The first huddle for you and your Inner Coach to practice is the Weekly Planning Huddle. I consider this huddle to be your Inner Coach's overall plan for you to win the game—staying on track for weight release each week. I cannot tell you how important a part of my week this session has become for my own weight mastery. During this weekly meeting with yourself (Sunday is usually the best day for most), you:

- Create a vision of ending the upcoming week masterfully.

- Set your specific weight-release goal for the week.

- Schedule exercise sessions on your calendar.

- Plan food prep for the week (meal ideas, shopping list, etc.).

- Troubleshoot upcoming weight-related challenges and create a plan for success.

"I like to wake up Sunday morning before the rest of my family is up and do my weekly huddle with my Inner Coach over with a steaming cup of coffee. It's a nice time with myself, and I have become organized with the rest of my life as well." Shane T. (Released 25 pounds, maintaining for 1 year.)

NOTE: During your *30-Day Thin Thinking Practice,* you will be guided through the steps of your Weekly Planning Huddle every seven days. You can also use the Weekly Weight Release Planner-Calculator online at www.FromFatToThinThinking.com or the one at the back of the book to guide you through the steps.

The Morning Meditation Huddle

Instead of jumping out of bed with a head still in fat thinking, this meditation only takes a few minutes and allows you to set a thin thinking roadmap for the day. While you are still in bed or in a quiet moment before your day begins, practice your morning meditation huddle to prime your mind for the day's weight-release success. I think of this as the "locker room session" before the game.

- Take a deep Shift Breath, close your eyes, and connect with your Inner Coach.

- Create your *End of the Day Vision.* How do you want your body to feel tonight as you go to bed? Imagine the wonderful feeling of lightness you are going to have from making healthy and light food choices all day. Imagine feeling good in your body because you exercised.

- Think your day through from start to finish. Think about what you might eat and when you will exercise, including how you will respond to the day's different food and exercise challenges. You may be reminded to set out exercise clothes or to bring food with you. This mental roadmap is key for being prepared.

- Visualize weight-challenged areas in your day. Think through how you can overcome the challenge. For example, instead of coming home and heading to the kitchen, imagine putting on your sneakers to go for a walk instead.

- Take another breath and open your eyes. That's it! You are much more prepared for a masterful day!

"As a caregiver for my elderly parents, I always rolled out of bed and got going to the one that needed me first. There was never any thought of how I was taking care of me. My morning meditation has made a huge difference. I'm finally showing up for me first." Bonnie M. (Released 18 pounds, maintaining for 6 months.)

NOTE: You will have access to the *Daily Vision Meditation mp3*—a short, guided meditation that takes you through this morning huddle. You can either download it at the Online Resource Center at www.FromFatToThinThinking.com or receive it daily in your *30-Day Thin Thinking Practice* email program.

The Shift Breath Huddle

How many times in your day do you stop and connect with yourself and ask "How am I?" In our fast-paced, super-charged world, the idea of taking a little breather seems like a joke. Use your Shift Breath for momentary reboots in the day when you are:

- Overwhelmed.
- Bored.
- Hit by a craving.
- Mindlessly reaching for a snack even though you aren't hungry.
- Eating so quickly you barely taste your food.

To take your Shift Breath break:

- Close your eyes and take a Shift Breath.
- Allow you Inner Coach to check in. "How are you doing? How are you feeling?"
- Ask yourself, "Do you need anything?" A longer break? Some healthy food? Some water? Many strugglers forget to eat, because they don't tune in to their body until it's too late.

- Eliminate items on your To Do list. Your expectations can often overwhelm you.

- Give yourself what you need and get on with your day!

"I used to overeat halfway through helping the kids with their homework. Now when I start to feel the stress coming on, I escape to the bathroom and do a Shift Breath Huddle instead of eating goldfish crackers. There are days when I may need three huddles during homework, and I take them. It's far more relaxing and far less fattening than stuffing my stress down with food." Carrie R. (Released 40 pounds, maintaining for 3 years.)

The Afternoon Refocus Huddle

The afternoon is when willpower starts to nosedive. This quick huddle allows you and your Inner Coach a moment to refresh your evening goals as well as make any adjustments that you need to stay on track with your plans. It is basically the same meditation as the Morning Meditation Huddle and can be done sitting at your desk, in your driveway before you head in for the night, or on the subway. It only takes a few moments.

Take a deep Shift Breath and close your eyes.

- Refocus your *End of the Day Vision*. How do you want your body to feel tonight as you go to bed—remember that light feeling.

- Refresh/adjust your plans to stay on track. Think about what you might eat and when you will exercise. You might have to adjust from this morning's plan, which is fine. Now is the time to do that!

- Visualize weight-challenged areas in your night. Think through how you might overcome the challenge. For example, you might put your dinner plate in the sink instead of going for seconds.

- Take another breath and open your eyes. That's it! You are ready for a masterful evening.

"I have been using this huddle every day for 30 days. I used to keep eating after dinner and into my night of television. During my huddle, I visualize finishing dinner and being finished with food. I call it 'Food free in front of the TV.' Getting

prepared mentally in the afternoon has made breaking the night eating habit much easier!" Stanley F. (Released 7 pounds in 30 days, maintaining for 2 years.)

NOTE: You can use the *Daily Vision Meditation mp3* in the afternoon as well…many of my clients use the recording in the afternoon instead of the morning. Some use the mp3 for both the morning and afternoon—you choose!

The Evening Learning/Review Huddle

Give yourself a few minutes at night to review the day. What went well? What didn't? This review enables your mind to make the necessary changes where they are needed and also reinforce what is going well. In addition, it gives you time to set yourself up for the next day.

- Find a quiet place to give yourself a few minutes to huddle.

- Review the day's food and exercise tracking. What behaviors and thinking patterns are serving your weight release? Also, notice the eating, exercise, or other habits and beliefs that are especially challenging.

- Think through your schedule for tomorrow, and plan your exercise time and food needs.

"I had a running conversation in my mind about how I didn't have time to exercise. After reviewing my days a few times with my Inner Coach, I realized that I could go for a walk at my son's baseball practice while he was on the field. I started walking every time my son practiced, and I broke the plateau that I had been experiencing. It wouldn't have happened if I hadn't taken the time to problem-solve in the evening." Gary P (Released 68 pounds, maintaining for 3 years.)

NOTE: You will find there is an Evening Review guide in the Index and in the Online Resource Center at www.FromFatToThinThinking.com that you can print out to keep in your journal. It is also a part of the daily email program.

WEEKLY PLANNING HUDDLE
1 x Week

- Set Vision for the Week
- Set Specific Weight Goal for Week
- Schedule Exercise on Calendar
- Plan Food Prep for Week
- Troubleshoot Challenges and Create Plan

DAILY VISION MEDITATION HUDDLE	AFTERNOON REFOCUS HUDDLE	EVENING REVIEW HUDDLE
• Connect with Inner Coach • Create End of Day Vision • Think Through Potential Challenges for the Day	• Refocus End of Day Vision • Refresh/Adjust Your Plans to Stay on Track • Think Through Potential Challenges for the Night	• Find a Quiet Place • Review Day's Food & Exercise Tracking • Think Through Food & Exercise for Tomorrow

S.H.I.F.T. BREATH HUDDLE
As needed throughout your day

2-Defensive Communications

Now, Apprentice, as you and I both know, the communications that you have with your Inner Coach are not only about weight release. Some of the most important communications are about getting back to releasing weight as quickly as possible should we get off track. (By the way, there will be times when you will get off track!)

The more you strengthen the habit of immediately getting back on track, the easier it is to continue releasing and then maintaining your ideal weight for good. Here are some ways that we can get off track:

- Fat thinking for a moment. You eat something you didn't intend to, and your Inner Critic says "You blew it!"

- Fat thinking for a day or two. You have company in town and your Inner Rebel takes over. You spend the weekend overindulging.

- Fat thinking for a week or more. You go through a period where you have been bored, stressed, or on vacation, and your fat thinking takes over. You know you've slipped back in that "being good or being bad," on-or-off Weight Struggle Cycle.

In the past, if you found yourself going off track, you may have given in to the "start over tomorrow" impulse. Starting over gives you permission to eat more until the day you get back on track. That kind of thinking puts you on that "being good or being bad" Weight Struggle Cycle very quickly. It goes like this:

- Get off track.

- Decide to start over tomorrow or Monday.

- Start over Monday but fall off again on Thursday and decide to start over next Monday.

- Start gaining weight back.

- Inner Critic gets louder with negative self-talk, saying "Pull yourself together!"

- Inner Rebel wants to escape with food, saying "Dieting is hard. I need a reward."

- Fat thinking mind is back and Weight Struggle Cycle resumes.

Now the steps back into fat thinking might not always look like this exactly, but you get the picture, right? When you go off track and make the decision to start over tomorrow, you are setting in play a series of beliefs and habits that quickly take you out of thin thinking and back into fat thinking and the Weight Struggle Cycle.

THE S.H.I.F.T FROM FAT TO THIN THINKING TECHNIQUE (HUDDLE)

Apprentice, as a Weight Master, your number one job if you go off track is to get back on track AS SOON AS POSSIBLE. How do we do this? The S.H.I.F.T. back into Thin Thinking Technique, of course.

We walked through the S.H.I.F.T. huddle earlier when you and your Inner Coach were introduced. Now, we revisit it because now you and your Inner Coach have learned some skills that will help you use the technique masterfully.

The S.H.I.F.T. to thin thinking huddle is a powerful defense to fat thinking. This mental interception stops the emotionally driven Inner Critic/Inner Rebel "you blew it, so screw it" mode and shifts you back into rational, problem-solving communication with your Inner Coach.

Let's use an apprentice named Mary as an example of using the SHIFT technique.

Mary has been releasing weight by shifting from fat to thin thinking. She has been releasing one pound a week by steadily burning 3,500 calories a week. She stays within her daily calorie budget of 1,400 calories and burns an extra 700 calories a week by walking 20 minutes at lunch time. She is banking those 700 exercise calories for the weekend and using it for dessert and a glass of wine when she goes out with her family.

One afternoon, Mary has a stressful meeting at work. Afterward, when she goes into the staffroom, she sees pizza leftovers from a birthday party on the counter. Without thinking, Mary grabs a slice and eats it. It tastes good for a few bites, but she eats the rest mindlessly without even enjoying it. On the way back to her desk, Mary impulsively grabs a few chocolates from the jar on her coworkers desk. She hadn't done that since she had started releasing weight.

Now, all of a sudden, the voice of her Inner Critic wells up in her. "Why did you eat all that crap? You really pigged out and fell off the wagon!" This stresses Mary even more, and now there is the voice her Inner Rebel of welling up inside her. "Since you blew it, you may as well eat more candy and pizza. You can start over tomorrow!"

Mary feels the urge to give in but recognizes that this moment calls for the S.H.I.F.T. technique and she begins:

- S—Shift Breath. Mary takes a deep inhalation and intercepts her fat thinking "start over and be perfect tomorrow" impulse.

- H—Harness the power of your Inner Coach. In that moment of pause, Mary reaches for her Inner Coach to begin thin thinking.

- I—Insert thin thinking and get the facts. Mary rationally assesses what has happened from a nonjudgmental place of curiosity. "What happened? I got stressed and ate a slice of pizza and two chocolates I hadn't intended on eating."

- F—Forgive yourself and find a solution.

  1. **Forgive.** Mary forgives herself right then and there. "I forgive myself for eating crap!" She immediately feels better. **NOTE:** Remember, no matter what has happened, no matter how much food you have eaten, or how many days or weeks you have been off track, forgive yourself and get on your own team.

  2. **Find a Solution.** Mary begins to use some of her Weight Mastery skills to find a solution. Below are three common problem-solving options Mary might use.

     NOTE: No matter how much damage has been done, there are always a few short steps you can take to get back to Weight Mastery.

Rework your food for the day. Alter your food plans for the day to allow you to come in at your Daily Calorie Budget and be on target for releasing weight.

Mary figures out the slice of pizza was 400 calories and the candies about 80 calories. Luckily, she had tracked her food earlier and knew she had eaten about 540 calories before she overate. With the additional pizza and candies she had consumed 1,020 calories. She subtracts her Daily Calorie Budget of 1440 from 1020 in her head and knows that she can just eat a lighter dinner that evening (380 calories) and still be on track for the day.

Focus on re-balancing later in the week. You can be okay with the fact you went over your Daily Calorie Budget for Weight Release and can make it up on some other day by altering your food intake or exercising a bit more.

Mary decides she will make up for going over her calorie budget by 540 calories by skipping her treat tonight (150 calories of ice cream) and using the calories from an additional hour-long walk that she will take on Saturday (390 calories) to compensate.

Or, Mary could decide to dip into her 700-calorie exercise savings and apply it to this calorie overage. She would still have 160 calories in her weekly exercise-calorie savings.

Be okay with going over. You don't have to meet your exact weight goal every week. You can still release weight for the week but maybe not as much, but that's okay. Releasing is releasing.

Mary realizes that if she stays on track the rest of today and the week she still will have released nearly 3,000 calories, which isn't quite a pound. She decides to be okay with it. She reminds herself it's more important to keep up the good habits and release slowly than go off track for the rest of the week and start over on Monday.

Apprentice, can you see how Mary used some of the Nine Skills to help her work out these solutions? Tracking her food and exercise helped her think things through and get right back on track.

T—**Take a lesson and step forward to weight mastery**. Mary thinks over what happened and realized that she was in the habit of heading to the staffroom when she was stressed. This realization allows her to think what she might do instead. She decides a better way to relax would be to go for a walk or sit at her desk and take a few Shift Breaths. Mary moves on with her day and has a masterful week and weight release.

S.H.I.F.T.
FROM FAT TO THIN THINKING TECHNIQUE

Shift Breath

Harness Your Inner Coach

Insert Thin Thinking

Forgive Yourself / Find a Solution

Take a Lesson / Move Forward to Mastery

During your *30-Day Thin Thinking Practice*, you will gain confidence in problem-solving and staying on track. While the mechanics of the S.H.I.F.T. Technique may seem time consuming, I assure you the time it takes to summon your Inner Coach and figure out a winning solution is far outweighed by the hours, days, or even weeks wasted in fat thinking and the Weight Struggle Cycle.

Remember, it is consistency and not perfection that keeps you on the road to Weight Mastery. Weight Masters got that way by putting one foot in front of the other and moving forward.

Case Study: Too Much Time?

It was almost time to break for lunch during a *Shift Weight Mastery Process* seminar when Debra raised her hand. She said, "These huddles make a lot of sense, but I don't have time in my day to do all of them. I wake up, and I am off to the races. How can I fit in this self-coaching? That's an extra half hour in my day that I don't have!"

I answered, "Remember, this positive way of communicating with yourself and guiding yourself through your day is replacing the time you used to spend struggling with yourself and your weight. How much time do you spend in the morning beating yourself up mentally about overeating the night before?"

Debra raised an eyebrow. "I definitely spend a few minutes doing that."

"The time you use talking negatively during the rest of your day probably adds up, too," I offered.

"Okay, I see what you are saying. It's not so much that I am adding to my day as I am changing the way I communicate with myself and take care of myself."

"Exactly," I told her. "It may seem like extra time, but it isn't. And in the long run, you'll save time. Can you give it 30 days to try on for size?"

Debra took the Inner Coach offensive strategy session by the horns over her *30-Day Thin Thinking Practice*.

....

"I can't believe I was worried about my time. Showing up for myself with positive self-coaching sessions throughout the day made me feel better. My huddles helped me follow through on health behaviors and release weight, and it saved me hours of feeling bad about myself. My new relationship with my

Inner Coach is addictive. I love the time we spend together setting myself up for success." Debra T. *(Released 47 pounds, maintaining for 2 years.)*

....

WEIGHT MASTERY SUM UP

SKILL 7: Communicating with Your Inner Coach

Communicating consistently with you Inner Coach is the most important skill of the Nine Skills, because it keeps you motivated and on track using the other skills to release and maintain your ideal weight.

There are two types of ways to communicate or "huddle" with your Inner Coach

- **Proactive "huddles"** focus on planning ahead and creating strategies for success. These huddles happen weekly, daily, even hourly if needed.

- **Defensive "huddles"** are interventions focused on intercepting going off track and falling into the old fat-thinking Weight Struggle Cycle and getting right back on track and into thin thinking.

APPRENTICE PAUSE: Are you beginning to see the potential for a beautiful relationship happening? You and your Inner Coach are embarking on the most important journey to Weight Mastery. When this skill is in place, all the others line up behind it and create a powerful synergy that stretches beyond your old way of being into a powerful way of self-care and self-respect. Are you willing to respect yourself? Are you willing to work powerfully with yourself? I bet you are.

_____

Great job, Apprentice, I hope it feels wonderful to have ignited the powerful coach within you. Now onto **Skill 8, Managing Your Inner Critic.**

CHAPTER 33
WEIGHT MASTERY SKILL 8

MANAGING YOUR INNER CRITIC

SKILL 8: Managing Your Inner Critic. This skill shifts you out of negative self-talk and overwhelming expectations that cause stress and emotional eating, sabotaging your success.

Have you ever noticed that more than half of the 80,000 thoughts that pass through your mind each day are negative? When you are stuck in fat thinking, those thoughts create a daily undercurrent of stress and anxiety. They eat away at your self-confidence and self-esteem, leaving you vulnerable to wanting to disconnect from the pain with food.

FAT THINKING AND THE INNER CRITIC

Your Inner Critic wields a lot of power over your relationship with yourself and weight management. Your Inner Critic is especially quick to take control of your beliefs and emotions with unrealistic goals and negative self-talk.

Overwhelming Expectations

Your Inner Critic holds you to standards that are impossible to live up to and overwhelms you with anxiety and a feeling of perpetual failure.

- "You must be perfect on your diet. If you aren't, you have to start over."

- "You are unlovable because you are not thin."

- "You need to lose 20 pounds this month."

Negative Self-talk

Your perfectionistic Inner Critic is in the habit of spewing zingers like these when you don't measure up:

- "You blew it!"

- "Why did you clean your plate? You're a greedy pig!"

- "No wonder you are fat! You're too lazy to exercise!"

Apprentice, don't take these comments personally. Oh wait, you already have! My guess is that negative self-talk has become such a part of you that you don't even hear it. You're stressed out, and guess what happens next? The fight-or-flight response kicks in, and you overeat to cope with the anxiety.

THIN THINKING AND THE INNER CRITIC

You can use the power of your relationship with your Inner Coach to counter your Inner Critic's influence. Look at the critic from a different perspective, one where the critic is no longer running the show. In fact, you can see that your Inner Critic is just a scared and disempowered part of you that has inherited some negative beliefs from the outside world and bought into them.

Are you ready to dismantle the power your Inner Critic? Great! You're going to learn how to:

1. Shift negative self-talk.

2. Overcome overwhelming expectations.

1-Shift Negative Self-Talk

Often the Inner Critic's voice becomes a combination of all the critics in your life:

- Parents

- Doctors

- Family

- Friends

- Media images

This voice becomes louder and louder until it's the voice waking us up in the morning, telling us we better be good today. The snarling disgust you hear when you look in the mirror or step on the scale is distressing. It's the same part of you that yells you to sleep at night. "You failed again! You are an out-of-control addict!"

Negative self-talk was the main driver of my client Sara's weight struggle when she came to see me.

CASE STUDY: SARA AND THE DIET DOCTOR

Sara spent several thousand dollars working with a diet doctor in one of the affluent areas of Los Angeles. The good news is this diet doctor gets great results! His patients are able to lose weight, which they hadn't been able to do previously. Sara lost 60 pounds in six months. Here is how his system works:

Visit One: You pay a lot of money to get on the scale, and the doctor tells you that you are overweight. He gives you a sheet listing the foods you can eat, according to his secret daily formula. Basically, it's a two-meal-a-day, 500-to-700-calorie diet that includes a few ounces of protein, several servings of vegetables, and a fruit serving. (The "secret" is the diet is very low in calories. Shhhh!) You eat only the foods on the sheet, nothing less, nothing more, or, in the doctor's eyes, you failed.

Visit Two: You return a week later, pay the doctor more money, and step on his scale. If you haven't lost weight, you have failed. The doctor admonishes you rather harshly and tells you to stick to the diet more carefully the next week. If you lost weight, you escape this scolding session.

Either way you take the doctor's food list and repeat the process again, returning to pay the diet doctor more money. Whether or not you are scolded depends on if you are "good" or "bad." On and on this process of paying, weighing, and being scolded or not keeps going until you reach your goal weight. Then, you continuing seeing him—and paying for those visits—to maintain your weight.

This sounds extreme, but isn't that how it goes? If there isn't a diet doctor yelling us down the scale, our Inner Critic is doing basically the same thing.

After six months Sara got tired of the very low-calorie diet and started to slip. She stopped going to the doctor, because she didn't want to get yelled at. "I started yelling at myself instead," she told me during our session. "I couldn't get through two days on the plan before I had somehow blown it. I was so stressed that all I could do was eat everything that wasn't on that stupid sheet of paper. I not only have an Inner Critic, I have an inner diet doctor and my super weight-conscious mother inside my head, and all three are disgusted with me."

She sighed. "I need to lose the weight for my health, but I can't get past this perpetual need to beat myself up and start over."

My response to Sara was "You don't need to pull yourself together. You need to shift the power struggle between you and this inner critical voice that has a chokehold on you and your ability to be masterful."

What if you listened to your Inner Critic through the ears of your Inner Coach? What if you experienced the Inner Critic's perfectionist expectations, negative beliefs, and unrealistic demands not as the truth but as the ramblings of an amusing character that just happens to be in your life?

Part of the "cognitive restructuring" that many Weight Masters use is learning to recognize their negative inner voice and separate themselves from it. When you poke holes in the Inner Critic's voice, it begins to immediately lose power.

I asked Sara to imagine that her Inner Critic was the over-the-top critical character in a movie or a real critic from her life. We gave the character a silly voice, and Sara imagined her Inner Critic saying a favorite criticism. With the following CBT technique, the Inner Critic seems silly and less of a voice of truth and more what it really is—a figment of the fat thinking mind.

PUT THE CRITIC BACK IN THE BACK SEAT EXERCISE

Apprentice, I am giving you the chance to show your Inner Critic who is boss. Get your pen and journal and complete this imagining process to wrest control from your Inner Critic. (I will use Sara's process as an example.)

If your Inner Critic were a character in a movie, who would they be? Or choose someone from your life that you don't like to play the part. (Sara chose the diet doctor to be her Inner Critic.)

What does your Inner Critic look like? (Sara's critic is a 67-year-old man. He's 5'5" tall and wears thick glasses and a white doctor's jacket)

What is a negative phrase that your Inner Critic tells you? (Sara's phrase for this exercise was "You have no self-control.")

Now close your eyes and imagine your Inner Critic saying your phrase in a silly voice like Donald Duck or SpongeBob SquarePants. Thank your Inner Critic for his opinion and tell him to take a nap. Put him to sleep in a tiny box in the back of your mind.

2-Overcome Overwhelming Expectations

Our Inner Critic likes to overwhelm us with unrealistic expectations. Many times, those who struggle with weight put themselves at the bottom of the totem pole, helping everyone except themselves in order to live up to our Inner Critic's perfectionistic standards.

- "I've got to be the perfect mom and do as much as I can for my kids. I don't have time to exercise."

- "My staff needs me, so I need to stay after hours to help them."

- "I have to get everything on my list done in order to be okay for today."

If your Inner Critic stresses you with expectations, you probably turn to food for soothing. It's a short-term fix and not a masterful one. Here's how to curb your Inner Critic's expectations.

1. **Notice the feeling of anxiety or being overwhelmed.** This means the Inner Critic is stirring up expectations.

2. **Take a Shift Breath.** Be present, and call your Inner Coach.

3. **Ask yourself "What are my expectations right now?"** Chances are your expectations are distorted and unrealistic, but you may think they are kind and sensible. For example, you might say to yourself "I have to work late and then go home and do the kids' dirty laundry and call my mom." The underlying expectation is "I have to be a perfect employee, mother, and daughter."

4.   **Enlist your Inner Coach for help taming the expectations.**
This might mean being okay with less-than-perfect options, ones that don't agree with your Inner Critic's standards. Take a Shift Breath and think those expectations through with your Inner Coach.

"Do I have to get all that work done for my staff today? Why don't I just get the things done that are a priority and leave the rest until tomorrow? I will have the kids help me with the laundry, so I'll have time to speak with mom and get the kids to bed at a decent hour!"

This little huddle takes seconds and shaves a huge amount of stress from your life.

CASE STUDY CONCLUSION

Over the week following our meeting, Sara made a point to huddle with her Inner Coach when unrealistic expectations loomed over her. As she huddled with herself, she realized the work quota she set for herself might make her look good to the company but was more than she could do. She also noticed that her expectations weren't even hers—they belonged to her perfectionist mother.

"I decided my ego and Inner Critic could take a break. I was going to look after Sara and change my sales quota. When I calmed down, I found that I made about the same number of sales as I expected to. I was able to connect with my customers and give them good service, not just sell them something. It was a win-win solve for me, my customers, and my health but not my Inner Critic."

Sara came back after a few months of shifting and had released 17 pounds. More importantly, she released over a thousand pounds of her old negative burden of high expectations.

....

"Learning to put my Inner Critic back in the closet, shut the door, and connect with my Inner Coach has made a huge impact on my weight and my life. I am loving myself down the scale without all the negative chatter. I am sure my Inner Critic is okay, too. If she gets bored in that closet, I am sure she will find a way to organize and make everything perfect!" Sara T. (Released 34 pounds and maintaining for 3 years.)

....

WEIGHT MASTERY SKILL 8 SUM UP: MANAGING THE INNER CRITIC

Your Inner Critic can be managed. It is important to separate yourself from the negative self-talk and perfectionistic expectations that keep you struggling.

- Separate yourself from that negative Inner Critic by making him or her a separate character from yourself. Hear that negative self-speak for the inaccurate, fearful, and distorted chatter it is.

- By tuning in and recognizing that the expectations creating stress and unpleasant emotions are overblown and unreasonable, you take control and make positive changes.

- As you learn to tame the fear, shame, and overwhelming expectations of the Inner Critic, you build confidence in yourself and your ability to succeed in the long-term.

APPRENTICE PAUSE: Do you think it's best to get rid of the Inner Critic altogether? Not so fast. Your Inner Critic may be causing you to stay in the Weight Struggle Cycle, but banishment isn't a good idea. The Inner Critic has some valid ideas from time to time. Your task is to prevent your Inner Critic from running the show. Let your Inner Coach manage your Inner Critic so both become your inner support team.

_____

Okay, is that Inner Critic being quiet? Good. Time to visit that other voice, the one that takes your power away with seduction— **Skill 9, Managing your Inner Rebel.**

CHAPTER 34
WEIGHT MASTERY SKILL 9

MANAGING YOUR INNER REBEL

SKILL 9: Managing Your Inner Rebel. This skill manages the big bold energy of the Inner Rebel who wants to resist embracing new healthy habits. The Inner Rebel seduces you to disconnect from your weight release vision and pursue momentary pleasures.

When I think of someone who symbolizes the Inner Rebel to me, I imagine the iconic black-and-white photo of James Dean taken from the 1955 movie *Rebel without a Cause*. The movie's poster shows James Dean leaning against a doorway and smoking a cigarette. It embodies this attitude: "Oh yeah? Try and make me do what you want. I don't think so."

FAT THINKING AND THE INNER REBEL

Your Inner Critic wants you to live by the rules and doles out punishment when you don't. In contrast, your Inner Rebel wants only to live outside the rules of dieting and weight loss systems and regimes. Your Inner Rebel is responsible for sabotaging your respect and trust in yourself and keeps you in the Weight Struggle Cycle by communicating through whining and seduction.

Resistant Whining

Your Inner Rebel wants things to stay the same and like a child throws a tantrum when change is enforced.

- "Losing weight is too hard."

- "I don't like sweating."

- "Food is fun why are you taking it away from me?"

Artful Seduction

Your Inner Rebel loves the feeling of letting loose and indulging, especially when feeling deprived. Like a sleazy car salesman, your Inner Rebel will say anything to close the deal.

- "Everyone else is indulging, why can't we?"

- "You worked so hard today you can't exercise. Sit down and have a treat instead."

- "Since the bag is opened, you might as well eat the rest, then we won't buy any more."

THIN THINKING AND THE INNER REBEL

This rebelliousness is interesting, isn't it? Like the Inner Critic, the Inner Rebel is not all bad. He or she is the interesting part of you that questions authority and has a red flag for any sort of idea or regime that seems oppressive to your soul. It's time to work with your Inner Rebel and use that creative energy in a productive way that will help not hurt you. For long-term success, you need to learn how to negotiate with this part of yourself.

Are you ready to disarm your charming Inner Rebel? You are going to learn to:

1. Overcome Inner Rebel Overtures.

2. Use the Think it Through Strategy.

1-Overcome Inner Rebel Overtures

My client Tom's Inner Rebel had him in a headlock when it came to his weight. I would like to walk you through how Tom learned to use his Inner Coach and shift the power struggle in his favor...

CASE STUDY: TOM AND THE DISAPPEARING PIZZA

Tom thought that being able to finish an entire pizza was a sign of manhood. "My friends and I would consider you a wimp if you left a piece of pizza on the plate. If you ate it all, you won!" Tom said at our consultation meeting.

Tom grew up in southern California and had been in the construction industry for a good part of his life. He had been a customer of the diet industry even longer. Tom had tried every weight loss program, fast, and cleanse out there…twice. "My mom always dieted and took me to my first Weight Watchers meeting when I was eight," he shared with me.

When I asked him what his biggest challenge to long-term success was, Tom replied, "I am not sure. I am very good at following a diet structure and releasing 30 of the 50 pounds I need to lose, but somewhere along the way, I get bored of the diet. Or I go out with the guys and eat pizza and drink beer. It's the devil sitting on my shoulder, and he's pretty hard to say no to when he wants something."

"I like to call that devil your Inner Rebel," I said.

"Whatever you call it, once I give in to it, a part of me snaps and doesn't want to return to the strictness of a particular diet. It's as if I'm on hiatus just as I am in between TV jobs until I regain the weight."

Have you felt like Tom? When a Weight Struggler is a slave to an Inner Rebel, he is a hapless victim of a rebel who wants to sabotage all attempts at weight release.

Remember how you learned to separate from your Inner Critic? You need to hear your Rebel's communications as desires and illusions and not as truth.

I invited Tom to participate in a CBT process similar to the one used to separate from an Inner Critic.

"Tell me one way your Inner Rebel tries to seduce you into sabotaging your weight-release efforts?" I asked Tom.

Tom laughed. "Just one? Okay. If I've started a diet and the weekend comes, I may go out with my family for dinner. If I see ribs on the menu, my Inner Rebel says, 'Hey, you worked hard this week, let's have the ribs, a beer, and a side of fries. We'll pull it together tomorrow.' In reality, that means restarting my program on Monday after eating a ton of food over the weekend."

I asked Tom to close his eyes and imagine that his Inner Rebel was a character outside him, a character in a movie or from his life.

Tom smiled. "I know exactly who my Inner Rebel is going to be. I just bought a new truck, and the guy that sold it to me was the ultimate salesman. I went in there wanting to buy a pre-owned model, and he talked me into buying a brand new model with a bunch of added details. This guy was smooth. He kept saying 'You work so hard, you deserve it.' I believed him, and I didn't know what hit me until I was driving home."

"Could you imagine this smooth talker saying 'Go ahead. You work so hard. Eat whatever you want, you can start again on Monday.'" I asked.

"Sure, easily."

"Now imagine that voice becoming silly and distorted like the voice of Homer Simpson or SpongeBob SquarePants."

Tom laughed.

"Does it take the edge off the seduction a bit?"

"Sure, I feel like I can hear my Inner Rebel from a mile away. He's not going to catch me daydreaming again," Tom said.

Next Tom shrank his Inner Rebel, invited him to take a nap, and put him in a box so Tom could take a break from all of his seductions.

OVERCOMING THE INNER REBEL EXERCISE

Now it's time for you to show your Inner Rebel who is boss and let him know that you're wise to rebel ways. As with the Inner Critic, you need to separate your Inner Rebel from you. Grab your pen and journal, and answer the following questions and follow along with the visualizations. Have fun!

If your Inner Rebel were a character in a movie, what character would he or she be? Or maybe choose a very seductive person from your life to play the rebel?

___

What does your Inner Rebel look like? (My Rebel is wild and unkempt with a cigarette hanging from her mouth.)

___

What is a seductive phrase that your Inner Rebel uses to sabotage you? (For me, one was "Oh, go on, you work so hard!")

___

Close your eyes and imagine your Inner Rebel saying that phrase but in a silly voice like Homer or Marge Simpson or SpongeBob SquarePants.

Now thank your Inner Rebel for his opinion, shrink him, and tell him to take a nap. Put him in a little box in the back of your mind.

Well done, Apprentice. Can you see how you and your coach can work together to become capable of managing even the most seductive Inner Rebels?

1-The Think it Through Strategy

Your Inner Rebel is very good at seducing you away from your weight-release intentions. The good news is that even though the seduction dance you do with your Inner Rebel has a powerful pull, ultimately it is predictable.

A typical Inner Rebel seduction attempt might be:

- Convincing you that you are too tired to exercise.

- Coming home from work when you are hungry and overeating.

- Overindulging at social outings, restaurants, and parties.

- Seducing you to get treats from the kitchen while watching TV at night.

The way to shift out of the seduction is with a CBT technique that I call the *Think it Through Strategy*. It involves turning the tables and seducing your Inner Rebel into making the healthier choice for you. According to psychologist Philip David Zalazo, PhD, "Our thoughts and the language we use to express them can remind us of bad consequences and guide us to other actions and reinforce the value of success."

What I am talking about is counter-seducing your Inner Rebel with an offer he or she can't refuse. Remember most of what drives our brain forward is the idea of perceived reward. The Inner Rebel is a master at making his reward seem better to you than sticking with your healthier option. What if you started marketing your healthier option in a more enticing way?

HOW TO THINK IT THROUGH

This technique allows you to shift your mind out of fat thinking impulsive pleasure seeking to thin thinking healthy action taking.

1. Take a Shift Breath and harness your Inner Coach.

2. Think through how taking the Inner Rebel's path will feel three hours from now after indulging. Really think about how that would feel in your body (full, bloated, lethargic) and your heart (regretful).

3. Next, think through what would happen if you made the healthier choice. How would you feel three hours later in your body (light, lean, energized) and heart (masterful, proud) at the end of the day?

Case Study Conclusion: Tom Romances His Inner Rebel

Let's look at how Tom used the Think it Through Strategy with his Inner Rebel during his morning vision meditation to prepare for an upcoming social outing.

Tom thinks forward to the lunch meeting he is having with friends at their favorite Italian restaurant. As Tom thinks about the lunch, he immediately thinks about the restaurant's fettuccini alfredo that he loves. Tom's Inner Rebel rears his head, thinking about the creamy noodles.

Tom's Inner Rebel says, "Wow, that fettuccini is so good, let's get that today. Come on, we never go to that restaurant, and your friend Joe is paying. I do not want a salad. That is for sure. A salad would just be…sad."

Tom takes a Shift Breath and begins to think through the Inner Rebel choice.

Tom says to himself, "Eating a plate of fettuccini would be amazing in the moment, but this afternoon I will feel bloated and gross with that fettuccini adding to the fat around my middle and pressing over the top of my pants. Do we really want to feel that way later?"

Tom's Inner Rebel responds, "Yikes, since you put it like that, um, I don't think so."

Tom now paints a seductive picture of a healthier option as he romances his Inner Rebel.

He says, "I can order the lemon chicken and veggies, and instead of a big plate of fettuccini alfredo, I can order a small side of fettuccini. I can eat a few bites and experience the fantastic flavors, and then I will put the plate on the table in the middle for the others to share. That way I can have the pasta and not become bloated. I can feel good about myself and good when I am done eating, because I ate healthfully, too."

Tom's Inner Rebel goes for it. "Okay, great, that is a plan I can sink my teeth into!"

"I have found a way to live my life not on the extreme of deprivation of a stupid diet or on the wild and crazy food fests my Inner Rebel relished. I have learned to enjoy life more since I'm in charge of what I put in my mouth. Yes, that sometimes includes beer and pizza. But I don't need to eat a whole pizza to feel like a man. I feel like a man because I am in touch with what I need to do to take good care of myself. That has been the biggest gift of all, and you can't smother it in mozzarella!" Tom D. Released 56 pounds, maintaining for 6 years)

WEIGHT MASTERY SKILL 9 SUM UP: MANAGING YOUR INNER REBEL

- By learning to separate yourself from your Inner Rebel's seductions, you can distance yourself from the unconscious pull that the rebel has over you and your weight.

- Using the Think it Through Strategy, you can allow yourself to recognize the negative outcome of rebel-based choices (Overeating indulgent foods, not exercising) and instead market the outcome of the healthy choice to your Inner Rebel—allowing this inner saboteur to see the healthy choice as the more seductive one.

APPRENTICE PAUSE: Most of what keeps the struggle for weight release going isn't eating something bad; it's how you choose to communicate with yourself before the temptation presents itself or after you have acted on it. By building the three Mind Skills, you are creating a strong inner communication system that results in more consistency with your weight release and more confidence in your mastery.

Now let's put the final nail in the structure of your Weight Mastery Home with the **NINE SKILLS HYPNOSIS SESSION.**

CHAPTER 35
HYPNOSIS SESSION

YOUR WEIGHT MASTERY HYPNOSIS SESSION

A T LAST, APPRENTICE, YOU HAVE completed your Weight Mastery Home with the powerful Mind Skills. You are now ready for the Weight Mastery hypnosis session that will guide your mind through the Nine Skills you have just learned and engage them on a deeper level.

INSTRUCTIONS

- Go to www.FromFatToThinThinking.com to access your hypnosis session.

- Listen only while in a relaxed position, not while doing the dishes or walking the dog.

- Listen to the Weight Mastery hypnosis session with an open mind expecting 100 percent success.

- DO NOT LISTEN TO HYPNOSIS WHILE DRIVING OR OPERATING HEAVY OR COMPLEX MACHINERY.

- Expect to feel relaxed. Don't expect to feel hypnotized.

- If you do go deep and feel like you are sleeping, try the session in a less relaxed position next time. You can get the impact of the hypnosis while in the sleep state.

When you finish listening, come back to the book to read the instructions for the final phase of your *Shift Weight Mastery Process*, your *30-Day Thin Thinking Practice*.

PART III

THE PRACTICE

Practice is the best of all instructors.

—*Publilius Syrus*

CHAPTER 36

INTRODUCTION

THE POWER OF PRACTICE

ONGRATULATIONS, YOU ARE NOW READY to begin your *30-Day Thin Thinking Practice*. I commend you again on coming this far on your journey from fat to thin thinking. To recap your progress in the *Shift Weight Mastery Process*:

Part 1: Orientation

You became educated in how your mind develops fat thinking and gets caught up in the frustrating Weight Struggle Cycle. You also learned how you can shift your mind from fat to thin thinking and begin living in the Weight Mastery Journey where you can achieve and maintain your ideal weight.

Part 2: The Shift

You began shifting your mind from fat to thin thinking by reading, doing the written exercises, and listening to the recorded hypnosis sessions.

You started your journey to weight mastery and did the following:

- You forgave yourself and moved beyond the self-distrust and resentment that kept you stuck in a negative relationship with yourself.

- You made the decision to be a weight mastery apprentice and learn from all that happens on your weight journey. For you, there is no more failure or starting over.

- You created powerful visions of the different milestones you will be achieving along the way to your ideal weight.

- You shifted your belief to 100 percent success by swapping your Weight Struggle Story for your Weight Mastery Story.

- You connected with your Inner Coach, the voice of weight mastery within you.

- You began mastering the Nine Skills and learned the Nine Skills in these three categories:

    1. The Physical Skills of weight release.

    2. The Environmental Skills that set you up for weight success.

    3. The Mind Skills of communicating with yourself to stay focused on your goal and moving forward consistently toward your ideal weight.

- You began to master the Nine Skills, learning from men and women who successfully released weight and kept it off.

Now you are ready to begin the last and final part of the *Shift Weight Mastery Process*—your *30-Day Thin Thinking Practice*.

GETTING STARTED

During your *30-Day Thin Thinking Practice*, you will use daily meditations, hypnosis, and coaching to continue wiring your mind for thin thinking. It takes 21 days for new habits to get wired into the brain, so by the end of the 30 days you should have:

- Daily and weekly practices that promote weight release at a rate you decide.

- A Weight Mastery way of life that is "yours." You are the owner and master. No one can take that mastery away from you.

- A powerful way of communicating with yourself that keeps you motivated and inspired.

- Eliminated the negative beliefs and habits that sabotaged you in the past and kept you struggling with food, exercise, and yourself.

I am now going to quickly walk you through the weekly and daily practices of the next 30 days to familiarize you with the 30-Day Practice

Huddles. Here's a reminder of how your huddles will work. A huddle is like a time-out where you and your Inner Coach take a moment, assess a situation, and make a plan. The five huddles we use over the *30-Day Thin Thinking Practice* are:

- Weekly Planning Huddle once weekly on the same day.

- Morning Huddle every morning.

- Afternoon Refocus Huddle every afternoon.

- Evening Review Huddle every evening.

- Shift Breath Huddles as needed throughout the day.

30-DAY THIN THINKING PRACTICE **SAMPLE DAY**

Here is an outline of how your daily *Thin Thinking Practice* is structured to flow through your day. You can see that you stay in communication with your Inner Coach throughout the day to set yourself up for success and follow through.

Morning

- Morning Huddle. Wake up and listen to the ten-minute Daily Vision Meditation. Take a moment to think about your day and plan for any challenges you expect.

- Read your daily coaching either online or in the email you received.

- Weigh yourself weekly or daily in the morning before eating.

During the Day

- Track your food and exercise. (See recommendations for setting up tracking in Chapter 37)

- Several times a day—hourly if possible—take a Shift Breath and check in with yourself.

- Do your Afternoon (pre-evening) Refocus Huddle to evaluate your day and plan for your evening.

Evening

- Evening Review Huddle. Review your day. What worked? What

didn't? (You can use the Evening Review questions as a guide—
see example Chart Y and see worksheet in Index.)

- Plan your food and exercise for the next day. (You can use the Planned Food Journal in the Index or print the PDF in the Online Resource Center.)

- Listen to your hypnosis session. For many people, the evening is the best time to listen to hypnosis but if you have time earlier in the day—that works just as well.

Here is an example of the kind of reflecting you might do during the Evening Review Huddle **(Chart BB)**. You can use the Evening Review page in the Index as a guide or print and use the Daily Journal provided in the Online Resource Center.

Evening Review Huddle

What are the three things that I did today to move towards Weight Mastery?

1. *Tracked my food.*

2. *Took a Shift breath instead of mindlessly eating.*

3. *Walked for 30 minutes*

What are the challenges that I faced today?
I was too hungry this afternoon at 5 pm.

Ideas to problem solve those challenges:
Save a third of my lunch to eat in the afternoon.

Chart BB: Evening Review Huddle

There will be days when you cannot fit all the steps of your daily practice in—do not fret! The idea of the *30-Day Thin Thinking Practice* is to try everything I've outlined and figure out what works for you and your weight mastery. Please do your best to at least listen to the morning meditation, track your food and exercise, and listen to one hypnosis session each day.

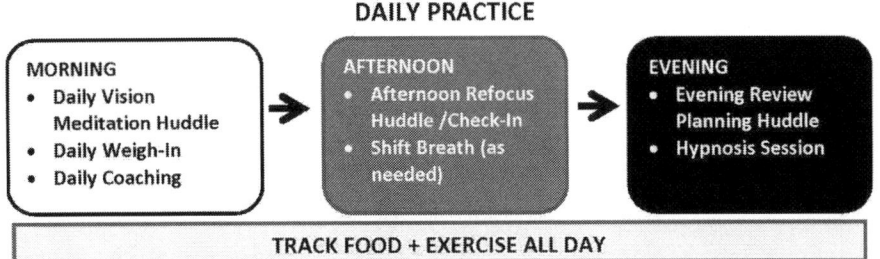

DAILY PRACTICE

MORNING
- Daily Vision Meditation Huddle
- Daily Weigh-In
- Daily Coaching

AFTERNOON
- Afternoon Refocus Huddle /Check-In
- Shift Breath (as needed)

EVENING
- Evening Review Planning Huddle
- Hypnosis Session

TRACK FOOD + EXERCISE ALL DAY

Now, Apprentice, you have your practice, let's get set up for it in **DAY 0—Setting Up for Success.**

CHAPTER 37
DAY 0

SETTING UP FOR SUCCESS

THERE IS ALWAYS A BUSTLE of excitement at the end of a *Shift Weight Mastery Process* seminar. The participants are chomping at the bit, ready to begin their *30-Day Thin Thinking Practice*. We spend the last hour talking about how they are going to make the most of the next 30 days, release weight at a rate they decide, and begin the Weight Mastery Journey.

You are going to do the same thing now. I call this Day 0 because it's the time you are taking to get everything set up to shift into your weight mastery. There will be two parts to Day 0:

Part 1: Setting up your *30-Day Thin Thinking Practice*
Part 2: Your first Weekly Planning Huddle with your Inner Coach

I highly recommend that you prepare for your week on Sunday and consider it Day 0. Otherwise choose whichever day works best for you.

As you are getting started, there is one other thing I will invite you to do for yourself today…

REMOVE THE "T" AND BEGIN YOUR MASTERY

When beginning a diet, our mindset is focused outwardly on the structure of the diet and wondering "Will it work for me?" Now that you are no longer dieting but are an apprentice of weight mastery, I'd like to SHIFT that idea of "will it work for me?" and remove the "T" from the equation and make it **"Will I work for me?"**

When you shift that one word, it shifts your life. You are now on a journey of shifting from the inside out. As you can see, this process is going to take some stretching, some work, and some rethinking of who you are. Are you willing to work for you? Are you willing to work for your health, your self-esteem, and your freedom?

I am going to remind you that you promised me you were ready to shift from fat to thin thinking, and now, as your coach working with both you and your Inner Coach, I will be asking you to continue to shift toward what you want.

Step up to the plate with me and don't half-heartedly "do" this process—**BE ALL IN TO WIN**—work for yourself. "Be the shift," and I promise you will never want to go back.

SETTING UP YOUR *30-DAY THIN THINKING PRACTICE*

Okay, Apprentice, let's get you ready to go. Follow these steps to prepare yourself for the next 30 days:

Step 1 Access your *30-Day Thin Thinking Practice* Resources
Go to www.FromFatToThinThinking.com. The Online Resource Center has everything necessary to successfully start and complete your *30-Day Thin Thinking Practice*. In addition to the meditation and hypnosis sessions, you can access the 30 days of daily coaching (online or as daily emails) support materials, and journal printouts. I urge you to take full advantage of this Online Resource Center for your best experience.

Step 2 Choose Your Food and Exercise-Tracking System
Over the next 30 days and on into your long-term weight release, I highly recommend that you track your food, exercise, and weight. I went into this in detail in Chapter 28. Let me just remind you of a few benefits that tracking your food and exercise will bring:

- Allow you to see that you are staying within your Daily Calorie Budget for Weight Release so you learn how to release weight at a rate you decide.

- Provide accurate data for you and your Inner Coach to rationally correct your course without going into "start over tomorrow" mode if you get off track or go over your Daily Calorie Budget.

- Teach you the calorie content and nutritional values (carbohydrates and proteins) of the foods you are eating and which ones nourish and stabilize your body best.

More reasons to track your food, exercise, and weight can be found in Chapter 28, Skill 4 Self-Monitoring.

MY EXPERIENCE WITH TRACKING MANUALLY

I have tracked my data in a journal for years. I write down my plan for the day's food on my to-do list in the morning and rewrite it as I eat during the day. I record my totals for exercise and food on the same weekly chart we use for your Weekly Weight Release Planner. (I print out many of these charts and keep an ongoing notebook of them.)

Tracking my daily food and exercise is such a part of what I do and who I am that I don't think twice about it. Like brushing my teeth, it's just something that I do, because it works. I treasure both my teeth and my weight mastery, so I have simply surrendered to taking the extra steps needed to attend to both.

Keep Tabs on Yourself

Monitor the following when you are tracking:

- **Calories consumed.** Keep it within your Daily Calorie Budget for Weight Release.

- **Food.** Become aware of the types of foods you eat and guide yourself toward nourishing and stabilizing foods.

- **Staying in the Mastery Zone.** I also recommend tracking the grams of carbohydrates and proteins in the foods you eat for at least 30 days. (The tracking apps I recommend will track fat, protein and carbohydrate grams automatically). This will allow you to make adjustments and feel free of the Carb Zombie! (Protein: at least 72 to 80 grams per day with calorie budgets under 1,600; for calorie budgets over 1,600, multiply your weight in pounds by 0.5 to determine the number of grams. Carbohydrates under 125 grams.)

- **Exercise.** Monitor how many calories you burn each day with exercise (the tracking apps will do this for you as well).

- **Daily and/or weekly weight.** Recording your weight will allow you to monitor your weight release and use the data to make adjustments and corrections in your food intake and exercise as you go along (provided in the tracking app). It is also very motivational!

Choose your tracking method. Consider two ways of tracking your food, calories, carbohydrates, exercise, and weight with either of the following methods that works best for you.

1. Track Manually
2. Track Digitally Online and/or with an app

You can track manually in several ways, including using the following:

- **A daily food journal.** I have provided both Planned and Actual Daily Food Journal pages to record your food and exercise (Index and Online Resource Center). Copy and/or print 30 of these journal pages and put them in a binder. You can also use the Weekly Weight Release Planner (In the Index and Online Resource Center) to track your ongoing data for the week.

- **A spiral notebook.** This is a super low-tech way of journaling. You simply record your food, the amount you ate, calories, protein grams, carbohydrate grams, and exercise in your notebook. You can also track the exercise you do and the length of time you did it for as well as the calories burned. Add these totals up each day to make sure you are staying within your calorie budget. Keep a running total of the net calories you have burned for the week, so you can stay on top of how much weight you are releasing.

- **A pre-printed food and exercise-tracking journal.** These are available for purchase at an online store, such as Amazon. Many of my clients have had success with these journals.

Pros: Many people find tracking their food and exercise manually in a journal comforting. One of the advantages of tracking by hand is that you can do it any place and any time. Obviously, it's also the first choice of people who don't like or use digital technology. Recording your food manually helps you become more familiar with the calorie counts and protein and carbohydrate contents of food, rather than relying on a database to do it for you. You'll quickly become well-versed in the calorie contents of the foods you eat regularly.

Cons: In the first few days to weeks of your practice, before you are familiar with the amounts of calories in foods you eat, you have to look each one up, which is time consuming.

NOTE: You'll find calorie contents on nutritional labels, online, and in nutritional tracking books, such as *Calorie King*. You can also find information on calories burned in exercise in apps, online, and in books. You can even ask your digital assistant, Siri or Alexa, to tell you how many calories are in an item! There are also devices that track your exercise calories.

You can track online or using a mobile app. This method of tracking is efficient if you are comfortable in the digital world. Thanks to technology, tracking is now as easy (sometimes) as a tap of your finger. There are now apps and websites that allow you to monitor and track your food, exercise, and weight. The two most popular apps available in the *Shift Weight Mastery Process* Community are *Lose It* and *My Fitness Pal*. You can find these free apps on your smartphone or access their websites.

Here are the steps to get started tracking digitally:

- Sign up for the service. You begin by entering your basic information, such as your weight, height, gender, and age, and your weekly weight-release goals. *Lose It!* or *My Fitness Pal* will then give you the calorie budget their algorithm indicates will achieve your goal.

- Adjust your Daily Calorie Budget for Weight Release in the app. The calculators for both the *Lose It!* and *My Fitness Pal* apps tend to give you a higher Daily Calorie Budget for Weight Release than the Shift Weight Release Calculator at FromFatToThinThinking.com. I find that the Shift Calculator gives you a more accurate Calorie Budget for Weight Release and will yield you more accurate results.

- Go to FromFatToThinThinking.com and access the Shift Weight Release Calculator. Put in your weight release information. The calculator will give you your accurate Daily Calorie Budget for Weight Release.

- Adjust your Daily Calorie Budget for Weight Release that was calculated in your *Lose It!* or *My Fitness Pal* account to the Daily Calorie Budget that you got in the Shift Weight Release Calculator.

To Adjust your Daily Calorie Budget in Lose It!

1. Click the **"Goals"** icon at the bottom of the interface
2. Click the **scale graphic** on next page
3. Click **"Edit"** on the upper right of the next page
4. Scroll down to find **"Daily Calorie Budget"** and adjust to the number given on the Shift Weight Release Page calculator

To Adjust your Daily Calorie Budget in My Fitness Pal

1. Click the **"More"** icon at the bottom
2. Click the **"Goals"** button on next page
3. Click **"Calories"** and adjust to the Daily Calorie Budget given on the Shift Weight Release Page calculator

Now you can start tracking your food and exercise! The database searches for the foods you input, presents serving size options, and provides the calories for the serving size you select. Most apps keep running tabs of your foods and meals so that the foods you typically eat appear quickly, and a tap of your finger records it. You track your exercise in the same way. The app keeps a running total of your daily data and shows you where you are within your Daily Calorie Budget for Weight Release. You can begin tracking your weight in the app, too. An app presents the data on a graph that shows your progress. This visual can be very motivating. Track your weekly progress, too. An app will also show your week in review, putting all your weight release data at your fingertips.

Pros: Many people find that using calorie-tracking databases make recording their food, calories, protein, carbohydrates, exercise, and weight seamless and easy. Many have said that recording becomes like a fun game they play on their phone. I also find it is easy to review past days to see what worked or didn't work and examine why.

Cons: If you aren't facile with your smartphone or don't have one or are not often online, you may find it inconvenient to track.

Tracking do's and don'ts. Regardless of whether you track manually or digitally, keep these do's and don'ts in mind:

> **Do** record everything as accurately as possible, using measuring devices, such as a food scale and cups and tablespoon measurers. Measuring accurately is especially important at the beginning of your *30-Day Thin Thinking Practice* when you're training your eyes for estimating.

> **Do** track immediately what you have eaten. (People often forget what they have eaten 15 minutes later.) Here's another system: Write what you plan to eat the day before. Then track as you go, changing amounts if you need to.

> **Don't** stop tracking because you went over your Daily Calorie Budget for Weight Release. Keep tracking as it will help you know exactly how much you went over. Love yourself, and keep tracking even if you go over your budget; chances are you can still maintain or even deficit some calories for that day.

STEP 3 Get Ready to Track Your Weight

Remember part of this process will be making the scale your friend by using it to help you and your Inner Coach track your progress. It's not all about the number on the scale, but accurate data is helpful in noting your progress.

- Make sure you have a scale that works.

- Weigh yourself in the morning.

- Be prepared to record your weight in your journal or on your app's weight chart.

- If you are recording manually print and use the Weight Release Tracker PDF available in the Online Resource Center.

STEP 4 Prepare to Exercise

Take the time to set yourself up for an active lifestyle. If you are already active, great. If not, think the following strategies through.

- Make sure you have the proper exercise equipment and workout clothes for your exercise plans.

- Join a gym, a dance class, a Sierra Club hiking group, or whatever active group meets regularly. (Check out www.meetup.com for groups meeting locally to exercise or play sports.)

- Get an exercise buddy, friend, or trainer lined up to work out with you.

- Plan walking routes around your home, work, or a nearby park.

- Check out apps and wearable tracking devices that record the calories you burn or steps you take. Information about them is in the Online Resource Center.

STEP 5 Prepare for Your Weight Release Eating Structure

Creating a healthy way of eating takes a bit of time and patience. Don't expect things to be perfect from the get go, but do expect to evolve a way of eating that honors you and allows you to release weight at the same time. You might want to review Chapter 26, "Skill 3 Creating a Masterful Relationship with Food." There you will find several strategies to get yourself started.

THE FOOD MASTERY ZONE

When you start eating in the Food Mastery Zone and getting adequate protein (Four 3-oz servings, at least 72 to 80 grams per day), fiber and nourishment from vegetables and fruit, and keeping your carbohydrate intake to a minimum (75 to 125 grams per day depending on your carb sensitivity) you will quickly be hibernating the Carb Zombie. The cravings and false hunger prompted by overeating refined foods will diminish, too.

NOTE: For the first three days of eating in this way, you may experience some mild feelings of blood sugar adjustment, such as a sensation that feels like hunger pangs or lightheadedness. If you are in good health otherwise, these sensations are your blood sugar insulin levels adjusting. That is a good thing. Think of these feelings as indications that you are putting the Carb Zombie in the Weight Struggle Prison. If you ignore him, the Carb Zombie will be forced to fall into a deep sleep, leaving you alone to enjoy eating more healthfully. Make sure you drink water and eat a form of healthy protein every few hours during this time.

If you have diabetes, please make sure you monitor your blood sugar levels and adjust accordingly during this process.

Review your weight release eating structure. If you didn't fill in the form in Chapter 26 yet, take a moment now to think about when you plan to fit meals, snacks, and a treat in your day—keeping within your Daily Calorie Budget for Weight Release. Check the Online Resource Center at www.FromFatToThinThinking.com for some daily meal plan structures that might be a good starting point for you.

Think through and have on hand easy, healthy meals, healthy pre-made products, and snacks that adhere to your meal structure. There are terrific suggestions for healthy meals with recipes online. You can often find low-calorie versions of your favorite meals online, too. Do some research. It will pay off in the long run. Here are some tips for healthy meal planning:

- **Research healthy fast food and eating out options.** Most chain restaurants and drive-throughs have nutritional information online and offer a few healthy options.

- **Have a healthy treat available for once a day.** Choose something that isn't a trigger food and stays within 15 percent of your Daily Calorie Budget for Weight Release.

- **While shopping, make sure you get plenty of protein options and a variety of vegetables and fruits**. Frozen vegetables are great because they don't spoil, and you can steam them in the microwave quickly. Add some protein and a sauce, such as marinara, teriyaki, or a curry-based simmer sauce, and dinner is served.

STEP 6 Prepare Your Environments for Stimulus Control
If you don't have a plan, the world has one for you, and it's not a slimming one. Be proactive and don't be a victim of your environments!

- Observe your kitchen, workplace, car, and any other environments in which you spend time every day. Are there any trigger foods that need to be removed?

- Do you need to ask others to keep their trigger foods out of your sight?

- Make sure you have healthy foods in your environment that you can reach for.

STEP 7 Assemble Your Weight-Release Support Team
It's time to get your team assembled for your *30-Day Thin Thinking Practice*. Don't take this step lightly!

- Review your support team list, and let each person know how to help you over the next 30 days and beyond.

- Encourage a supporter or two to go through the *Shift Weight Mastery Process* with you! This process is a great group project. If you assemble a group, you can begin being a leader, which will elevate your own chances of long-term success. The process works great for families and groups of friends or colleagues.

STEP 8 Set Time Aside Daily for Hypnosis and Huddles
The *30-Day Thin Thinking Practice* is obviously going to take some time each day. Before you begin, think through how you will make time for these important mental processes. The following is the best time you will ever spend making positive change:

- You will need about eight minutes for your Daily Vision Meditation Huddle in the morning.

- You will need a few minutes throughout the day for reading the coaching emails and doing some Shift Breath Huddles.

- A few minutes in the afternoon and evening for your Afternoon and Evening Huddles.

- About 20 minutes for your Hypnosis Session in the evening.

Now you are set up for your 30 days. It's time to officially huddle with your Inner Coach for your first week of mastery practice.

2-Your First Weekly Planning Huddle with your Inner Coach

Since you already have done all the heavy lifting with setting up your *30-Day Thin Thinking Practice*, this first Weekly Planning Huddle will be short, sweet, and to the point. I want you to get used to the idea of sitting down with your Inner Coach for a Planning Huddle every week to set a vision, goals, and strategies to meet those goals.

1. Take a deep Shift Breath and connect with your Inner Coach for this session.

2. Go to www.FromFatToThinThinking.com and find the Weekly

Weight Release Planner-Calculator. Go ahead and use the calculator provided to determine:

- Your weight release goal for the week.

- The Daily Calorie Budget for Weight Release that allows you to meet that goal.

- The specific exercise you will be doing to help you meet that goal

Print your Weekly Weight Release Planner. The planner-calculator is a great tool that makes planning your week easy and you can print it and use it all week long to guide you.

NOTE: If you don't want to use the online planner-calculator, you can use the one in the Index to guide you.

1. Look at the coming week on your personal calendar and do the following:

- Create your exercise appointments—and plan to keep them!

- Think through upcoming social events and other possible challenges, like the business lunch or the book group feast. How are you going to set yourself up for success?

- Mark in meal ideas and even remind yourself of the times you should eat if you tend to forget.

2. Close your eyes and imagine yourself at the end of the week, feeling lighter, leaner, and happy with yourself and proud of all you and your Inner Coach have accomplished. Take a Shift Breath and lock that vision in!

You are done preparing, now relax and have a good night's sleep so you can be ready for Day 1.

DAY 0 CHECK LIST

Follow these steps to prepare yourself for the next 30 days:

STEP 1: Access the *30-Day Thin Thinking Practice* Resources Online

www.FromFatToThinThinking.com. Click on the tab marked "Start Email Coaching" and sign up to begin your 30-Day Thin Thinking Practice emails. You will immediately get an email for "Day 0" that will walk you through these steps you are going through.

The next Day you will receive your Thin Thinking Practice Training Day 1. Each daily email will contain the hypnosis and mediation sessions for that day along with written coaching for that day's practice.

If you do not receive the email check your spam folder—it could end up there.

STEP 2: Choose your Food and Exercise-Tracking System

- **Manual Tracking:** Get a notebook, or print out 30 Daily Food Journal PDFs from the website or copy 30 Daily Food Journals from the index.

- **Electronic Tracking:** Sign up for Lose It! Or My Fitness Pal either online or in the App Store. These services are free of charge.

Remember: You will want to adjust the Daily Calorie Budget in these systems to the Daily Calorie Budget given to you by the Shift calculator.

STEP 3: Prepare to Track your Weight

- Digital Scale
- Weight Tracking system (app or manual print out)

STEP 4: Prepare to Exercise

- Attire—Music—Schedule—Gym or other location ready

STEP 5: Prepare to Eat in your Food Mastery Zone

- Plan meals, snacks, and treats for the week.
- Create a shopping list of healthy options. (See website)
- Create an eating out plan. Think about healthy take-out options and look at restaurant websites ahead of time to know what choices you can make ahead of time.

STEP 6: Prepare your Environments

- Remove trigger foods / Add healthy food options

STEP 7: Create your Support Team

- Make sure you are ready to make yourself a priority.
- Enroll family and friends in supporting you.

STEP 8: Set Aside Daily Meditation and Hypnosis Times

- Morning—10 minutes—Daily Vision Meditation
- Evening—20 minutes—Hypnosis (can be in afternoon or at bedtime)

Do's And Don'ts

- DO see yourself as an apprentice. This is not about perfection but about learning and creating your new thin thinking mind.
- DON'T give into limiting beliefs, such as:
  - "I don't have time!"
  - "This is hard."
  - "I'll start over Monday."
- DO expect to be overwhelmed, confused, and have other emotions at times. Emotions are fine. Allow them to wash over you and know that you are learning.
- DO expect to start feeling confident and free.
- DON'T stop or start over.
- DO keep moving forward on your journey of weight mastery.

Common Q's And A's About The 30-Day Thin Thinking Practice

Q: What if I skip a few days or get off track from my practice?

A: Keep going wherever you are. Do not start over. If you missed a few days, you can review the materials later, but just keep going. Break the "start over pattern."

Q: What if I don't listen to the hypnosis for a few days?

A: Keep going and begin listening again. Do all the meditation and hypnosis sessions that you can. Keep moving forward!

There are more Q's and A's on www.FromFatToThinThinking.com.

CASE STUDY: Jackie's Insight

Jackie is a hairstylist and works long, busy days. One of her clients released weight with the *Shift Weight Mastery Process* and recommended Jackie try it. Jackie loved the idea of hypnosis but was a bit slower to embrace the "thinking process" of shifting from fat to thin thinking. You may feel like Jackie: "Just give me the hypnosis and fix me." The following is Jackie's experience.

"I have struggled with my weight since I was a kid. When I signed up for *the Shift Weight Mastery Process,* I thought *What the heck, lie back and let the hypnosis do the work, and I will shake these 40 pounds.* So I was a bit intimidated when I realized that I was going to be 'practicing' daily mindsets. I thought *Crap! I am going to be spending so much time thinking and working things out! I don't have time for this!"*

I invited Jackie to step up to the plate and give it a try. After a week of practicing the process, Jackie said, "I am glad I didn't give up. I realize now that the few minutes a day I spend practicing shifting from fat to thin thinking can't compare to the hours that I spent obsessing about my food and weight and feeling bad. I save so much time and heartache with these simple daily tools. Anyone can do it. The hypnosis helps make thin thinking easy."

....

"I have released 40 pounds and feel confident and in control, because I am creating my success. No one but me can do it. This process gave me the best and least expensive weight loss coach in town…ME! Give Shifting a shot. You are worth it!" Jackie T. (Released 41 pounds, maintaining for 6 months.)

....

Now Just Begin

The secret to releasing weight and shifting from fat to thin thinking with the *Shift Weight Mastery Process*—drum roll, please—is to begin. Yes, that's right. Many people will buy something and then put it aside, saying "Oh I'll start later," and then they never follow through. Start when you say you are going to start and really commit to that day, your Day 0.

As my high school social studies teacher Mr. Prepazac used to say: "The best term paper is a completed term paper." Well, the best *Shift Weight Mastery Process* is one that is completed. There is no perfect time, mood, or season. Life is never going to line up for you to do your process perfectly, and that is good!

You are not here to be perfect; that is a word for dieters. Success comes from consistently showing up for yourself day after day. The perfect time is now. Give yourself the wonderful gift of showing up for yourself and participating 100 percent.

If you have any doubts about the process or already feel as if you are not going to be able to do it or stick with it, I understand. That's your resistant unconscious speaking to you already. Remember, the unconscious hates change, and what you are thinking about right now is change.

You are readier than you will ever be. Your mind is primed for success and mastery. I believe in you, Apprentice, and I am here with you every step of the way to your ideal weight. Let's begin your first day of practice.

FROM FAT TO THIN THINKING
GLOSSARY OF TERMS

Basal ganglia: The part of the brain responsible for such functions as control of voluntary motor movements, routine behaviors or habits, and emotions.

Carb Zombie: The overstimulated craving brain and body state initiated by consuming a diet high in refined carbohydrates.

Cognitive Behavioral Therapy (CBT): A form of therapy that uses cognitive techniques to help people become aware of when they make negative interpretations and engage in behavioral patterns that reinforce that distorted thinking.

Daily Body Burn Calories: The total number of calories the body burns during a 24-hour period (*resting metabolic rate + sedentary calories*).

Daily Calorie Budget for Weight Release: The number of daily calories you choose to consume that will allow you to release weight at your chosen rate.

Diet: Any way of eating with the intention of losing weight, including low carb, low fat, Weight Watchers, Jenny Craig, Paleo, clean, vegan, no sugar, and gluten-free.

Fat thinking: The deeply rooted, limiting belief and habit systems that keep one struggling with their weight.

GAK: Food that is highly refined and gives your body no nourishment.

Hypnosis: A conscious but relaxed mental state in which changing beliefs and habits in the subconscious mind is possible.

Inner Coach: The wise, rational, strategy-seeking and problem-solving inner voice.

Inner Critic: The perfectionistic and condemning inner voice that holds a person to abnormal standards, prompts negative self-talk, and undermines the ability to succeed in changing behavior.

Inner Rebel: The impulsive and sometimes childish inner voice that resists healthy change and drives a person to make unhealthy choices.

Mastery Zone: Daily protein intake of 72 grams or more and daily carbohydrate intake of less than 125 to 150 grams. This maintains physical stability and mental focus and prevents craving.

Meditation: Spending time in quiet thought for relaxation, problem-solving, and reflection.

Metabolism: The energy expended by the chemical reactions taking place within a living organism.

Neocortex: The part of the brain responsible for higher-order brain functions, such as sensory perception, cognition, language, and generation of motor commands.

Neural pathways: The pathways on which information travels along nerve cells (neurons) in the brain.

Neurotransmitters: Chemicals that transmit signals from one nerve cell to another.

National Institutes of Health (NIH): Twenty-seven separate national institutes and centers that conduct research in various biomedical science disciplines.

National Weight Control Registry (NWCR): A research study that includes people who have released at least 30 pounds and have kept it off for over a year.

Resting metabolic rate (RMR): The amount of energy (number of calories) that your body expends in a resting state over a 24-hour period.

Sedentary calories: The amount of calories that you burn performing daily, non-exercise related activities.

Stimulus control: Minimizing or eliminating foods or situations that prompt a reaction. For example, proactively creating an environment free of trigger and problem foods and keeping healthy food choices available.

Thin thinking: Powerful, mastery-based thinking that prompts the positive beliefs and behaviors that lead to long-term weight release.

Weight Master: A person who has learned the skills and mindset of long-term permanent weight release and maintenance.

Weight Mastery: The ongoing, gratifying journey of honing the skills and mindset for permanent weight release and maintenance.

Weight release: The act of letting go of weight.

Weight Struggler: A person who has been in a perpetual battle with weight, regardless of whether it's five pounds or 500 pounds.

Weight struggle: The frustrating and cyclical battle with weight gains and losses in which a person constantly struggles with consistency regarding food, exercise, their body, and most of all himself.

Weekly Weight Release Rate: The amount of calories a person chooses to burn each week in order to release a specific number of pounds.

ACKNOWLEDGMENTS

No weight release happens in a vacuum, nor does a book on weight release! I owe a debt of gratitude to many generous and amazing people who have been a part of my own journey to weight mastery. My journey led to creating the *Shift Weight Mastery Process* and ultimately to this book, *Fat to Thin Thinking*. What an amazing journey it has been.

First, I would like to thank my amazing husband, Simon Black, who has been by my side as a partner, a mentor, a cheerleader, and a friend. Simon is always there to help me through the fat and thin of it all. Thank you for giving me permission to become obsessed and allowing my mission to be a part of our lives. What would I do without you?

I would also like to thank my children, Archie and Vivien, who drew pictures of healthy foods for my early seminars. Also, I am very thankful for my mother-in-law, Margaret Black, and my sister-in-law, Kate Khaleel, who bravely attended early seminars as guinea pigs.

I am grateful for my friends and family who patiently cheered me along.

I would not have written this book if not for my fabulous, life-changing clients, all of the *Shift Weight Mastery Process* participants, the beta-tester clients who participated in research for the book, and the pioneer team of eight brave clients who participated in the pilot *Shift Weight Mastery Process* in 2007. Your stories, your struggles and successes, your ideas and feedback, and your generosity of heart, tenacity, courage, intelligence, and wisdom move me so much. I wake up every day thinking how grateful I am that you have allowed me to make a difference in your lives and for what a difference you have made in mine.

I'm also grateful to Mickey Marraffino, Mark Schubb, Deb Magit, Genia Quinn, and other clients and friends who loaned me their professional insights on business and marketing in the early days.

I would like to humbly bow down before my amazing team. Without their incredible talent, commitment, and patience, this book would not be possible. Dianne Lange, thank you for guiding me through the process of my first book. Your coaching and editing have made an enormous difference. Mary Burch, thank you for coming on board with the SHIFT and whipping the company and this book into shape. I truly appreciate you and your dedication to me and the book. I couldn't have done it without you. Kelly Hartigan at xterraweb.com who brought her keen eye to the proofreading. Catherine Aguilar who lent her artistic talent for the drawings. Pam Patterson and her design team at 14-Forty, thank you all for your design and branding contributions, friendship, generosity, and pivotal insights—from day one, you have been helping SHIFT (and me, too) to thrive and grow. I am forever grateful.

I would also like to express my gratitude to both my sets of beta test readers who fearlessly went through reading the book and testing the effectiveness of the 30-day process. I appreciate your pioneering spirit, your intelligent notes and, above all, your support. A special thanks to Maureen Burkhardt who went through the final draft with an amazing attention to detail that went above and beyond anything that I could have hoped for.

Finally, dear reader, thank you for taking the journey of making the shift from fat to thin thinking. I appreciate your willingness to make a deep change in your life. I believe that if we learn to show up for ourselves in a positive powerful way and get healthy, that our transformation will inspire others to make a similar transformation and in time make the world a much healthier and happier place to exist.

Alone we diet—Together we SHIFT
Rita Black

INDEX

What you'll find in the index:

- Weekly exercise planner
- Weekly weight release planner
- Exercise Calories Burned List
- Planned Food Journal
- Actual Food Journal
- Weight Tracking Chart
- Evening Review Huddle
- Weekly Review Huddle
- Online Resource Center

Note: These index resources exist as downloadable PDF files in www.fromfattothinthinking.com under "Resources".

Weekly Exercise Planner

My Weekly Exercise Calorie Burn Goal is: _____ calories.

Day	Time	Exercise Type	Minutes of Exercise	Calories Burned
Mon				
Tue				
Wed				
Thu				
Fri				
Sat				
Sun				

Total Weekly Calories Burned =

Weekly Weight Release Planner

	MO	TU	W	TH	FR	SA	SU	Weekly Totals
Daily Body Burn								
+ (Add) Actual Exercise Calories								
= Total Daily Burn Calories								
- (Less) Actual Food Calories								
= Net Calories Burned								
= Net Calories Running Total								

Exercise Calories Burned List

Exercise/Physical Activity: Calories Per Hour

Weight	120	140	160	180	200	220	240	260	280	300
Aerobics	229	265	305	343	381	419	457	495	533	571
Biking (mod. 11 mph)	332	387	442	497	552	607	662	717	772	827
Bootcamp	351	423	495	567	639	711	783	855	927	999
Circuit Training	380	430	480	530	580	630	680	730	780	830
Elliptical	400	467	534	601	668	735	802	869	936	1003
Jogging 5 mph	418	487	554	621	688	755	822	889	956	1023
Hiking	286	333	381	429	477	524	571	618	665	712
High Intensity Interval	325	380	435	490	545	600	655	710	765	820
Pilates	164	191	218	245	272	299	327	354	381	408
Power Yoga	220	250	270	310	340	370	400	430	460	490
Singles Tennis	351	417	483	549	615	681	747	813	879	945
Spin	360	400	440	480	520	560	600	640	680	720
Stairs Climber	457	533	609	685	761	837	913	989	1065	1132
Swimming Laps	274	320	366	412	458	504	550	596	642	688
Treadmill (mod. incline-4 mph)	320	373	427	480	533	586	639	692	745	798
Walking Moderate	263	307	351	395	439	483	527	571	615	659
Water Aerobics	257	300	343	386	429	472	515	558	601	644
Weightlifting	165	192	219	246	273	300	327	354	381	408
Zumba/Dance	314	367	419	471	523	575	627	679	731	783

Planned Food Journal

30-Day Thin Thinking Practice
Planned Food Journal Day __

Today's Date: Weight:

TIME	PLANNED FOOD	PROTEIN	CARBS	CALORIES
Planned Food Grand Totals:				

PLANNED EXERCISE

	Planned Exercise Calories:	

PLANNED TOTALS

My Daily Body Burn	
Exercise Calories Burned (+)	
Total Daily Calories Burned (=)	
Food Calories (-)	
Daily Net Calories Burned (=)	

Actual Food Journal

30-Day Thin Thinking Practice
Actual Food Journal Day ___

Today's Date: _____ Weight: _____

TIME	ACTUAL FOOD	PROTEIN	CARBS	CALORIES
Actual Food Grand Totals:				

ACTUAL EXERCISE _____

Actual Exercise Calories: _____

ACTUAL TOTALS

My Daily Body Burn	
Exercise Calories Burned (+)	
Total Daily Calories Burned (=)	
Food Calories (-)	
Daily Net Calories Burned (=)	

Weight Tracking Chart

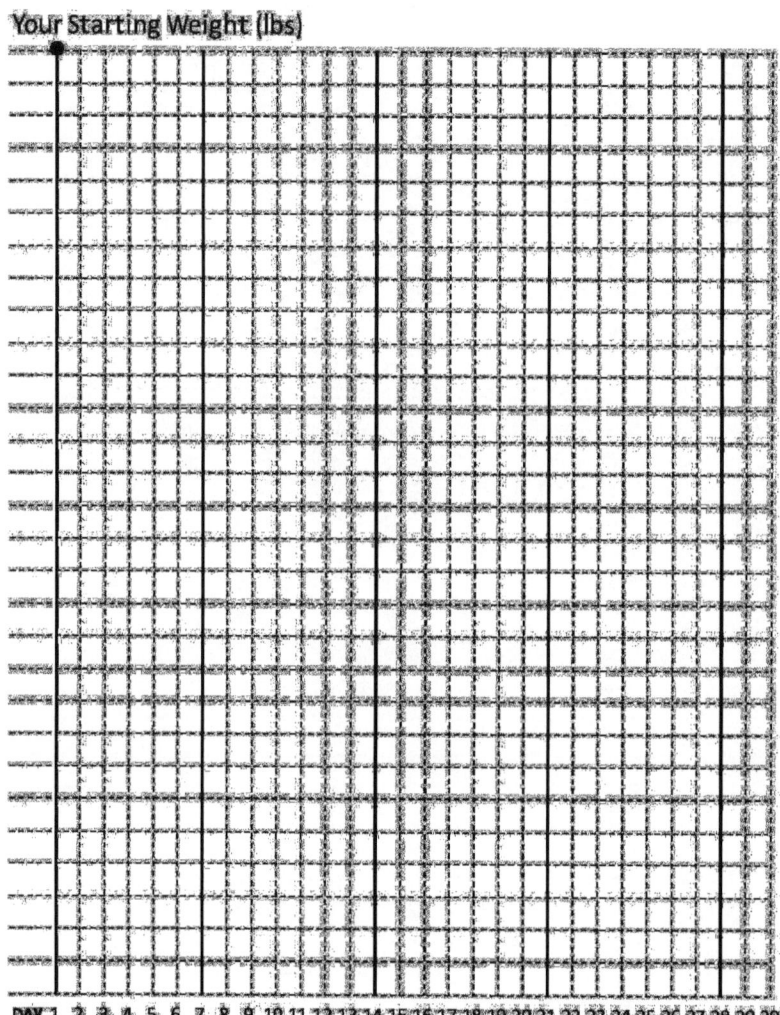

Your Starting Weight (lbs)

DAY 1 2 3 4 5 6 7 8 9 10 11 12 13 14 15 16 17 18 19 20 21 22 23 24 25 26 27 28 29 30

Evening Review Huddle

What are the three things that I did today to move toward Weight Mastery?

1. _____

2. _____

3. _____

What are the challenges that I faced today?

_____

_____

_____

Ideas to problem solve those challenges:

_____

_____

_____

- Remember to plan out your food and exercise for tomorrow.

- Listen to your hypnosis session.

- Congratulate yourself for another day of moving towards mastery.

Weekly Review Huddle

Use these questions to help you reflect on last week:

Which goals did you achieve (weight, exercise, calorie budget and others) for this week?

_____

_____

Why did you achieve them?

_____

_____

Which goals did you not achieve?

_____

_____

Why did you not achieve them?

_____

_____

Which of these skills needs more attention and/or improvements?

- Planning ahead
- Staying within your Calorie Budget for Weight Release
- Exercise
- Mastery Zone: More protein? Less refined foods? More vegetables and fruit?
- Tracking your food and exercise
- Keeping trigger foods out and healthy foods around
- Seeking support from others
- Removing negative self-talk
- Taking a Shift breath and refocusing
- Strategizing with your Inner Coach
- Getting back on track rather than starting over the next day

Is there anything else that needs to improve?

_____

_____

Do you need to be more consistent with the hypnosis and meditation sessions (they have a cumulative impact so it helps to keep up with them)?

_____

_____

What would you like to acknowledge yourself for?

_____

_____

ABOUT THE AUTHOR

Rita Black is a certified clinical hypnotherapist specializing in long-term weight loss and smoking cessation. She is the director of Shift Hypnosis and Motivational Resources and has led the highly successful *Shift Weight Mastery Process* seminars for over a decade. She is the creator of *Shift In A Box* (an online 30-day hypnosis-based weight loss program) and the *Shift Monthly Mastery Membership Program*. Rita lives in Los Angeles with her husband and two children.

ONLINE RESOURCE CENTER

Access Resource Center:
www.fromfattothinthinking.com

Orientation Video:
http://www.fromfattothinthinking.com/i-the-orientation/

Hypnosis and Meditation Sessions:
http://www.fromfattothinthinking.com/hypnosis-sessions/

Bonus Resource Videos:
http://www.fromfattothinthinking.com/ii-the-shift/

Weight Calculator:
http://www.fromfattothinthinking.com/weight-calculator/

Worksheets from the Book:
http://www.fromfattothinthinking.com/worksheets/

Sign up for 30-Day Thin Thinking Practice:
http://www.fromfattothinthinking.com/start-email-coaching/

For more information about Shift Weight Mastery:
www.shiftweightmastery.com

Made in the USA
Monee, IL
23 April 2023

32290541R00206